Promiscuous Feminist Methodologies in Education

The book marks the circulation of the term "promiscuous feminist methodology" and registers its salience for educational researchers who risk blundering feminist theories and methodologies in chaotic and unbridled ways. The sexism embedded in language is what makes the notion of promiscuous "feminists gone wild" tantalizing, though what the book puts forth is how the messy practice of inquiry transgresses any imposed boundaries or assumptions about what counts as research and feminism. What can researchers do when we realize that theories are not quite enough to respond to our material experiences with people, places, practices, and policies becoming data? As a collection, the book shows how various theories researchers put to work "get dirty" as they are contaminated and re-appropriated by other ways of thinking and doing through (con)texts of messy practices. In this way, gender cannot simply be gender and promiscuous feminist methodologies are always in-the-making and already ahead of what we think they are.

This book was originally published as a special issue of the *International Journal of Qualitative Studies in Education*.

Sara M. Childers, PhD, is an independent scholar currently residing in Dublin, Ohio, USA. She received her doctorate in Social and Cultural Foundations of Education from Ohio State University, USA. Her research utilizes qualitative methodologies, including ethnography, sociocultural policy analysis, and critical race, feminist, and post-structural theories. Her current project looks at how teachers in an underprivileged elementary school in the South define what counts as "data" and how they use it to make instructional decisions in the classroom. In 2010 she completed an ethnographic case study of a high achieving, high poverty high school in the Midwest to understand both the successful policy negotiations by students, parents, and teachers, as well as how racial inequality effected these negotiations.

Jeong-eun Rhee is an Associate Professor in the College of Education, Information, and Technology at Long Island University, Post, NY, USA. Her scholarly interests include decolonizing research methodologies, postcolonial inquiry in education, and issues of subjectivity, identity, and knowledge. She is currently working on a project that examines changing meanings and operations of race and racism vis-à-vis neoliberalism, which she calls the neoliberal racial project.

Stephanie L. Daza is a Fellow at the Education and Social Research Institute, Manchester Metropolitan University, Manchester, UK. She is a Research Methodologist and Critical Ethnographer interested in empirical and theoretical inquiry of boundaries – cross-cultural, cross-disciplinary, local-global, and PK-20. With an emphasis on difference and in/equity in education and society, her research examines institutions, policies, and practices. Her in-progress book on grant-science and STEM culture reflects six years of research on two National Science Foundation grants. Her new project explores digital affective technologies (DAT) as social science methodologies for a digital age of big data.

Promiscuous Feminist Methodologies in Education
Engaging Research Beyond Gender

Edited by
Sara M. Childers, Jeong-eun Rhee and
Stephanie L. Daza

First published 2015
by Routledge
2 Park Square, Milton Park, Abingdon, Oxon, OX14 4RN, UK

and by Routledge
711 Third Avenue, New York, NY 10017, USA

Routledge is an imprint of the Taylor & Francis Group, an informa business

© 2015 Taylor & Francis

All rights reserved. No part of this book may be reprinted or reproduced or utilised in any form or by any electronic, mechanical, or other means, now known or hereafter invented, including photocopying and recording, or in any information storage or retrieval system, without permission in writing from the publishers.

Trademark notice: Product or corporate names may be trademarks or registered trademarks, and are used only for identification and explanation without intent to infringe.

British Library Cataloguing in Publication Data
A catalogue record for this book is available from the British Library

ISBN 13: 978-1-138-80994-9

Typeset in Times New Roman
by RefineCatch Limited, Bungay, Suffolk

Publisher's Note
The publisher accepts responsibility for any inconsistencies that may have arisen during the conversion of this book from journal articles to book chapters, namely the possible inclusion of journal terminology.

Disclaimer
Every effort has been made to contact copyright holders for their permission to reprint material in this book. The publishers would be grateful to hear from any copyright holder who is not here acknowledged and will undertake to rectify any errors or omissions in future editions of this book.

Contents

Citation Information vii
Notes on Contributors ix

1. Introduction: Promiscuous (use of) feminist methodologies: the dirty theory and messy practice of educational research beyond gender
   Sara M. Childers, Jeong-eun Rhee and Stephanie L. Daza 1

2. Promiscuous feminisms for troubling times
   Rick Voithofer 18

3. Wild reading: this madness to our method
   Aparna Rita Mishra Tarc 31

4. Working on a failed research: promiscuity of wanting and doing both ways
   Jeong-eun Rhee 47

5. Much more than power: the pedagogy of promiscuous black feminism
   M. Francyne Huckaby 61

6. A promiscuous (feminist) look at grant-science: how colliding imaginaries shape the practice of NSF policy
   Stephanie L. Daza 74

7. The materiality of fieldwork: an ontology of feminist becoming
   Sara M. Childers 93

8. Was Jane Addams a promiscuous pragmatist?
   Becky Atkinson 104

9. Promiscuous feminists postscript
   Maggie MacLure 119

Index 123

Citation Information

The chapters in this book were originally published in the *International Journal of Qualitative Studies in Education*, volume 26, issue 5–6 (June–July 2013). When citing this material, please use the original page numbering for each article, as follows:

Chapter 1
Introduction: Promiscuous (use of) feminist methodologies: the dirty theory and messy practice of educational research beyond gender
Sara M. Childers, Jeong-eun Rhee and Stephanie L. Daza
International Journal of Qualitative Studies in Education, volume 26, issue 5–6 (June–July 2013) pp. 507–523

Chapter 2
Promiscuous feminisms for troubling times
Rick Voithofer
International Journal of Qualitative Studies in Education, volume 26, issue 5–6 (June–July 2013) pp. 524–536

Chapter 3
Wild reading: this madness to our method
Aparna Rita Mishra Tarc
International Journal of Qualitative Studies in Education, volume 26, issue 5–6 (June–July 2013) pp. 537–552

Chapter 4
Working on a failed research: promiscuity of wanting and doing both ways
Jeong-eun Rhee
International Journal of Qualitative Studies in Education, volume 26, issue 5–6 (June–July 2013) pp. 553–566

Chapter 5
Much more than power: the pedagogy of promiscuous black feminism
M. Francyne Huckaby
International Journal of Qualitative Studies in Education, volume 26, issue 5–6 (June–July 2013) pp. 567–579

CITATION INFORMATION

Chapter 6
A promiscuous (feminist) look at grant-science: how colliding imaginaries shape the practice of NSF policy
Stephanie L. Daza
International Journal of Qualitative Studies in Education, volume 26, issue 5–6 (June–July 2013) pp. 580–598

Chapter 7
The materiality of fieldwork: an ontology of feminist becoming
Sara M. Childers
International Journal of Qualitative Studies in Education, volume 26, issue 5–6 (June–July 2013) pp. 599–609

Chapter 8
Was Jane Addams a promiscuous pragmatist?
Becky Atkinson
International Journal of Qualitative Studies in Education, volume 26, issue 5–6 (June–July 2013) pp. 610–624

Chapter 9
Promiscuous feminists postscript
Maggie MacLure
International Journal of Qualitative Studies in Education, volume 26, issue 5–6 (June–July 2013) pp. 625–628

Please direct any queries you may have about the citations to
clsuk.permissions@cengage.com

Notes on Contributors

Becky Atkinson is an Associate Professor in the College of Education at The University of Alabama, USA. She teaches courses in cultural and social foundations. Her interests, teacher knowledge research, pragmatic semiotics, feminist materialism and critical theory, seed her current research. Presently she is involved in a project studying how teachers deal with multiple forms of data. She has published articles in *Educational Theory*, *Qualitative Inquiry*, *Educational Studies*, *The Journal of Educational Research* and *The Journal of Teacher Education*.

Sara M. Childers, PhD, is an independent scholar currently residing in Dublin, Ohio, USA. She received her doctorate in Social and Cultural Foundations of Education from Ohio State University, USA. Her research utilizes qualitative methodologies, including ethnography, sociocultural policy analysis, and critical race, feminist, and post-structural theories. Her current project looks at how teachers in an underprivileged elementary school in the South define what counts as "data" and how they use it to make instructional decisions in the classroom. In 2010 she completed an ethnographic case study of a high achieving, high poverty high school in the Midwest to understand both the successful policy negotiations by students, parents, and teachers, as well as how racial inequality effected these negotiations.

Stephanie L. Daza is a Fellow at the Education and Social Research Institute, Manchester Metropolitan University, Manchester, UK. She is a Research Methodologist and Critical Ethnographer interested in empirical and theoretical inquiry of boundaries – cross-cultural, cross-disciplinary, local-global, and PK-20. With an emphasis on difference and in/equity in education and society, her research examines institutions, policies, and practices. Her in-progress book on grant-science and STEM culture reflects six years of research on two National Science Foundation grants. Her new project explores digital affective technologies (DAT) as social science methodologies for a digital age of big data.

M. Francyne Huckaby is the Director of the Center for Urban Education and Associate Professor of Curriculum Studies at TCU, USA. Her scholarship and teaching merge theoretical, philosophical, and historical knowledge with an attentiveness to tacit knowledge formed by culture, context, and current realities to create openings and space for anti-oppressive discourses and practices. Her current research focuses on the ways communities resist neoliberal education reform.

Maggie MacLure is a Professor of Education in the Education and Social Research Institute, Manchester Metropolitan University, UK, where she leads the Theory and Methodology Research Group. She is the Founder and Director of the international Summer Institute in Qualitative Research.

NOTES ON CONTRIBUTORS

Jeong-eun Rhee is an Associate Professor in the College of Education, Information, and Technology at Long Island University, Post, NY, USA. Her scholarly interests include decolonizing research methodologies, postcolonial inquiry in education, and issues of subjectivity, identity, and knowledge. She is currently working on a project that examines changing meanings and operations of race and racism vis-à-vis neoliberalism, which she calls the neoliberal racial project.

Aparna Rita Mishra Tarc is an Assistant Professor at the Faculty of Education, York University, Canada. Her current research and scholarship conducts a series of philosophical, ethical, and pedagogical investigations into the problem of representing the lived experiences of others. Her articles have appeared in *Educational Theory*, *Changing English*, *Curriculum Inquiry*, *Curriculum and Pedagogy*, *Race, Ethnicity and Education* and *Pedagogy, Culture and Society*.

Rick Voithofer is an Associate Professor in the Faculty of Education and Human Ecology at Ohio State University, USA. His research interests lie in the intersections of culture, equity, technology, and learning.

INTRODUCTION

Promiscuous (use of) feminist methodologies: the dirty theory and messy practice of educational research beyond gender

Sara M. Childers[a], Jeong-eun Rhee[b] and Stephanie L. Daza[c]

[a]Educational Studies in Psychology, Research Methodology, and Counseling, University of Alabama, Tuscaloosa, AL, USA; [b]College of Education, Information and Technology, Long Island University, Post, Brookville, NY, USA; [c]Education and Social Research Institute, Manchester Metropolitan University, Manchester, UK

> This editor's introduction narrates how we as researchers trained in qualitative and feminist methodology came to read our own work as promiscuous and interpret the terms "feminist" and "feminism" through both practice and theory. It marks the circulation of the term "promiscuous feminist methodology" and registers its salience for educational researchers who risk blundering feminist theories and methodologies in chaotic and unbridled ways. The use of the phrase "promiscuous feminist" to describe methodology is not merely an attention-seeking oxymoron, though we hope that its irony is not lost. The sexism embedded in language is what makes the notion of "feminists gone wild" tantalizing, though what we put forth is how the messy practice of inquiry transgresses any imposed boundaries or assumptions about what counts as research and feminism. Because the theories we put to work "get dirty" as they are contaminated and re-appropriated by other ways of thinking and doing through (con)texts of messy practices, promiscuous feminist methodologies are always in-the-making and already ahead of what we think they are. Set in motion by anxieties, disappointments, and frustrations of feeling out of place in the academy and in feminism, we examine our personal, academic, and political engagement with these contradictions that became the springboard for this special issue.

Introduction

What does it mean to claim a feminist position in educational research today? The researchers in this issue, whose work tries to understand the complexities of diverse (con)texts and practices, might not quite fit readers' (or even our own) taken-for-granted assumptions about what counts as feminist research – and that is the point. This issue demonstrates how the messy practice of inquiry transgresses any imposed boundaries or assumptions about what counts as research and feminism. Often re-appropriated through the (con)texts of messy practices, the theories we put to work "get dirty" as they are contaminated by other ways of thinking and doing. Methodologies-in-practice cannot be neatly defined or expected to stay in place on a grid or continuum graphic (Lather, 2006). Methodologies, the integration of dirty theory and messy practice, are in the making and "on the move" (Childers, 2012). Because (fortunately) human beings continuously imagine and create fictions of all kinds, including stories that repeat, are mistaken, and extend ontological and epistemological engagements (Spivak, 2012, p. 121), methodology-in-practice is always already ahead of what we think it is.[1] Thus, rather than defining promiscuous feminist methodologies per se, this editor's introduction explores how we came to read our work as promiscuous[2] and interpret the terms "feminist" and "feminism" through both practice and theory.

The use of the phrase "promiscuous feminist" to describe methodology is not merely an attention-seeking oxymoron, though we hope that its irony is not lost. "Promiscuity" is a racy, sexy, pejorative, and even punitive term denoting "bad" girls. Around 1600, "promiscuous" meant "mixed and indiscriminate," but it was not recorded as referring to sexual relations until 1900 (*Online Etymology Dictionary*, n.d.; see also Voithofer[3]). The sexism embedded in language is what makes the notion of "feminists gone wild" tantalizing, though what we put forth is about the wild becomings implicit in feminist methodologies in-the-making. So, like deconstruction (Derrida, 1997; Spivak, 1999), promiscuous feminist methodologies are not necessarily a way to do research but a kind of a new metaphor, grounded in the engagement of materiality, for understanding what is always already happening.

Our notion of what it means to be promiscuous with feminisms worked its way through rhizomatic channels of casual conversations, business meetings, and conference papers over the last four years. As researchers trained in qualitative and feminist methodology, we were set in motion by anxieties, disappointments, and frustrations of feeling out of place in the academy and in feminism. Yet the illicit desire, excitement, and energy of experiencing/living out-of-bounds of the spaces we thought were our own catalyzed us and our work. While feminist methodologies partially liberated us, and some forms of knowledge production, from patriarchal ontology and male-dominated epistemology, it also relegated us to the margins of the academy. This we expected. But, in various ways, we found ourselves and our research (con)texts retrained, unexpectedly and perhaps unintentionally, by discursive boundaries of feminist methodologies (especially around gender). Our personal, academic, and political engagement with this contradiction has produced this issue. It marks the circulation of the term "promiscuous feminist methodology" and registers its salience for educational researchers who risk blundering feminist theories and methodologies in chaotic and unbridled ways.

At different points, we interrupt our narrative to exchange dialog. Sometimes taken verbatim from our discussions about this issue, the dialog is meant to interject our different voices and everyday positionalities. It shows how we came together to think about promiscuous methodology from different backgrounds and contexts. Because each of us came to this project from different positions, research trajectories, and ways of seeing the world, no one framework took hold. Our dialog may be too neat and confessional. While we wish it were more promiscuous, we also note promiscuity in re-appropriating "testimonial narratives" through standpoint epistemologies (Matias, 2012; Moraga & Anzaldúa, 1984) to highlight our current working conditions when promiscuous feminism is expected to do otherwise.

Sara: I began rethinking how I conceptualized feminist methodology in 2008, while conducting fieldwork for my dissertation (see Childers). I cautiously presented conference papers on what I was then calling a "not-so-feminist" feminist methodology. Trained and mentored by feminists inside and outside the academy, I somehow felt disloyal, because I was not researching gender/women/girls. I was surprised at how the tension and anxiety I struggled to articulate in claiming the feminist in my fieldwork resonated with others. Collaborations with other (feminist and not-so-feminist) feminist-identified researchers followed, and the term promiscuous took hold.

Stephanie: Although I considered myself a feminist by values and training, and was experiencing gender discrimination and sexism on a daily basis, I had all but given-up on doing any kind of research that I thought would be considered as contributing to feminist methodology in education. I thought I had "moved on" to queer theory and trying to read my research with NSF engineering grants through Gayatri Spivak. Then, Sara, who I absolutely considered one of those "real feminist feminists" hailed me as feminist, too (!) when she invited me to participate in a panel where we would begin articulating this promiscuous position.

Sara: When I organized the symposium for American Educational Research Association (AERA) in 2010 (*Promiscuous Feminisms: The Application of Feminist Methodologies and Epistemologies to Curriculum Theorizing Beyond Gender*[4]) that included some of the contributors to this issue, I had no idea that you felt this way. After the session, both you and Jeong-eun approached me about growing it into a special issue.

Jeong-eun: I have continuously and constantly used various feminist theories and methodologies in my work. Yet, I would not have participated in this project had it been framed as feminist research methodology sans promiscuity due to my ambivalent relations with feminist work in education, in particular and US feminisms, in general. My observation of feminist work in education has been predominantly white. Go to any AERA session entitled with "feminism" and check out the presenters and audience. Also, US feminism of color can be very nationalistic (Alexander, 2005). During Sara and Stephanie's AERA session, I sensed a strange space opening up by your provocation with promiscuity, that I was willing to occupy to re-member myself as (promiscuous) feminist. At the same time, I still think we should publicly wonder about why another immigrant woman of color said no to this project despite her commitment to emancipatory research.

While our "upbringing" in the academy is produced in and through a legacy of feminist educational scholarship and a lineage of feminist mentors, we see ourselves as a new generation of scholars working within a different terrain, a terrain made possible by the work of those before us, and still (im)possibly different from their experiences. Many of the contributors to this issue express ambivalence with feminist research as an effect and affect of "living differently," after the ruins of feminism and research have been excavated. We also argue that while feminism has been undone by critiques from inside and outside of its discipline, a particular discursive construction of what counts as feminist research, in part an inevitable response to ongoing sexism, manages to re-territorialize its center. Our interactions with the field, material negotiations of doing grants and research, and of our lives outside of the academy have shaped our research practices as much as, or maybe even more than, our theoretical training and engagements. While ambivalence has been an effect of wrestling with such re-territorializations and (re)marginalizations, promiscuity is what keeps our wrestling continuous. Therefore, ambivalence is a potential symptom of our own promiscuous work.

Outside-in feminist methodology

Feminist research is outside-in the academy, contentiously working within the constraints of the teaching machine (Spivak, 1993), producing scholarship as critique of the universities and disciplines that paradoxically provide homes and support for the work. Similarly, feminist research also has its own outside-in, its own centers and margins, and its own multiplicities. In broad strokes, feminist theorizing itself is articulated as heterogeneous, complex, and even conflictual; be it critical, racial, phenomenological, psychoanalytic, autobiographical, queer, post-colonial, or post-foundational, these variegated ontological, epistemological, and methodological positions commonly endeavor to "center and simultaneously problematize conceptions of the categories woman and gender identity, for example, and the various situations, embodiments, contexts, and institutions that frame diverse lived realities" (Miller, 2010, p. 371). While feminism is often defined in opposition to male-dominated epistemologies (around the concept of gender and for gender equality), the researchers who have developed feminist methodology and the ideas they contributed are not homogenous. Queer feminists (e.g. Britzman, 1998; Butler, 2004, 2011), US feminists of color (e.g. Hill Collins, 1991/2008; Villenas, 1996), indigenous feminists (Smith, 1999/2012), postcolonial feminists (Coloma, 2008, 2012; Lorde, 1984/2007; Spivak, 1999, 2008, 2012), and queers of color (Anzaldúa, 1987/1999) have worked against white, heterosexual, Euro-US-centric versions of feminist methodology and male-dominated critical race theory.

Feminist philosophers and methodologists have consistently argued against a "distinctive method" (Harding, 1987) of feminist research to resist the possibility of exclusion inherent in fixing criteria. Rather, Harding and others have drawn attention to its distinctive features and challenges to traditional methodologies. Features such as interdisciplinarity, intersectionality, privileging the epistemology of disadvantaged groups, advancement of social justice, attention to relations of power, and researcher reflexivity have been identified as distinguishing features of feminist research (Fonow & Cook, 2005; Harding & Norberg, 2005; Pryse, 2000). These broader characteristics are posited alongside attending to the significance of gender and gender disparities in social life.

A review of feminist methodological literature across the fields of feminist research for "what counts" provides examples of how its discursive articulations share this common core of attention to gender/women/girls/sexuality. Fonow and Cook (2005, p. 2230) articulate feminist research within Women's Studies as having moved:

> well beyond the analysis of bias and exclusion and toward more contextual forms of theorizing about the intersection of gender with other categories of social difference and with place and time, and this, inevitably, has led to more sophisticated discussions about method.

In education, Miller (2010) positions feminist theorizing within curriculum studies as diverse and multiple in its approach, and most commonly bonded by its necessary attention to gender, women, and girls, however, troubling and problematic these categories may be. Feminist methodologists Hesse-Biber and Leavy (2007) propose that feminist research challenges the structures and ideologies that oppress women to foster empowerment and emancipation in the name of social change (p. 4). From the position of feminist policy analysis, Mazur (2002) argues that feminist research aligns itself in some way with a desire for social justice for women and the elimination of gender-based oppression for both men and women (p. 31). Campbell (2000) similarly frames "feminists [as] dedicated to discerning, defining, and changing structures of exclusion, marginalization, social isolation, and subordination based on gender wherever and however they occur" (p. 37).

We argue that because of its discursive articulations and institutional practices such as publications, faculty lines, and funding directives, feminist theorizing and research, regardless of critiques, is most legible and legitimate when contained within the parameters of gender/sex/women's issues and re-categorized or pushed out into other theoretical and methodological boxes when it seeks to be otherwise. For example, Childers and Daza discuss the illegibility of their research to feminism, but the ease at which their studies fit other spaces, such as policy studies, urban research, anthropology, or qualitative methodology. Part of this is not the fault of feminist methodology but that sexism and male-domination permeate all societal institutions–politics, capitalism/neoliberalism/globalization, education, religion, and even/especially gender. In response to patriarchy, feminist research has maintained its own essence, one that is provisionally necessary, yet potentially exclusive and hegemonic (Abu- Lughod, 1991). Its discursive construction circumscribes the practice of feminist methodology within an ontological boundary of a certain or salient way of being/doing. It is the breaking of this ontological boundary, and ab-use[5] of the legacy of feminist methodology, that we attempt to articulate in this issue. To separate from it, while also embracing it, an ab-use of feminist methodology is what is becoming of the traces of feminisms' legacy from below. Our violation, or what Spivak calls ab-use, is what enables promiscuous feminisms.[6]

Genealogy, lineage, and legacy: working the ruins of feminist methodology

> At one time, feminist researchers were on the outside looking in, but now many feminist scholars of our generation have become the gatekeepers (Cook & Fonow, 1984) of a much richer array of resources that are needed to produce and distribute feminist knowledge. We are training the next generation of feminist researchers and deciding who will receive grant funding, who will publish, and who will be awarded tenure. This is both an important responsibility and valuable opportunity to advance the field by championing and mentoring the work of newer scholars, some of whom are questioning the feminist work – including our own – that came before them. (Fonow & Cook, 2005, p. 2230)

Our promiscuous feminist methodologies and promiscuous use of methodologies do not emerge from nowhere, but from a lineage and legacy of feminist theory, feminist methodology, and qualitative research in education. Indeed, advisors/mentors of contributors to this issue – Britzman (1986, 2003, 2009, 2012); Lather (1986, 1997, 2007); Lincoln and Guba (1985); Lincoln (2010); Denzin and Lincoln (2011), Danowitz (Danowitz, Hanappi-Egger, & Mensi-Klachback, 2012; Dickens & Danowitz Sagaria, 1997), and Adams (2003, 2005) – defined, and continue to define, the very fields of engagement, not just through their publications, but also through their teaching and mentorship of graduate students, speaking engagements, and their leadership. Our idols and icons, many cited in this issue, also continue to define what it means to be a feminist and do feminist research. We also acknowledge male academic allies, such as Voithofer, who are feminists and who have supported feminist methodology and continue to support our work in various ways.

More than a decade ago, St. Pierre and Pillow (2000), also products of this lineage, named "the ruins" (Lather, 1991) of positivism in feminist and educational research and began to articulate what it means to interrupt and work out of those ruins. Because of their work, feminist methodology in education has been imagined as "working the ruins" of male-dominated positivism in one way or another. Therefore, contributors to this issue represent a generation of feminist educational researchers well-schooled, but not in homogeneous ways, in working the inadequacies of an inefficient social science. We have been warned carefully, thoughtfully, and rigorously about the ruins of feminism, education, and methodology (Lather, 2007; St. Pierre & Pillow, 2000). No longer needing to articulate the loss of foundations, we accept that we work and live on shaky ground. Some may wonder, then, what is left to discuss in the face of the death of science, ruins of feminism, and violence of research already declared. Others may contest that promiscuity is already a new norm in this post-foundational, post-proliferating paradigmatic research field (Abu-Lughod, 1990; Behar & Gordon, 1995; Pillow, 2000).

Sara: What does it mean to work in "the ruins" after the ruins have been excavated? Can "feminist" educational research focus on subjects beyond gender and still be considered "feminist"? Our task is to articulate how living, working, and finding a place within the ruins has impacted our research and our becoming as feminists and researchers.

Jeong-eun: Especially, how does this discursive work of ruins meet our everyday material reality of living and working as researchers who must interact with participants, schools, grant agencies, etc?

Stephanie: Maybe because feminist research has been defined in relation to what is assumed to be "mainstream research," as the ruins of enlightenment (or male) ways of knowing, feminist methodology is limited as an effect of sexism and male domination. Albeit in different ways and degrees, feminism, along with sexism and male domination, is internalized and institutionalized, especially through the Westernized concept of gender in the US (Abu-Lughod, 1991; Spivak, 2012). Thinking about this helps me understand how our lives and research exceed feminism and in effect move feminist methodology outside of itself.

Sara: This issue presents an unruly group – emboldened by our training and intensely driven to contribute to our fields, but simultaneously ambivalent about our location, and therefore unruly, within feminist research. We set out here to show how our emerging promiscuous feminist methodological lenses offer possible futures for educational research. In a way I feel like we are also "coming out" about the politics of location inside and outside the academy and feminism, living not-quite-on the edge of recognizability for both. But I see this uncertain edge now as a given quality of the materiality of my life, but it has taken writing this issue to figure that out.

Stephanie: I think my unruliness is a direct benefit of the legacy of feminism that I especially learned through feminists – community activists, teachers, and academics in undergraduate and graduate school. It helped me see how I could be engaged beyond and across various boundaries – cross-cultural, transnational, and interdisciplinary. This way of working has become the hallmark of my research. I don't think we set out to re-imagine or re-theorize feminist methodology in education but also we could not *not* do it. Promiscuity is the consequence of incompatibilities between imagined research and real life and places. In this way, promiscuous methodology is more than a metaphor (Tuck & Yang, 2012).

Jeong-eun: I also think that it is important to note that this move is not to reject ontology of being women in our work. Perhaps this is to recognize how existing feminist methodologies have been more interested in a certain ontology of being women because of particular materiality at their particular historical junctures. This move can be useful for any socially constructed difference-based work (Rhee, 2008). Our attempt is to articulate how we had to face our lived material reality of being non-feminist feminist researchers (Childers) – e.g. how are fieldwork, everyday interactions with colleagues, students, neighbors, and working conditions – exceeding the current discursive practices of feminisms and how we see promiscuity as a way to suture them. Acknowledging our unduly indebtedness to feminist researchers who have prepared our generation to work in the ruins, what does it mean to do research now, on a terrain changed by those who came before us?

Becoming promiscuous: the materiality of feminist methodology

This section points towards a (dys)functional coming to and conceptualization of "promiscuous feminist methodology" that is very much about making sense of the uncertainty that contextualizes what it means to live and work as feminist researchers in the academy today. As various feminist researchers have discussed, research is always, already a partially failed and violent attempt to represent the world and others within our current symbolic systems of languages and methods of science and social science – built on a colonial legacy. Living in the unredeemable "ruins" of social science, many feminist researchers have embraced the failures as productive, and even longed for them. Since research is already undone in feminist methodology, we were taught by Patti Lather and others to "do it and trouble it simultaneously," perform the "doubled move," "work the double bind," "work the ruins," "work the hyphen," "do good enough research," and "work within and against." However, in these strategies to keep the center unsettled, feminist research becomes its own vicious circle (see Sandoval, 2000, p. 183).

Once we began conducting our own research in the field we realized these moves were not quite enough to respond to our material experiences with people, places, practices, and policies becoming data (St. Pierre, 2011). For example, our promiscuous methodological engagement involves interrogating our employment in academia. As Rhee writes in this issue, accepting and working the ruins as the task was not enough when she had to face "the materiality and 'conditions of employment and research funding' (MacLure, 2011, p. 998)" as a nontenured faculty member. Who have access to and can (afford to) do "work the ruins" moves? Who(se moves) get hired, tenured, published, and funded? How do we engage this material issue of researchers' employment conditions as a (necessary) component in feminist research methodology? On a different note, Childers also discusses how merely interrogating the ruins of urban schooling through feminist post-structural analysis was not only insufficient but also unethical to respond to the materiality of the field. Our generation has not experienced failure as a technique, romance, or despair, rather we live it. We are the ruins; failure is our context, the only constant, the foundation of our slippery landscape. Thus, we promiscuously mix with the ruins of the ruins, or the failure of the failures. Here, our emphasis is not the ruins themselves but our indiscriminate mixing with other ways of thinking, doing, and being for promiscuous work.

Forsaking and feeling forsaken by feminisms, contributors to this issue narrate an ambivalent embrace of feminism/theory/research and all that those signs hold in their meanings. We narrate what it means to work out of these ontological tensions in practice and not just in theory, and to simultaneously experience a break with the legacy of feminisms – a legacy without which we would not exist. Not a romance of failure, we find such ambivalences disconcerting in many ways: when we live outside-in many centers (our feminisms, science, departments, and institutions); occupy libidinal spaces between our training and "real"-world experiences as researchers, (m)others, grand/daughters, and so on; and bear the toll of exile, whether self-imposed or not. Our loss of place, of failing to fit-in, becomes a pretext for a different ethos of working outside-in the academy. It is in the materiality of loss, violation, homelessness, and failure that we claim our wild and promiscuous becoming.

Our promiscuous feminist methodologies emerged from our persistent encounters with histories/herstories, fieldwork, pedagogy, and (con)texts, where the interplay of ourselves, others, and the world were inseparable and simultaneously constitutive of race, ethno-linguistic affiliation, class and socioeconomics, gender, sexuality, nationality, and so on. In this way, gender cannot simply be gender (Alexander, 2005; Mohanty, 2003; Trinh, 1989). Our engagements and inquiries can be wild, unbound, and illicit; and we/they transgress, displace, and change our subjectivities.

Consequently, affective notions of madness, vulnerability, failure, collisions, betrayals, resistances, excess, loss, alienation, and isolation accompany promiscuous feminist methodologies. Tarc "theorizes the possibilities of a qualitative method committed to….what Virginia Woolf (1922/1992) claims is 'the wild horse in us'… the 'promiscuous' aspects of human existence and difference …. that the 'scientific' methods underlying normative humanistic inquiries are oriented towards disavowing." In one example, Daza discusses how colliding subjectivities mis/interpret grant policies resulting in a modified research design. In another, Huckaby theorizes power through relations of vulnerability. Tarc's use of literature and Rhee's use of folktale to do promiscuous feminist science are other examples.

Working within and against what we read as the bounded and mainstream discourses of what "counts" as feminist research, we neither attempt to reconcile our approaches with the mainstream nor the margins, but rather accept unfitting and edgework. Promiscuous feminisms do not represent a desire for inclusion or synthesis or to assert a new center or margin. Rather coming to see our work/selves as promiscuous has become a source of energy and survival in our institutions and research lives. It has been the link to our "selves" and others, a reminder that vulnerability, contamination, wildness, excess, and being pushed-out (or existing between), though painful, can be powerful. We differentiate promiscuity from a margin-vs.-center binary. We use this reconceptualization of promiscuity as an unfixed becoming of feminist methodology – to drive it beyond its limits, exasperate it, and there see its usefulness that has yet to be thought. Not an antidote to the melancholy that ails us (MacLure, 2010), it is a way to view and navigate the complicit complexity (Daza, 2012) of our relations outside-in. When we step out of the bounds of what counts as feminist, our promiscuities are the enablements of these violations, our wild energy. As (im)possibilities, different sources of pleasure, and wild energy can feed such work when we step out of the bounds of what counts as feminist.

Living promiscuously: towards "wild" writing and "un/containment"

> To recover promiscuity is to repair the damage done to human existence demeaned by the term and to revitalize its force as a source of thinking and acting. (Tarc)

Our foremothers trained us to be "good girls," to carve out spaces for ourselves and our radical work while conservatively negotiating the tenure-grant-research machine that is the academy. The mantra has been to work both within and against "the hands that feed us" – educational research/ers, research participants, and feminism and feminists as well as universities, journals, funding agencies, and conferences – and not jeopardize these spaces and places as they also offer security and refuge – for our "different lovely knowledge" (Rhee).

Sara: But I think we've become something different. I don't see myself as a "good girl" or a "bad girl" for that matter, though I think the mentors that have invested in my training would prefer I err on the side of "good" because it protects me from damaging consequences that they have experienced first-hand. I believe I was schooled in how to live inconspicuously in the academy, run under the radar, and these are important lessons for making it. I am in a privileged space made possible by the feminist researchers that came before me – they taught me what they learned the hard way. We have all heard many stories of the kinds of institutional oppression women and feminist faculty have faced and continue to deal with in the academy. Because of them, I have been afforded the space to do my work; I don't have to fight as hard for it. I've got the flexibility to line up and "do as I'm told" (i.e. publish, serve, teach) to preserve my position as a junior faculty, but I'm not loyal to the academy in the ways it wants me to be. For the most part, I fall in line, or as Stephanie says, I'm complicit, but I am also willing to jeopardize this safety if the academy threatens my politics or my beliefs. When I speak up against the academy or against male and/or white hegemony, it's because, after all I've learned, I can't not speak, even if it means looking like "the bad girl." I feel like I'm confronted with these decisions on a regular basis – in department meetings, classrooms, when I get dressed in the morning. The materiality of this academic life is at once wild, promiscuous, and a disorderly space where there is no right answer.

Stephanie: Can queer colored single-moms be "good girls"? To be both uncontained and contained in academia cannot be reconciled. As Chicana feminists have reimagined La Malinche and the Virgin to interrupt such whore/virgin binaries (Calvo, 2004; Petty, 2000; Pratt, 1993), the concept "promiscuous feminist" is a methodology of otherwise, what Moraga and Anzaldúa (1984) call a "theory in the flesh" (cited in Sandoval, 2000, p. 7). Through incompatibilities, however painful, open-endedness, complexity, and innovation survive; thus, here difference is a methodology, not an object (Sandoval, 2000). The pleasure that comes from my pain of uncontainment is itself from surviving containment.

Jeong-eun: A funny thing is that I have not even considered myself as suitable for the category of good girls or bad girls in US academy. For an illegitimate child whose presence is constantly demanded to be as inconspicuous as possible, sometimes having a name, even if it is a "bad girl," can be desirable. Desiring uncontainment can risk the erasure of one's hard-fought presence. If a metaphor of borderlands has allowed me to make sense of a subjectivity of in-between locations, I see promiscuous methodology as a vehicle to move back and forth between containment/marked and uncontainment/unmarked for full engagement with material realities and un/marked desires.

Stephanie: Promiscuity is a method of surviving impervious un/containments.

Sara: Because of these experiences I think we've all had to negotiate our subjectivities in the workplace and lives away from the academy. Because of my background as a first-generation college student, I have knowingly engaged in a process of assimilation and passing – covered my accent, learned white middle class cultural expectations, leashed the radical enthusiasm I embraced as a feminist to be more strategic – but never quite fitting in and sometimes being read as "too big for my britches" so to speak in and out of the university. As we write this, I also admit that trying to perform a fitting-in is a big waste of time, because it's always already unsuccessful, in part because eventually, and maybe in spite of my whiteness, I irrupt in ways I cannot control or imagine. Eventually I'm found out, I out myself. But part of the politics of difference is making the space for others to irrupt the mainstream. So we have to interrupt, irrupt, and "be" or become ourselves.

Stephanie: When we first started working on this, I remember thinking that Sara may choose to fit or not and this is not a choice people of color often get to make (see Daza, 2008, 2009). Working with Sara on this issue has helped me better understand my own internalized racism. It made me think about how researchers can and must find ways to work with diverse populations (diverse ethnically, racially, linguistically, economically, politically, and so on) and methodologically prepare researchers of different backgrounds to do research. Sara confronts race in her project on the terms of the racialized and interrogates and changes her methodology. Along with Pollack (2004), Dyrness (2011), and Brown (2012), who engage race politics in their scholarship, Sara is leading the way for how White-identifying scholars and feminist methodologists in education might interrogate and race methodology in order to engage race and White privilege in US schools, society, and research.

Jeong-eun: I must agree as that is where I become tantalized by Sara's promiscuous feminism. Yet is it possible not to try to fit in? When we completely stop trying, or fail a fitting-in/assimilation/passing at least in a certain degree, can we exist in any institution whether it is academy, religion, family, or feminism? Promiscuity incites new imagination through which we can want and do bad girls, good girls, in-between and even no-girls. As researchers, we are as guilty as charged in our complicity of reproducing the US teaching machine. Through our promiscuity, at the same time, our work and our presence become dirty, messy, and wild enough to interrupt certain containments.

To be uncontained is to be uncoded – free from the coercive training of our own desires – from our training as subjects of temporal-spatial, sociocultural, political, economic, psychological, and historical worlds – even free from our training as feminists and as methodologists. In our entanglement with the enlightenment, to be free to produce autonomous knowledge is a glamorous and impossible notion, but there is also little pleasure in being an asylee. To be out-of-bounds, "free" in exile, and an asylee is often an experience of pain, shame, isolation, and revulsion – we may experience exceeding our containment as an experience of desire *for* containment, legibility, and some measure of success in the face of falling apart: when we are confounded by failure when researching with Korean immigrants and research partners (Rhee); when the materiality of the field disrupts taken-for-granted assumptions of what it means to do feminist work (Childers); when the hope of social justice risks infiltration and complicity through NSF grants (Daza); by (re)locating Jane

Addams somewhere in between pragmatist and feminist philosophy and therefore critiquing both (Atkinson); for narrating our science work as "wild" (Tarc); and for re-theorizing the "high" theory of Foucault through valuing familial knowledge as a pedagogical methodology (Huckaby).

But held within a desire for un/containment, is a desire for containment. A "strategy of containment" (Bhabha, 1994, p. 31) tries to keep agents and ideas as the subjects of power by setting up a false choice between what it considers dichotomous categories of sanity and madness (Tarc), of power and vulnerability (Huckaby), of what is inside and out-of-bounds (Rhee). This also includes depicting people and ideas who reside in the uncontained contours of the center and margins as mad, wild, and promiscuous in order to control desires, resistance, counter-movements, and the margins. Containment is dangerous when it is either the center or the periphery trying to maintain its hold.

But promiscuous desires for un/containment also acknowledge the desire to be contained by the very mechanisms that we critique, for that containment might provide momentary respite from the experience of exile. We want our work to be legible but pushing the edges of scholarship; we want collegiality at our institutions, but acceptance for our different ways of being; we want tenure and promotion, but on our own terms; we want to take risks, but not be isolated or ignored; we want to engage in respectful critique of our feminisms but not lose our sense of place in the process. To be promiscuous is to be overwhelmed, perhaps even overcoded by legacy, and simultaneously not fitting-in. As Rhee states we want it "both ways." Or as Daza articulates, we want to be un/contained. There is a wildness to such desires, a madness that wrecks expectations, especially our own. What happens when researchers "can take into account the messiness of not knowing the secret desires or imperatives residing within recognizable forms of thought" (Tarc)? What happens when we exceed not only our material realities but our desires, hopes, and dreams? What the authors in this issue capture is the possibility of possibilities embedded in the desire for, and reality of, un/containment.

Conclusion

> Life does not accommodate you; it shatters you. Every seed destroys its container, or else there would be no fruition. (Scott-Maxwell, 1968)

Drawing on Sandoval (2000), feminist methodology is often misrecognized and underanalyzed when it is translated as a demographic constituency *only* (e.g. confined to gender and gendered issues) and not as theoretical and methodological approach in its own right. The conflation of feminist methodology – understood as a theory, method, practice, and becoming – with the demographic or "descriptive" and generalized category of "women" or "feminist" is not just a textual, metaphorical, or philosophical problem, but, indeed, a political and methodological problem. It depoliticizes and limits the specificity of the politics and ways of living, being, working, and becoming developed by "feminists" but which is not gender-dependent. Promiscuous (use of) feminist methodologies re-politicizes these theoretical and methodological strategies (ways of knowing and naming what is becoming that is embedded in lived practice) beyond gender. This issue is the result of needed collaborations (Subedi & Rhee, 2008) – "many of us speaking at once" – that Behar described in her introduction to *Women Writing Culture* (Behar & Gordon,

1995, p. 13). This collection of feminist anthropology was inspired by Moraga and Anzaldúa's (1984) *This Bridge Called My Back: Writings by Radical Women of Color* and written in direct response to the notable absence of feminism, indigeneity, and race in Clifford and Marcus' (1986) *Writing Culture*:

> *This Bridge* not only called attention to white feminist oversights but also signaled the importance of creating new coalitions among women that would acknowledge differences of race, class, sexual orientation, educational privilege, and nationality. That the divisions between women could be as strong as the ties binding them was a sobering, and necessary, lesson for feminism. Placing *This Bridge Called My Back* side by side on the bookshelf with *Writing Culture*, feminist anthropologists felt the inadequacy of the dichotomies between Subject and Object, Self and Other, the West and the Rest. (pp. 6–7)

Promiscuous (use of) feminist methodologies is a methodology of "differential consciousness" (Sandoval, 2000) in an era of accountability, efficiency, and productivity. It embraces the wild, inefficient and unaccountable, and it engages the consequences of failure differently, through the pleasure and pain of "wanting both ways" (Rhee). So, vulnerability is power (Huckaby), "cheating" on feminism is feminist methodology (Childers), complicity is infiltration (Daza, 2012), herstory is history and philosophy in addition to feminism (Atkinson), and wildness is logical (Tarc). Promiscuity in research is an exposé of the excesses of material life, of secret desires, vulnerabilities, failures, complicities, contaminations, and infiltrations that is the becoming of promiscuous feminist methodologies. Promiscuity is not just about disrupting convention; it is what becomes of the dilemma of writing and being written. It is the re-politization of feminist methodology in the negotiation of desires and material realities.

To practice promiscuous feminist methodology is to attend to paradoxes and aporetic suspensions that comprise it – to want what we cannot want – to fit in, to have a place, to make sense – and to learn to live with such wanting that must not be fulfilled. In the face of un/containment (when material life always already exceeds its boundaries), promiscuous feminist methodology asks what might be our response-ability (Spivak, 1999, 2008) for composing a life (Bateson, 1990) – for improvisation, for combining un/familiar components in response to new situations, for making something in/coherent from conflicting, unexpected elements, and for the displacements that happen when attempting to have it both ways, to be un/contained? As Childers states, for a promiscuous feminist methodology, "its displacement is an investment in its becoming."

Acknowledging that readers have their own investments, we expect different responses to our introduction and the special issue itself. Readers with commitments to certain kinds of feminisms and methodology may feel uncomfortable, because we appear unfaithful and refuse to stay on the map of the field laid out for us. Instead, we are interrogating the map (Lather, 1996). We hope the issue is neither too palatable nor too illegible, which really is what we mean by promiscuous.

This editors' introduction, if we have done our job, lays out how we have come to read our work as promiscuous and puts forth the articulation of promiscuous feminist methodology as a conceptual position with material implications. Next, Rick Voithofer, who served as discussant for our original panel, provides opening remarks for the issue. The opening is followed by the six main manuscripts sequenced in reverse alphabetical order. A postscript by Maggie MacLure, also a discussant on the original panel, concludes the special issue.

As we compiled and edited this issue, we have attempted to disrupt "business as usual" in the academy that overemphasizes competition and hierarchy. Prior to sending the manuscripts out for blind review, all editors and contributors participated in a voluntary internal review process where we read each other's work, provided feedback, and had a larger conversation around the ideas of the issue. This process contributed not only to the development of the editor's introduction and the issue as a whole, but also to other individual and joint conference, writing, and research endeavors among us. With the many types of writing, subject positions, and philosophical orientations brought to bear and the conversations and interruptions equally apparent when read together, there was no one "right" way to sequence the articles. Therefore, reverse alphabetical order was chosen as a way to flatten the power relations between editors and contributors. Lastly, we would like to note that as co-editors we shared equally in writing, editing, and development of the special issue while at the same time acknowledging Sara's conference presentations early on that led to this collaboration and the development of the concept of "promiscuous" before we began.

Acknowledgements

In closing, we would like to thank Aparna, Becky, and Fran for participating in and supporting this different kind of process and intervention in the academy, and Rick and Maggie for thoughtfully and carefully reading our readings of feminist research. We are thrilled to showcase all of this work here. We would also like to acknowledge (in no certain order) folks who have provided encouragement, critique, and labor as friends, mentors, colleagues, and peer reviewers, all of which were integral to this process: Kimini Mayuzumi, Magda Lewis, Chinwe Okpalaoka, Lisa Mazzei, Tasha Smith, Jessi Hitchins, Chloe Brushwood Rose, Bernadette Baker, Crystal Laura, Wanda Pillow, Riyad Shahjahan, Kate McCoy, Alecia Youngblood Jackson, Kathleen Quinlivan, Magda Lewis, Nirmala Erevelles, Lisa Cary, Jerry Rosiek, Roland Sintos Coloma, and Nina Asher.

Notes

1. For example, as we finalized the editor's introduction in January 2013, we became aware of a conference being held at Columbia University, New York, NY, USA in March 2013 entitled "Thinking Feminism at the Limits" which sets out to examine how feminist and queer thinkers are extending feminism beyond the limits of gender analysis. See http://irwag25.com/feminism-at-the-limits for more information.
2. In addition to this introduction, the issue includes Rick Voithofer's opening remarks that offer a close reading of each article. His piece will orient the reader to the wide variety of promiscuous methodologies performed in this issue.
3. When a contributor is cited without a date, we are referring to the contributor's work in this issue.
4. This panel included Childers, Daza, Sophia Sarigianides, Maggie MacLure and Rick Voithofer. We would like to acknowledge Sophia's early contributions to the discussion of this idea.
5. According to Daza, "(Ab)-use" is a term employed by (Spivak, 1999, p. 142, note 43) that roughly translates "to use from below" but not be outside of; it is meant to convey more than simply "abuse" and to be distinct from other attempts to use the Enlightenment critically. According to Spivak, "the Latin prefix 'ab' says much more than 'below.' Indicating both 'motion away' and 'agency, point of origin,' 'supporting,' as well as 'the duties of slaves,' [the (*ab*)-use of European Enlightenment] nicely captures the double bind of the postcolonial and the metropolitan migrant … the public sphere gains and the private sphere constraints of the Enlightenment" (Spivak, 2012, pp. 3–4).
6. In her 1988 essay "Defining Feminist Ethnography," Visweswaran (1994) argues that "the project of feminist ethnography [is] one that continually challenges the very notion

of a canon" (p. 39). Here Visweswaran foreshadows promiscuity in offering "a series of experiments ... for the practice of feminist ethnography" (p. 10). While women and gender remain objects of study, Visweswaran's statement – "if I have not told you anything of the women with whom I worked, I have at least told you something of why it was that I attempted to work with them" – marks an epistemological shift "where gender ceases to hold the center of feminist theory" (pp. 112–113). Visweswaran argues that feminist ethnography based on the failure of feminist thinking and the failure of ethnography's "fieldwork" "will not produce a substantially different (or 'decolonized') ethnography, but a feminist ethnography characterized by 'homework' might" (p. 113). For Visweswaran, the praxis of feminist ethnography is the result of the breaking down of conditions for producing an ethnographic monograph of practice, people, and context before the theoretical essay (p. 11), of when "experience directs us to ask certain questions of theory that theory alone may not enable us to ask" (p. 137). In the concept of "identifying ethnography," she takes up "the difficulties and challenges that arise from being accountable to multiple audiences" (p. 11) as the problem of recognition both in/of genres and subjects (pp. 114–140).

References

Abu-Lughod, L. (1990). Can there be a feminist ethnography? *Women & Performance: A Journal of Feminist Theory, 5*, 7–27.

Abu-Lughod, L. (1991). Writing against culture. In R. Fox (Ed.), *Recapturing anthropology: Working in the present* (pp. 466–479). Santa Fe, NM: School of American Research Press.

Adams, N. G., & Bettis, P. (2003). *Cheerleader!: An American icon*. New York, NY: Palgrave Macmillan.

Alexander, M. J. (2005). *Pedagogies of crossing: Meditations on feminism, sexual politics, memory and the sacred*. Durham, NC: Duke University Press.

Anzaldúa, G. (1987/1999). *Borderlands, La frontera: The new mestiza* (2nd ed.). San Francisco, CA: Aunt Lute Books.

Bateson, M. C. (1990). *Composing a life: Life as a work in progress – the improvisations of five extraordinary women*. New York, NY: A Plum Book.

Bettis, P., & Adams, N. G. (2005). *Geographies of girlhood: Identities in-between*. Mahwah, NJ: Lawrence Erlbaum Associates.

Bhabha, H. K. (1994). *The location of culture*. London: Routledge.

Britzman, D. P. (1986). Cultural myths in the making of a teacher: Biography and social structure in teacher education. *Harvard Educational Review, 56*, 442–457.

Britzman, D. P. (1998). Queer pedagogy and its strange techniques. In J. L. Ristock & C. Taylor (Eds.), *Inside the academy and out: Lesbian/gay/queer studies and social action* (pp. 49–71). Toronto, ON: University of Toronto Press.

Britzman, D. P. (2003). *Practice makes practice: A critical study of learning to teach*. Albany, NY: State University of New York Press.

Britzman, D. P. (2009). *The very thought of education: Psychoanalysis and the impossible professions*. Albany: State University of New York Press.

Britzman, D. P. (2012). What is the use of theory? A psychoanalytic discussion. *Changing English, 19*, 43–56.

Brown, A. (2012). A good investment? Race, philanthrocapitalism and professionalism in a New York City small school of choice. *International Journal of Qualitative Studies in Education, 25*, 375–396.

Butler, J. (2004). *Undoing gender* (eBook). New York, NY: Taylor & Francis/Routledge.

Butler, J. (2011). Remarks on "Queer Bonds". *GLQ: A Journal of Lesbian and Gay Studies, 17*, 381–387.

Calvo, L. (2004). Art comes for the Archbishop: The semiotics of contemporary Chicana feminism and the work of Alma Lopez. *Meridians: Feminism, Race, Transnationalism, 5*, 201–224.

Campbell, N. (2000). *Using women: Gender, drug policy, and social justice*. New York, NY: Routledge.

Childers, S. (2012). Against simplicity, against ethics: Analytics of disruption as quasi-methodology. *Qualitative Inquiry, 18*, 752–761.

Clifford, J., & Marcus, G. E. (1986). *Writing culture: The poetics and politics of ethnography*. Berkeley: University of California Press.

Collins, P. H. (1991/2008). *Black feminist thought: Knowledge, consciousness, and the politics of empowerment*. New York: Routledge.

Coloma, R. S. (2008). Border crossing subjectivities and research: Through the prism of feminists of color. *Race Ethnicity and Education, 11*, 11–27. doi: 10.1080/13613320701845749

Coloma, R. S. (2012). White gazes, brown breasts: Imperial feminism and disciplining desires and bodies in colonial encounters. *Paedagogica Historica, 48*, 243–261. doi: 10.1080/00309230.2010.547511

Cook, J. A., & Fonow, M. (1984). Am I my sister's gatekeeper? Cautionary tales from the academic hierarchy. *Humanity & Society, 8*, 442–452.

Danowitz, M. A., Hanappi-Egger, E., & Mensi-Klarbach, H. (Eds.). (2012). *Diversity in organizations: Concepts and practices*. New York, NY: Palgrave Macmillan.

Daza, S. (2008). Decolonizing researcher authenticity. *Race Ethnicity and Education, 11*, 71–85.

Daza, S. (2009). The noninnocence of recognition: Subjects and agency in education. In R. S. Coloma (Ed.), *Postcolonial challenges in education* (pp. 326–343). New York, NY: Peter Lang.

Daza, S. (2012). Complicity as infiltration: The (im)possibilities of research with/in NSF Engineering Grants in the age of neoliberal scientism. *Qualitative Inquiry, 18*, 773–786.

Denzin, N. K., & Lincoln, Y. S. (2011). *Handbook of qualitative research* (4th ed.). Thousand Oaks, CA: Sage.

Derrida, J. (1997). *Of grammatology* [De la grammatologie]. (Correct ed.). Baltimore, MD: Johns Hopkins University Press.

Dickens, C. S., & Danowitz Sagaria, M. (1997). Feminists at work: Collaboration among women faculty. *Review of Higher Education, 21*, 79–101. Reprinted in J. S. Glazer-Raymo, B. K. Townsend, & B. Ropers-Huilsman (Eds.). (2000). *Women in higher education: A feminist perspective*. Boston, MA: Pearson Custom Publishing.

Dyrness, Andrea. (2011). *Mothers united: An immigrant struggle for socially just education*. Minneapolis, MN: University of Minnesota Press.

Fonow, M., & Cook, J. A. (2005). Feminist methodology: New applications in the academy and public policy. *Signs, 30*, 2211–2236.
Gordon, D. A. (1995). Conclusion: Culture writing women: Inscribing feminist anthropology. In R. Behar & D. A. Gordon (Eds.), *Women writing culture* (pp. 429–441). Berkeley: California University Press.
Harding, S. (1987). Introduction: Is there a feminist method? In S. Harding (Ed.), *Feminism and methodology: Social science issues* (pp. 1–14). Bloomington: Indiana University Press.
Harding, S., & Norberg, K. (2005). New feminist approaches to social science methodologies: An introduction. *Signs, 30*, 2009–2015.
Hesse-Biber, S. N., & Leavy, P. L. (2007). *Feminist research practice*. Thousand Oaks, CA: Sage.
Lather, P. (1986). Research as praxis. *Harvard Educational Review, 56*, 257–278.
Lather, P. (1991). *Getting smart: Feminist research and pedagogy with/in the postmodern*. New York, NY: Routledge.
Lather, P. (1996). Postcolonial feminism in an international frame: From mapping the research to interrogating the mapping. In R. G. Paulston (Ed.), *Social cartography: Mapping ways of seeing education and social change* (pp. 357–373). New York, NY: Garland.
Lather, P. (1997). Validity as incitement to discourse: Qualitative research and the crisis of legitimation. In V. Richardson (Ed.), *Handbook of research on teaching* (4th ed., pp. 241–250). Washington, DC: American Educational Research Association.
Lather, P. (2006). Paradigm proliferation as good to think with: Teaching qualitative research as a wild profusion. *International Journal of Qualitative Studies in Education, 19*, 35–57.
Lather, P. (2007). *Getting lost: Feminist efforts toward a doubled science*. Albany: State University of New York Press.
Lincoln, Y. S. (2010). "What a long, strange trip it's been …": Twenty-five years of qualitative and new paradigm research. *Qualitative Inquiry, 16*, 3–9.
Lincoln, Y. S., & Guba, E. G. (1985). *Naturalistic inquiry*. Beverly Hills, CA: Sage.
Lorde, A. (1984/2007). *Sister outsider: Essays and speeches*. Trumansburg, NY: Crossing Press.
MacLure, M. (2010). The offence of theory. *Journal of Education Policy, 25*, 277–286.
MacLure, M. (2011). Qualitative inquiry: Where are the ruins? *Qualitative Inquiry, 17*, 997–1005.
Matias, C. (2012). Beginning with me: Accounting for a researcher of color's counterstories in socially just qualitative design. *Journal of Critical Thought & Praxis, 1*, 122–143.
Mazur, A. G. (2002). *Theorizing feminist policy*. Oxford: Oxford University Press.
Miller, J. L. (2010). Feminist theories. In *The Sage encyclopedia of curriculum studies* (pp. 371–375). Thousand Oaks, CA: Sage.
Mohanty, C. (2003). *Feminism without borders: Decolonizing theory, practicing solidarity*. Durham, NC: Duke University Press.
Moraga, C., & Anzaldúa, G. (1984). *This bridge called my back: Writings by radical women of color* (1st ed.). Watertown, MA: Persephone Press.
Online Etymology Dictionary. n.d. s.v. "promiscuous." Retrieved October 6, 2012, from Dictionary.com website: http://dictionary.reference.com/browse/promiscuous
Petty, L. (2000). The 'dual'-ing images of la Malinche and la Virgen de Guadalupe in Cisnero's The House on Mango Street. *Melus, 25*, 119–132.
Pillow, W. S. (2000). Deciphering attempts to decipher postmodern educational research. *Educational Researcher, 29*, 21–24.
Pollock, M. (2004). *Colormute: Race talk dilemmas in an American school*. Princeton, NJ: Princeton University Press.
Pratt, M. L. (1993). "Yo soy la Malinche": Chicana writers and the poetics of ethnonationalism. *Callaloo, 16*, 859–873.
Pryse, M. (2000). Trans/feminist methodology: Bridges to interdisciplinary thinking. *NWSA Journal, 12*, 105–118.
Rhee, J.-e. (2008). Risking to be wounded again: Performing open eye/I. *Race Ethnicity and Education, 11*, 29–40.

Sandoval, C. (2000). *Methodology of the oppressed* (Vol. 18). Minneapolis: University of Minnesota Press.
Scott-Maxwell, F. (1968). *The measure of my days*. New York, NY: Penguin Books.
Spivak, G. C. (1993). *Outside in the teaching machine*. New York, NY: Routledge.
Spivak, G. C. (1999). *A critique of postcolonial reason: Toward a history of the vanishing present*. Cambridge, MA: Harvard University Press.
Spivak, G. C. (2012). *An aesthetic education in the era of globalization*. London: Harvard University Press.
St. Pierre, E. A. (2011). Post qualitative research: The critique and the coming after. In N. K. Denzin & Y. S. Lincoln (Eds.), *The Sage handbook of qualitative research* (pp. 611–625). Los Angeles, CA: Sage.
St. Pierre, E., & Pillow, W. (2000). *Working the ruins: Feminist poststructural theory and methods in education*. New York, NY: Routledge.
Subedi, B., & Rhee, J.-e. (2008). Negotiating collaboration across differences. *Qualitative Inquiry, 14*, 1070–1092. doi: 10.1177/1077800408318420
Trinh, T. M.-H. (1989). *Woman, native, other: Writing postcoloniality and feminism*. Bloomington: Indiana University Press.
Tuck, E., & Yang, K. W. (2012). Decolonization is not a metaphor. *Decolonization: Indigeneity, Education & Society, 1*. Retrieved from http://decolonization.org/index.php/des/article/view/18630
Tuhiwai Smith, L. (1999/2012). *Decolonizing methodologies: Research and indigenous peoples*. London: Zed Books.
Villenas, S. (1996). The colonizer/colonized Chicana ethnographer: Identity, marginalization, and co-optation in the field. *Harvard Educational Review, 66*, 711–731.
Visweswaran, K. (1994). *Fictions of feminist ethnography*. Minneapolis: University of Minnesota Press.
Woolf, V. (1922/1992). *Jacob's room*. New York, NY: Penguin Classics.

Promiscuous feminisms for troubling times

Rick Voithofer

Cultural Foundations, Technology, and Qualitative Inquiry, Department of Educational Studies, Ohio State University, Columbus, OH, USA

> Looking across the six articles in this issue, this paper argues that promiscuous uses of feminist methodologies offer a unique constellation of conceptual, pragmatic, material, and ethical strategies with which to understand and engage some of the social and cultural tensions that are occurring within and outside schools. It presents a promiscuous etymology of the word "promiscuous" in which a varied set of definitions provide a backdrop against which to study the project of these six scholars. Seven areas are developed with which to cluster the main themes of the articles including: (1) post-critical, (2) feminisms becoming, (3) productive unease, (4) not bound by gender, but always grounded in gender, (5) always already historical, (6) bodies that still matter, and (7) post-representational. These clusters illustrate how the authors are always becoming, sometimes intentionally and sometimes serendipitously, scholars and women who are willing to reconsider, reposition, reclaim, and rewrite a past, present, and future method, angle perspective, or identity.

Introduction

I had the pleasure, along with Maggie MacLure, to be a discussant at the American Educational Research Association conference in 2010 when Childers and Daza first presented their work on promiscuous uses of feminist methodologies. I was grateful to engage with their scholarship then and was thrilled when they proposed to expand and refine their work and invite other scholars to develop their thoughts on feminist methodologies in a special issue of *QSE*. My goal for this paper will be to pull some common themes from across the six papers that appear in this issue by Tarc, Rhee, Huckaby, Daza, Childers, and Atkinson. It will be one reading of the many possible and equally plausible readings that are thinkable and doable across this scholarship.

One of the first things that you might observe after reading each of these papers is that scholars who use feminist methods promiscuously resist any easy definitions or fixing characterizations. As some of them noted, they are always becoming, sometimes intentionally and sometimes serendipitously, scholars and women who are willing to reconsider, reposition, reclaim, and rewrite a past, present, and future approach, angle perspective, or identity. They are scholars always already working in the ruins of feminisms, Marxism, the science wars, the philosophical debates between and within post-structuralism and positivism, the crisis of representation, the limits (and always present possibilities) of gender, and identity politics driven by the curiosities of the material world that have changed before the latest interview, observation, and data point is recorded for analysis. These scholars show that ambiguity, contingency and ambivalence can be productive, and, in fact, needed at this historical moment.

Troubling times

Educational researchers in 2013 must confront a number of social and cultural dynamics in US schools that are occurring in the context of a host of financial, pedagogical, social, and cultural tensions. For example, the rate of ethnic and racial diversification among teachers is not keeping pace with the increasing diversity in student populations, creating the potential for a growing number of sociocultural and educational disconnects between teachers and their students. To address the ever-present financial pressures on public schools, the privatization of public education made possible by the national common core students is in the midst of a process that will transform education across all levels in the coming years. The private sector is gearing up to target a K16 market that comprises 9% of the US gross domestic product. Educational researchers must study what kinds of accountability this privatization will bring as the desire to cut costs and raise profits becomes a louder discourse in education. Who will be disadvantaged when the threat of profitability creates systemic cracks for students to fall through as new and dangerous forms of meritocracy, tracking, and neglect arise?

Across broader contexts, women's reproductive and healthcare rights are still under attack from various segments of society. The nuclear family has become a fading myth that is being replaced by other more fluid and diverse family structures that can be equally nurturing and supportive environments to raise children, but that need to be better understood and articulated to educators who must meet students at the lives that they actually lead rather than lives that they might imagine their students to lead.

This is a time of the myth of logocentric certainty where social, cultural, economic, and environmental problems are invested with technical solutions, where STEM subjects (Science, Technology, Engineering, and Math) have been anointed as the solution to many of the social, economic, educational, and environmental problems that society is confronting. The myopic attention to STEM, to the detriment of the humanities and the arts, has led to a vicious cycle in which the blind spots of humanity, those unconscious and unacknowledged places in the human psyche, construct a false certainty that creates a fragile foundation on which to build solutions to the material suffering that is occurring.

How will educational researchers respond to these existing dynamics and possible futures? How will feminist researchers adapt to the hostilities that they will likely encounter as they name the ethical, material, and discursive transgressions that they will bear witness to in their scholarship? Promiscuous uses of feminist methodologies offer a number of conceptual, pragmatic, material, and ethical strategies with which to engage a range of important issues in troubling times.

This raises the question of how are promiscuous uses of feminist methods different from other feminist interventions and perspectives like queer theory, hybridity, interdisciplinarity, and intersectionality. The answer to that question is complex because all of these perspectives intersect and co-create one another in ways that are situated for a particular inquiry. In that spirit I will locate a response within the limited conceptual space of this paper.

Being promiscuous is not tied to any specific intervention; it benefits, however, from the theoretic, methodological, and political work that all feminist methodologies have undertaken. For example, promiscuous uses of feminist methods are closely related to queer theory, which destabilizes social categories like gender and renders their normativity visible (Butler, 1990, 1993). They are inherently consistent with intersectionality, which traces its origins to Black feminist scholars and studies how social and cultural categories like class, sexuality, race, and gender interact to construct subtle and overt forms of oppression (Crenshaw, 1989, 1991). Being promiscuous accepts as a given that subject positions like gender are constructed; that oppression can be identified and addressed at the intersections of difference; that hybrid spaces between identity constructions are places to create agency; that physical, conceptual, and methodological border crossings are routine; and that feminist research is always already interdisciplinary and working the ruins of past and emerging frameworks.

Negotiating these spaces promiscuously shifts the conversation to commitments that lie within the material lives of research participants and researchers, instead of adherence to particular frameworks, methods, or theories. To begin illuminating and endarkening (Dillard, 2000) these strategies, I undertake a promiscuous reading of the word "promiscuous" in the following section.

Divining "promiscuous"

Promiscuous is a provocative word. Most commonly it is a label given to someone who is undiscriminating in sexual relations. While no word is culturally neutral, without an evolving set of definitions and connotations, this one in particular carries a distinctly strong cultural charge in US culture, traditionally more negative when it is applied to women, compared to when it is used to label men. Yet, the etymology of promiscuous reveals a much more nuanced and varied set of definitions that provide a suitable backdrop against which to study the project of these six scholars and the broader work that they are gesturing toward.

Following this etymology I decided to do a promiscuous reading of the OED definition of promiscuous (Oxford University Press, 1989). A promiscuous reading is more closely tied to the current context of the word than to a rigid adherence to static definitions. It is undertaken with the awareness that the OED epitomizes the apex of Eurocentric, paternalistic, and static representations of the English language.

The first definition of "Promiscuous" in the OED states:

(1) (a) Done or applied with no regard for method, order, etc.; random, indiscriminate, and unsystematic.
 (b) Of an agent or agency: making no distinctions; undiscriminating.
 (c) Of a person or animal: undiscriminating in sexual relations. Also (of sexual intercourse, relationships, etc.): casual, characterized by frequent changes of sexual partner.

While (c) offers the most widely used definition of promiscuous, (a) and (b) reveal a word that can be used to modify a number of research components that should be considered. Social science research is defined by a set of structuring methods that work towards establishing the authority of a research study, most often ensuring some form of reliability, trustworthiness, and validity. The justification for promiscuous methodologies may appear at first to be random, indiscriminate, or unsystematic. This, however, is a strategic position by the researcher to highlight other priorities beyond a strict logocentrism. The second definition (b) suggests the concern of many feminist researchers to address issues of equity, while engaging in the tricky and contingent nature of equity, without drawing hard lines (i.e. discriminating) between social and culture categories (i.e. male/female, urban/non-urban, privileged/under-represented, agential/suppressed, and material/discourse). Finally, (c) notes a frequent change in sexual partners. As can be seen in these six papers, these scholars do not adhere to some monogamous fiction in their relationships with feminisms, they continuously change partners (e.g. methods, theories, assumptions, and questions) in order to serve their deep ethical commitments.

> (2) Consisting of assorted parts or elements grouped or massed together without order; mixed and disorderly in composition or character; (with plural noun) of various kinds mixed together.

Based on its most static definition, the goal of research is to bring (impose) order onto some aspect of a chaotic and multi-dimensional world. Learning, for example, is a profoundly complex process complicated by social, cultural, and cognitive factors with an almost infinite number of "independent" and "dependent" variables. Promiscuous uses of feminist methodologies acknowledge this complexity by not trying to tame and discipline understandings and representations of learning, but by highlighting and at times celebrating, its limits and limitations. This does not mean the traditional practice of pointing out the limits of a study against some notion of validity or reliability, but instead a promiscuous methodology discovers the most interesting findings within its limitations.

> (3) Of common gender; of either sex, of both sexes.
> (4) That forms part of a mixed or undifferentiated company.
> (5) Casual, careless.

Feminist scholarship has been at the center of thought that questions the false binaries around gender, sex, and sexuality. A promiscuous treatment of gender as demonstrated in these papers, applies the deconstruction of gender to other social categories like race. Definitions 3 and 4 suggest this capacity. Some scholars who evaluate these promiscuous uses of feminist methodologies may attribute a careless or casual approach to methodology and theory as expressed by definition 5. They should not, however, confuse a willingness to shift theories, methods, political commitments, research questions, and findings at any point of a study with a lack of commitment or care – quite the opposite. This willingness to adapt promiscuously is the willingness to appear casual, and possibly enduring the social stigmas that come with that, while strengthening commitments that may fall outside the acceptable discourses of the academy or even particular forms of feminism.

> (6) (a) Of a protein, organism, etc.: able to infect or interact with, or bind non-specifically to, a variety of hosts or targets.

(b) *Genetics*. Designating a DNA sequence common to more than one of the genomes within a eukaryotic cell.

While rarely used, this final definition of promiscuous is related to particular biological mechanisms including the capacity of certain organisms to engage with a variety of other organisms. On a cellular level, promiscuous gene expression refers to the capacity of some bacteria to inherit a part of their genetic code from different distant relatives and even other species of bacteria. Within feminist methodologies and philosophies, there is not a clean and clear lineage and progression of thought. As can be seen from the authors in this issue, each scholar has assembled a historical and conceptual bricolage of feminist thinking. Some lineages are clear, while others assemble their DNA from both distant and current codes.

In the following section, I will look more closely at the work of Tarc, Rhee, Huckaby, Daza, Childers, and Atkinson as the foundation for trying to uncover some of the genetic code and assembled DNA that make up these promiscuous uses of feminist methodologies.

Clusters, codes, and codifications

In what follows, I identify some of the conceptual clusters that emerge across the six papers. These clusters are by no means exhaustive, nor mutually exclusive. I will begin with a brief sketch of each author's thesis and then show how these papers fit within seven broad categories that can be associated with aspects of promiscuous feminist perspectives.

Drawing on her research in a high-performing, high-poverty urban public school, Childers develops a portrait of the ways that race is silenced and fixed within this setting. She overcomes an initial reticence to shift away from gender, inspired by a renewed commitment to materialism. Revisiting the life and scholarship of Jane Addams, a feminist pragmatist philosopher, Atkinson discovers the conflicting and conflicted spaces between the life lived and the life represented (through her scholarship) by Addams. Like Childers, she finds a way to reconcile them through a new feminist materialism. Entering the realm of federal grants, difference, and policy, Daza maps the ways that the practice of diversity policies within scientific discourses petrifies the most well-intentioned policy aims around diversity in the STEM fields. Situating herself within her own post-colonial history and identity, Rhee calls upon a promiscuous feminist methodology in order to move between her commitments as a feminist researcher and her desire to have her research be recognized by peer reviewers, despite the violent epistemic apartheid that exists between these often conflicting discourses. Huckaby shows how "relations of vulnerability" grounded in post-structural theories of power are a fertile ground for black feminists who remain deeply connected with their biological and cultural foremothers. Tarc illustrates how "wild reading," the primal sense of wonder and dependence that an infant first experiences as she navigates her most fundamental desires with her mother's response, provides a foundational experience that can be accessed during subsequent readings and authorings of all texts including research. She argues that fiction can function as an important genre to represent the complex unknown and unknowable interactions between the unconscious and conscious.

While there are inevitable overlaps, I have clustered the promiscuous feminisms presented by these scholars within seven areas: (1) post-critical, (2) feminisms becoming, (3) productive unease, (4) not bound by gender, but always grounded in gender, (5) always already historical, (6) bodies that still matter, and (7) post-representational.

Post-critical

There are various responses and correctives that have been offered to address the limitations of critical theory in its assorted incarnations. Discussing the evolution of critical and post-critical approaches to research, Lather observes:

> As critical practices derive their forms and meanings in relation to their changing historical conditions, positions of resistance can never be established once and for all. They must, instead be perpetually refashioned to address the shifting conditions and circumstances that ground them. (Lather, 1992, p. 121)

Following this reasoning, a post-critical perspective is one that engages promiscuously with critical theory and its offshoots in order to acknowledge the material histories and realities of research participants while anticipating that these histories and materialities flow and change within the problematic nature of resistance, without abandoning the possibility that resistance can make positive and material changes in lives.

Both Daza and Childers position their papers as post-critical. Daza situates herself as a "post-critical-feminist-ethnographer of color" who understands culture as an ongoing negotiation and her ethnographic work as a continuous process of unpacking, "the complex social, political, and historical relationships that undergird policy outcomes." Childers on the other hand suggests a post-critical feminist perspective allowed her, within her whiteness, to situate the representation of race in her study as a stuck place and still "trouble voice, agency, and emancipatory goals to move beyond constructions of essentialized, romanticized subjects." For her this involved engaging in a doubled move that entailed her both doing the research, despite a number of tensions, while also troubling the research process. From this post-critical feminist perspective, she did not shy away from partial, complicated, and nuanced representations of the narratives that she collected.

As part of this post-critical perspective, these scholars are developing new perspectives based on renewed feminist commitments to materialism that give equal footing to the discursive and the material, the ontological and the epistemological. Inspired by Barad (2006), Childers and Atkinson both considered a "new feminist materialism." According to Barad, objects do not precede interactions; they are a result of interactions; agency is a relationship; and scientific work is always ethical and political. Eschewing the division between material and discourse, she describes an agential realism in which human and non-human interact and exert their own agency through interactions. A consistent theme throughout these papers is that when feminists engage in the materiality of their research subject they, "move promiscuously through and beyond gender." As Childers concludes: "Qualitative inquiry, be it feminist or otherwise, is an engagement with the material, and yet due to the crisis of representation there has been a privileging of how representations are pure discursive constructions of power and knowledge."

Feminisms becoming

Promiscuous feminisms are always becoming. The concept of "becoming" has been a common thread in the life's work of Deleuze and one that many feminist scholars, including some in this issue, have found productive. According to Deleuze, when elements (e.g. individuals, words, objects, and places) come together (i.e. an assemblage) in a context (e.g. research site, academic paper, policy, etc.), something new always occurs – they are always becoming. Becoming is open-ended and emergent in space and time, an ontology of transformation and change. Deleuze developed the concept as a way to, "overturn philosophy's traditional 'dogmatic image of thought' and to open up new pathways down which thinking and living can travel" (May, 2003, p. 151). Despite the protests that some feminists have leveled at his notion of becoming-women in "A thousand plateaus" (Butler, 1987; Jardine, 1986), it remains a productive concept to frame the always, already changing nature of gender, research, race, equity, etc. Childers captures this perspective when she observes that "feminist research as a site of promiscuous becoming."

Grappling with the complex history and philosophy of Jane Addams, Atkinson concluded that:

> We who read and engage her life and work today see how she is still becoming, a becoming that challenges us to think about our own becomings – becomings in which we are all entangled that compel us to deliberate on how we become.

Here, Atkinson points out a central dynamic within an individual becoming, a conceptual becoming, or a methodological become – all becomings are interconnected, rhizomatic. Thus, in rewriting Addams' history, the histories that are written about her are always deeply influenced by the historian's methodological and personal becomings. The historian and history are always promiscuously co-created.

In her paper, Daza positions policy as becoming. She notes, "policy is not simply a document or a directive but a living practice of ongoing interpretation." She warns that when policies become fixed within disciplining discourse (e.g. technocratic) they may at the least be ineffective and at worst work against their own aim. Citing the NSF's stated policy on social justice, she warns that, "technocratic worlding of grant-science and STEM's culture of neoliberal scientism may persist in spite of NSF's social justice policies that contradict or at least complicate them." Instead she argues for a policy of becoming where:

> The contours of imaginaries through which policy is mis/interpreted are made visible but without fully formulating, determining, or justifying policy practice. In this way, irony (complicities, contaminations, contradictions) and uncertainty give way to the possibility of being otherwise that more chaste approaches to knowledge production – those that would avoid and deny uncertainty – do not.

Productive unease

All of these authors in one way or another demonstrate a productive unease with aspects of feminisms, their positionality, and their research site and methods. Some of the authors like Daza and Rhee started their papers with a conflict that they identified within their research site or within themselves. Accepting a history of certain exclusions in white feminisms, Daza is able to situate herself as feminist of color " – that has always already been colonized by feminisms." She goes on to say, "I am 'outside' but also complicit within grant-science so that my decolonizing struggle continues but in different ways." She is complicit in that she is part of an NSF grant that is driven by neo-liberal policies that value, "accounting, efficiency, austerity, utility, and measured effectiveness," values that often contradict her commitments to studying equity issues relevant to women of color. The change in focus allows her to advocate for a "promiscuous science" that decolonizes the certainty and containment of science. One specific way she suggests that can take place is by making visible, as she does in her paper, the power relations of the world of grants and science.

As a feminist of color, Huckaby must contend with the unease produced by both the legacies of paternalism and racism that often diverge from the struggles of white feminists and black men. Given this history of exclusion and discrimination against black women, some might think it would be easy for her to narrow her political commitments and theoretical leanings, yet she finds it necessary to utilize male continental philosophers like Foucault, scholars who neither paid attention to gender, nor race, to theorize power. In the process of doing this she rejects certain feminist concepts of power, instead asserting that an idea like Foucault's power/knowledge, "is more useful in theorizing actions in the world than conceptions of power as invested in certain kinds of bodies (e.g. white, male) more so than other bodies (e.g. black, female)."

As Childers' data started to point her attention towards the racial inequities that she found at her research site, she initially experienced ambivalence about diverting her focus from gender and more promiscuously applying feminist theories and methods toward race and policy, particularly in light of her being white. She wondered, "… was I cheating on feminism?" She found resolution through the feminist commitment to paying attention to the materiality of her participants and the research context. Later in her paper she writes:

> The very debates in feminist research that pushed me away from studying the effects of racial inequity in schools, also became useful in bringing me back. Once the materiality of the field drove me back to confronting race and dealing with my outsider position, it was also feminist work that held my feet to the fire.

Rhee invokes the Aesop parable of the bat that is neither bird, nor beast to illustrate the tensions that emerge as she navigates the performative spaces of the academy and other performative geographies defined by various hybridities and third spaces (e.g. non-white, non-native English speaker). In the parable, the bat, questioned by both the bird and beast about its identity, asserts that it is neither bird, nor beast, but bat. Confronting her desire to be a bat, bird, and beast, Rhee must consider the pressure to live in the dark cave of shame because she wants to "have it both ways." She reconciles that she not only is the dutiful daughter (in-law), she is a bat to feminism, concluding, "The Beast and the Bird are defined through each other. Their boundary is regulated by both rejecting a Bat."

Not bound by gender, but always grounded in gender

Researchers and their participants are always in some ways informed by their gendered histories, physical experiences, and performances. Feminist theorizing has explored the complex ways that gender informs the lived experiences of various gender identifications and constructions. Over the course of this history, feminist scholars have mapped how women share divergent and convergent experiences that are grounded in the ways that their gendered identities are positioned within social discourses and contexts and the choices that they make in relationship to those positionings. Often these histories deviate when they intersect with race, class, ability, ethnicity, sexuality, etc. Sometimes they converge as they navigate the social demands on their bodies when they are reduced to reproductive entities. Divergences and convergences, however, are never predetermined or fixed because they are always situated, contingent, and fluid. Used promiscuously, gender becomes a metaphor for the ways that aspects of an individual's identity are invested with a false sense of stability and containment.

Within these papers, gender, in this metaphorical guise, functions as the beginning point for the researchers in this issue, as well as a resting place to return to in the midst of writing and research that can, at times, be unsettling for the authors. All of the authors make explicit references to their training as feminist scholars. Some aspect of gender always informs a feminist scholar. A promiscuous feminist scholar, on the other hand, is never structured by this attention to gender. For promiscuous feminists, gender becomes the signifier for social and cultural power differentials, for fluid and hybrid identity construction, for histories that are always being (re)written, and for the lived, embodied, and material experiences of individuals and groups across all contexts.

This treatment of gender can be clearly seen across these papers. Atkinson chooses to contextualize some of the choices that Addams makes that appear to reinforce gender inequities in light of the time in which she lived and her broader personal and ethical commitments. In this move, she promiscuously troubles the false binary of feminist/non-feminist. Similarly, Huckaby embraces male, continental scholars like Foucault, to theorize power despite the fact that, "Foucault's work rarely attends to gender." Following Spivak's lead, she takes a more strategic approach and chooses theories and methods based on how they support her project rather than basing it on the gender or geography of origin. She takes it one step further and notes that not only is continental philosophy a resource for black feminists to understand power and agency, but, "black feminism is equally its resource." Her promiscuous use of European post-structuralists illustrates the dynamic bidirectional process of theory building.

Always already historical

Historicizing research contexts, questions, participants, methods, and theories has been a consistent commitment of feminists who have worked to (re)claim and (re)write histories that were often never written or were grossly distorted. Promiscuous feminists maintain this commitment. All six papers are deeply grounded in the histories of women, of the authors, of power, and of inequity. Perhaps, what distinguishes their approach to history is the urgency with which they highlight the process of always reclaiming and rewriting history as part of the scholarly writing process. One clear example of this is the psychoanalytic approach to reading and writing offered by Tarc.

According to Tarc, the first history written by an individual comes "from the infant's first reading of (m)other." In other words, history is first unconscious and pre-discursive. She argues this space is one place that women can write themselves back into histories in which they have been excluded. These promiscuous histories are, "intimate, libidinal, abject, and excessive." From this psychoanalytic perspective, history is structured by unruly and secret desire. "The primal scene of reading founds every subsequent scene of thinking/writing."

Huckaby recounts that many early black feminists in the USA were engaged with recovering the histories and cultural productions of black people and women. In recreating this history and (re)creating the complexity of the identities of black women who work both for black liberation and gender equality produced by deep historical oppression, she observes that while the experience of black women is central to a black feminist project, she warns of the dangers of relying solely on experience as evidence of truth. She cautions that this practice "is dangerous, particularly for marginalized groups." The danger comes from the use of experience to reify unequal power relations (e.g. white privilege) and social groups as natural and real, rather than discursively constructed.

Bodies that still matter

The experience, construction, positioning, movement, representation, and reclamation of the body are at the center of feminist ontologies and epistemologies. Feminist research is never disembodied. Promiscuous uses of feminist theories reinforce and revisit the importance of the body by considering it both as an ontological touchstone and as a discursive construction.

As pointed out by Atkinson, bodies and particularly women's bodies matter and continue to matter to feminist researchers. She asserts citing Barad that the woman's body matters as a phenomenon to understand the ways that ontology cannot be separated from various forms of agency that are produced by interactions of multiple material and discursive practices. Looking at Addams' philosophy, Atkinson praised her scholarship for its capacity to show the embodied and material experiences of women and families suffering as a result of an industrial economy and noted that these experiences cannot be untangled from ideological, psychical, and physical pressures. The suffering that she documented transcended philosophical and theoretical hand-wringing. Speaking of the research that she conducted with Korean immigrants, Rhee comes to a similar conclusion:

> This was not about the crisis of representation, failure of Enlightenment project, or a discursive discussion on human agency. The task was to face squarely every day structural-physical hunger, pain, and exhaustion of other immigrants within the complete inability of science and research.

Arguing against a harsh disembodied rationalism, Tarc's "wild reading" allows feminist writers to break out of phallogocentric structures, to write in ways that are, "less or differently rational and incoherent" to find new forms of representation. According to Tarc, an individual's sense-making capacity begins in infancy when she interacts with her mother's body for food and comfort. During this "first reading" the infant must find a way to relate to her mother in the midst of often dire, violent and primal needs, desires, and drives. In the process, the infant begins to learn the differences between the inner and outer world. This relationship between two people at vastly different levels of development is the basis for the bodies' most deeply held understandings and, according to Tarc, is the foundation for all other understandings and relations in a person's life. Even after the child learns how to separate from her mother by learning to speak and then to name, the separation is an illusion, because all understandings are based in some need of others. Tarc concludes:

Each time we struggle to make meaning of something difficult we are reminded of our need. Our need of the other is embedded in the formation of the self even while language (of self) gives us the illusion of separateness, of sovereignty.

Similarly, Huckaby shows how the relational vulnerabilities can be productive sources of agency.

Breaking the false binary of strength (e.g. action) and vulnerability (e.g. inaction), Huckaby takes a promiscuous turn to show how the vulnerability of the body provides a unique position for the researcher to build understandings. She goes further, invoking Butler, to say that vulnerability does not mean lacking in power:

> Vulnerability is an openness to being affected by others and also affecting others in ways that are not simply negative, but also positive. Unfortunately, the quest for power and more power only produces (pro-ducere) a negative, undesirable vulnerability. But as a condition of potential, other conditions are possible because of vulnerability – suffering, harm, love, pleasure. These are conditions that both limit and enable.

Post-representational

All of the scholars in this edition position their work within a post-representational world that exists in the shadow of the crisis of representation in research in which the capacity of research to represent a world that is inherently unstable, fluid, and therefore unrepresentable in any definitive way is questioned. This crisis brought about the linguistic turn in which it was asserted that the world can never be known directly, it can only be approximated through discursive constructions. In other words, research cannot exist outside of one or more signifying systems. The disengagement of the chain between experience and the representation of experience questions the foundational assumptions of research and presents a host of challenges with which promiscuous uses of feminisms are equipped to grapple.

In this final section, I would like to return to the original premise of this paper that promiscuous uses of feminist theories and methods are uniquely equipped to address the many complications that are being presented to researchers committed to achieving a measure of equity in these troubling times. One social movement that has navigated the challenges of political action in a post-representational world is the global Occupy Wall Street Movement (OWS or simply Occupy movement). According to Tormey:

> Liberal-democracy is being hollowed out by the growth of often-unaccountable global institutions and processes, such as the IMF, the World Bank and most recently the bond markets. In this sense, OWS is not just a gesture in opposition to representation. It is a gesture marking the slow yet seemingly inexorable collapse of representative democratic governance as a practice and as the paradigmatic 'end of history'. Representative governance is, on the contrary, increasingly seen as complicit in the emptying out of democracy, and in the perpetuation of gross inequalities. OWS is part of the generalised revolt against representation. (Tormey, 2012, p. 136).

Each author in her own way enacted a unique revolt against representation in the face of the inequities that she represented.

According to Tarc, the limits of words and representation can be attributed, in part, to the limits of language and conscience to bring meaning. She advises: "We ought to attend to and bear our uncertainties in interpreting the world rather than rush too quickly to name our feelings for others and objects," suggesting that researchers engage in wild readings and interpretations that are grounded in primal interdependence rather than "systematic" writing that disavows the person's first act of sense making.

Childers and Atkinson demonstrate how in a post-representational world the discursive and material are co-created. Childers concludes that feminist methodologies must became promiscuous so that they can, "circulate and infiltrate across boundaries" in order to interact with the materialities of the world. Atkinson shows how even the representations of histories are becomings in which the materiality of the history is always interacting with the discursive representation of that history and that these interactions are enmeshed with each person's becomings that compel individuals in their various identities and roles to reflect on how they come to be.

Huckaby identifies the shared vulnerabilities of embodied lives that offer a common representational gesture away from the impossibilities of representations, even if those lives can never be known. This gesture of vulnerability sidesteps the representational in order to open the possibility for other conditions that both limit and enable in ways that often cannot be controlled. Similarly, Rhee reconciles her promiscuous desire to be bird, bat, and beast, by patiently and persistently hacking the representational fixity of all three. To continually break them apart and reconstitute them, she must constantly find new seams in which to suture them together, rather than living in the well-established chasms that separate them.

Challenging the presentational certainty of grant-science and neoliberal ideology through positivism and technoscience, Daza presents a way to map the "complicities, contaminations, contradictions" of policy "through the prism of a feminist imaginary, [that] also has the potential to be promiscuous. Promiscuous (feminist) ethnography maps the contours of worlding in such a way that both containment and uncertainty are revealed."

Conclusion

The promiscuous feminist scholars in this issue work within the performative spaces of research, academics, and the various roles and identities that they have as women – mothers, daughters, granddaughters, women of color, etc. They do not, however, allow the expectations of these subject positions to confine and define them. All of the scholars in this issue have made productive the overlaps and border crossings in which they work and live. Reconstituting the once/still pejorative term "promiscuous" Daza notes, "Promiscuous feminism(s) is not the denial or death of feminism but rather setting its legacy to work."

Moving forward, it is important to point out the limits of the materiality of the journal and academic publishing process in relationship to the work of these six scholars in particular and to promiscuous uses of feminist methodologies in general. From the moment that these authors pressed "save" for the last time when writing these papers so many months ago, the thoughts, ideas, and arguments in this form of representation congealed as the authors continued to promiscuously develop their ideas. The conditions of academic publishing do not allow for documents that are constantly being rewritten. Instead, there are mechanisms for citational tracing in place that enforce a rigid intertextuality between scholarly works. These mechanisms are hostile to the ideas being presented here in that they are grounded in deep and fluid interactional, contextual, temporal, embodied, and contingent landscapes. The promiscuous turn, however, offers a response to this dilemma because the individual text or groups of texts, in this case, are always, already being rewritten through your becomings as a reader. What the assemblages of these six scholars have accomplished is to provide you with a set of maps, that do not show you where to look, but suggest ways to reflect on how to look as you become.

References

Barad, K. M. (2006). *Meeting the universe halfway: Quantum physics and the entanglement of matter and meaning.* Durham, NC: Duke University Press.
Butler, J. (1987). *Subjects of desire: Hegelian reflections in twentieth century France.* New York, NY: Columbia University Press.
Butler, J. (1990). *Gender trouble: Feminism and the subversion of identity.* New York, NY: Routledge.
Butler, J. (1993). *Bodies that matter: On the discursive limits of 'sex'.* New York, NY: Routledge.
Crenshaw, K. (1989). Demarginalizing the intersection of race and sex: A black feminist critique of antidiscrimination doctrine, feminist theory, and antiracist politics. *University of Chicago Legal Forum, 14*, 538–554.
Crenshaw, K. (1991). Mapping the margins: Intersectionality, identity politics, and violence against women of color. *Stanford Law Review, 43*, 1241–1299.
Dillard, C. (2000). The substance of things hoped for, the evidence of things not seen: Examining an endarkened feminist epistemology in educational research and leadership. *International Journal of Qualitative Studies in Education, 13*, 661–681.
Jardine, A. (1986). *Gynesis: Configurations of woman and modernity.* Ithaca, NY: Cornell University Press.
Lather, P. (1992). Post-critical pedagogies: A feminist reading. In C. Luke & J. Gore (Eds.), *Feminisms and critical pedagogy* (pp. 120–137). New York, NY: Routledge.
May, T. (2003). When is a Deleuzian becoming? *Continental Philosophy Review, 36*, 139–153.
Oxford University Press. (1989). *Oxford English dictionary.* Oxford: Oxford University Press.
Tormey, S. (2012). Occupy Wall Street: From representation to post-representation. *Journal of Critical Globalisation Studies, 5*, 132–137.

Wild reading: this madness to our method

Aparna Rita Mishra Tarc

Faculty of Education, York University, Toronto, ON, Canada

> My paper theorizes the possibilities of a qualitative method that engages with promiscuous aspects of human existence and difference foreclosed by established research methods and representations. I locate the not known of knowledge in the unconscious time of the maternal relation where the infant is put upon to wildly and without symbolic resources make sense of others and the world around her. Engaging with the "wild" aspects of interpretation can provide us with an analytical space to forge a sustained inquiry into suppressed desires producing dominant representations of human existence. I look to J.M. Coetzee's short story, "The Humanities in Africa," as a text that might support feminist researchers' unorthodox efforts to commune with the less rational processes of thinking and being driving representation. Reflexive to what remains unthought in our representations of knowledge, we might develop new modes of analysis that are open to unconventional and unorthodox research orientations and methods.

Blame it or praise it, there is no denying the wild horse in us. (Virginia Woolf)

In an interview conducted by Francois Ewald entitled "A certain madness must watch over thinking," Jacques Derrida articulates an incredible insight: one's reasonable means of faithfully representing the world defend against unfathomable dimensions of human thought and action. Derrida (1995) suggests that the "scientific" methods underlying normative humanistic inquiries are oriented towards disavowing what Woolf (1922/1992) claims is "the wild horse in us" (p. 123). He further argues that empiricism masks irrational dimensions of thought in the scholar's account of the world and others. "As with reason, a certain madness," Derrida (1995) insists, stalks our[1] efforts for truthful representation and threatens to undo the presumed coherence of normalized narratives of human life (p. 291).

The suggestion that our knowledge accounts contain the "wild horse" and mask our illicit desire for self and others gives scholars, researchers, and social actors some pause and has been the source of division in educational research (Denzin, 1994; Lather, 2004, 2006; Wright, 2006). My article grapples with this problem of interpretation through psychoanalytic and postcolonial theories of subject formation.

It theorizes the possibilities of a qualitative method committed to acknowledging the effects of the "promiscuous" aspects of human existence and difference that defy easy representation. Interpretation, in my paper, describes the complex frameworks of intelligibility supporting one's capacities to symbolize and represent a particular understanding of the world. Ragged psychical processes of interpretation find "seamless" symbolic form in our representations of the world and others (Cameron, 2012). A close analysis of the "wild" practices of interpretation constructing representations of the other's life can provide educational qualitative researchers with a method of inquiry into the conflicted logics driving normative, intelligible, and categorical representations of human existence.

Wild in my paper refers to unruly, passionate dimensions of interpretive practice effaced in dominant representations accounting for sentient life and external realities. As an adjective, promiscuous is used to diminish openly sexual and sexualized bodies and expression. In Western ontology, wildness is associated with the primordial and is used to describe and demean the existence of animals, women, children, and non-normative and/or racialized others (Haraway, 1991; Spivak, 1999). Feminist scholars have recently reclaimed promiscuity as a defiant stance against female and other sexualized bodies diminished by the term (Attwood, 2007; Ringrose, 2012). Along with a general understanding that wildness accompanies our every attempt to interpret, I argue that inner unwieldy feelings of aggression and hatred can be projected out onto the bodies of those we study and examine. I theorize promiscuity as a quality of human existence that paradoxically manifests in creative *and* destructive forms of thinking and action. Following Freud (1930/1989), I suggest that wild thoughts interfere with our efforts to forge a "civil" social response to the world and others. A wildness held tightly within requires acknowledgment, expression, and containment in order for the self to exist well with others. To recover the promiscuous in my work, then, is not limited to an act of defiance or a struggle for power for female and/or dehumanized bodies. Rather than celebrating or disparaging the wildness of our thought or projecting it onto the bodies of others, we might learn to compassionately harness this potentially creative and destructive aspect of human capacity and relation. To recover promiscuity is to repair the damage done to human existence demeaned by the term and to revitalize its force as a source of thinking and acting. My work also reclaims passionate qualities of human existence to uphold the maternal, base conditions of sentient existence grounding human experience and reality. With a return to the unconscious dimensions of the maternal relation as the grounds of subject formation and social and political life, my paper highlights the role promiscuity plays or might play in our interpretations of others and the world. Through the development of analytical, self-reflexive, and deparochialized interpretive practices, we might begin to do justice to representations of our objects of enquiry and in doing so learn to manage and "live with" our wild readings of ourselves and others (Butler, 2005).

In this paper, I turn to the work of particular literature to explore highly charged spaces of libidinal desire and fantasy lurking in dominant and legitimized representations of human life and others. I suggest that primal, libidinal desires for others affect what we imagine are "objective" interpretations and representations of the other's lived reality. The poetic methods and affective language of literature seem more adept at engaging what social scientific method seems unwilling to address: the messier, unruly aspects of human interiority and its distorting symbolic effects. With literary devices and sharp analysis the novels of Woolf, for example, remarkably depict the conflicted mind in the process of thinking when faced with the fact of the other's existence. As I demonstrate, researchers' engagements with the methods of literature, psychoanalysis, and literary criticism have implications for social science research: literary engagements might supplement the researcher's efforts to qualify the other's inner processes of teaching, learning, and being.

An unascertainable wildness, then, accompanies one's attempt to represent one's sense of the world to others. The methods of social science work to silence affect through appeals to the possibility of achieving objectivity. Along with offering the development of a trained practice of close and analytic reading, literature can provide educational researchers with much needed insight into unconscious dimensions of knowledge production. Along this vein, the first section of my paper explicates the notion of wild reading through the psychical and intersubjective mechanism of projective identification. I suggest that an affective capacity to make identification and to project our feelings of ambivalence for others on the "reality" of differently situated others makes interpretive practice difficult when studying human subjects. To support my theoretical claim that wild reading is an unacknowledged dimension of both ordinary and scholarly interpretive practice, in the third section of the paper I turn to a fictional account to reconstruct the interpretive dynamics at play in the scholarly arguments on the human and humanism adopted by two fictional sisters depicted in Coetzee's (2003) short story "The Humanities in Africa." In this story, the sisters wage conflicting positions on the "true" nature of humanity through a "reasoned" debate on the role that the humanistic sciences and their methods have played in the "humane" construction of the human. To make their case, the sisters then exploit the figure of Joseph, an "African" convert who, through the ravages of traumatic history, is ironically subject to the violating effects of the competing colonial theories of the human they make. The fictional account offers a living example and evidence for the shaky basis of each sister's claim to humanism from which researchers might learn. The story parallels my argument that without a psychoanalytic and postcolonial approach to interpretive methods, our representation of others risks harmful violation and gross misrepresentation of the other's existence. Literature and its devices can support qualitative researchers' efforts to heed the creative and destructive potential of the wildness inherent in interpretive practice and foster ethical attentiveness to the lived realities of its subjects.

Projective identification: psychoanalysis, postcolonial studies, and interpretive practice

Sigmund Freud found that objective methods for narrating our "true" selves and our relation to the world are plagued by psychical interference containing unseemly thoughts and actions towards others. Our attempts to narrate our sense of others to ourselves (through myriad forms of interpretation and representation) are not simply a reflection of our knowledge of another's social reality. These narrations of others also articulate the great pains we take to contain wild feelings, desires, and thoughts that others animate within. Freud (1938) characterized interference to knowledge formation in the form of defensive psychical mechanisms circulating within projective identifications.

From a psychoanalytic perspective, the faltering capacity to take in and project out one's sense of others is initiated in infancy. One's capacities for identification and projection are animated in the baby's first sensuous interactions with maternal others. Wild reading is grounded in feminized qualities of response, care, and nurture because the maternal environment plays a vital role in the development of the felt interpretive capacity of the baby (Irigaray, 1993; Klein, 1930/1984; Kristeva, 2001). In contrast, the capacity to symbolically represent one's sense of one's self and the world is oriented toward the maintenance of a patriarchal sociality, toward what Jacques Lacan terms the "law of the father." Interpretation is an inner and chaotic practice of framing intelligibility while representation, through the auspices of logos, makes symbolic order from the ravages of inside and unkempt feelings and thought.

Representation in the social sciences refers to the researcher's claim to mirror reality (Britzman, 1995). Britzman (1995) argues that such a notion forecloses deeply subjective processes underlying the researcher's interpretation of the world and other. According to Britzman (1995), our processes of interpretation, before, during, and after an event, interrupt and de-stable the notion of a fixed or essential representation. Attending to conflicts in interpretive practice, we are given insight into the fragile quality of our representations, into the process by which knowledge of others is shakily produced (Britzman, 1995).

Psychical dynamics of identification and projection animated in infancy are intertwined in the capacity to think ourselves in relation to others. Klein (1930/1984) depicts the space of the maternal relation[2] as one of epistemological newness, uncertainty, and reproduction. The maternal relation marks the infant's first unintelligible experiences of the other and the world. Wild reading characterizes the infant's first staggering attempts to make wordless sense of a sensually felt world. Kristeva (2001) describes wild readings as semiotic, infused with qualities of flesh and sensation, of motherhood and infantile potential and of creation and destruction. Klein recovers these femininized qualities of being, however, from the domesticated and normative, idealized and disparaged forms with which we have come to associate motherhood and woman. The maternal relation is fraught with the wildness of first readings as the mother[3] tries to negotiate competing desires dictated by the social and the infant unevenly and without a preformed, rigid method upon which to depend. If the mother is conditioned by her own memories of care and social rituals of motherhood, these too can become both triggered and destabilized by the newness and uniqueness of the infant to whom she is entrusted to care. Half haphazardly and through the faltering, interpretive effort of trial and error the mother begins to tend to the newborn being in her midst.

According to Klein (1946/1975) we know ourselves through our first, sensate experience of (m)others. In infancy, internal feelings are taken as the reality of others. A war of infantile feeling of love and hate for the mother sets the stage for the baby's capacity to make identification with others. But as identification is made the infant projects her sense of the other, posed as both necessary and threatening to her survival, outward onto mother. In her introduction to Klein's work, Segal (1973) explains: "In projective identification parts of the self and internal objects are split off and projected into the external object, which then becomes possessed by, controlled and identified with the projected parts" (p. 27). Bad feelings, in particular, experienced by the baby are projected and later attributed to the (m)other to support the baby's unmanageable feelings threatening to destroy her self. Klein

(1946/1975) writes, "Much of the hatred against parts of the self is now directed towards the mother. This leads to a particular form of identification which establishes the prototype of an aggressive object-relation" (pp. 7–8).

Our adult relations with other are tinged with unconscious traces of infantile need, warring affection and violent aggression as described by Klein. These unconscious affects instantiate the internalized template by which we begin to make real, symbolic sense of the world. Projective identification is an internal form of affective interpretation, a type of deeply felt intrasubjective communication embedded in intersubjective communication via gestures, emotional expression, and bodily contact. The practice is wild, silent, and confused and based on one's sense of external reality as felt from the inside out. The precariousness of interpretation depends on the symbolic form through which the mother accepts the baby's aggression and returns to the baby a renewed sense of herself. Miraculously and wildly through gesture and utterance the infant makes her felt need known to (m)others. The mother is somewhat limited to make sense of the existence of the child and feels put upon to make "wild" interpretations of what the foreign and speechless being is trying to express. "She's hungry" we think, when the baby wants to be held. "She's a fussy baby" we exclaim, when fussiness is the only mode of expression the baby has to express her need. This primal miscommunication of our own needs in perpetual conflict with the other's interpretation sets us on a lifelong existential conflict with both symbolic representation and the fact that we are subject to the other's determinations of ourselves (Derrida, 1998).

Our social relationships to others bear a trace of the originary, primitive aggression the baby learns to manage through the development of an interpretive apparatus that supports and protects the formation of an intelligible self. How the mother interprets and responds to the unintelligible projection of baby is crucial to the infant's capacity to begin to distinguish her feelings of herself from her feelings for the mother from the actual person. Narratives of the child written by the (m)other's personal and socialized interpretations are superimposed on the child's unique subject formation. Subjecting one's self to the interpretations of (m)other marks one's first impression of a self overwritten by social representations (Britzman, 2009b).

In her essay "Psychic space and social melancholy" Kelly Oliver argues that the social reception of the child through word and deed is intrinsic to her sense of well-being. Loving one's self is critical to one's interpretation of the self through hospitable representations of one's social existence:

> The alienation of oppression is not analogous to the existential alienation of a subject thrown into a world not of his own making. Rather, the alienation of oppression is what I call a double alienation insofar as it results not just from finding yourself in a world of ready-made meanings but from finding yourself there as one who has been denied the possibility of meaning making or making meaning your own without at the same time denying your own subjectivity. Oppression presents that subject with the paradoxical choice of not existing or existing as object, animal, as less than human. (2002, p. 56)

With Oliver I also wish to make a link – not an equation – between the "originary" (psychic) alienation that the self feels in being born to the mother's interpretation and the secondary alienation the self experiences in being colonized by a dominant representation and society which makes one "Other." Extreme hatred and fear projected onto "Others," as that experienced by the colonized in the colonial scene, monstrously and comic-tragically mimic the ordinary dynamics of projective identification necessary to forge attachments and make relations to others (Bhabha, 1994). Bhabha (1994) finds that stereotypes, for example, are symbolic forms of wild readings where our heightened sense of the other's lived expression is returned to the world in distorted or hyperbolic form. He writes, "terrifying stereotypes of savagery, cannibalism, lust and anarchy [...] are the signal points of identification and alienation, scenes of fear and desire" (p. 25). Stereotypes become frames of intelligibility and, at worst, normative social categories by which we come to know and relate to the other's experience. While the social form of projection is not the equivalent of the psychical process of projective identification – there is a perpetual mismatch between internal and external feelings and actions setting the stage for the construction and translation of knowledge – aggressive, infantile affects are wildly at play in our interpretations of others and can be grossly projected onto representations of the other's body, making them monstrously "Other" than human. Bhabha (1994) describes the writing of the colonial scene as one beset by the originary dynamics of projective identification and infused with a wild and secondary mix of fantasy, fetish, and misappropriation. The psychosocial dynamics of identification and projection plague interpretative practice and impede our findings, qualifications, and reconstructions of the other's life.

Our first infantile readings of the world and other are irrecoverable. Lost to the unconscious are our desperate efforts at making sense of the world without the support of coherent symbolic language. Wild reading in adulthood erupts when we find ourselves in conflict with the truth of experience narrated to us in the other's words. Or when we experience hatred of ourselves in facing the unfamiliar reality of others. Or when we experience the hatred of others suddenly and without reason. At these times, we can feel as if we are grasping for words and flailing around for (in)credible representations that can bring order to our confused sense of things. To rid ourselves of the wildness within, we can project our feelings for ourselves wrongly onto our interpretations of the existence of others. And we are also subject to the same mistreatment from others in their projections onto our selves. We can make others "Other" than we are. We can also be made to be "Other" than we are. Projective identifications crash into the social through our intense interpersonal conflicts with others that, when left unchecked, can escalate into larger forms of social hatred and genocide. At those moments that we experience social conflict, confusion, or breakdown as a threat posed by others to self, we are reminded of the precariousness of the interpretive apparatus and the difficulties we undertake in making sense of a life unfamiliar and strange to our own. The unwieldy dynamics of projective identification in the researcher/researched relationship have profound implications for qualitative researchers. As Mehan (2012) suggests, the fraught relationships between self and other might be part of a new "socially conscious" social science movement that acknowledges the complex historical-political and interpersonal dynamics at work in the co-construction of knowledge.

To give a sense of the incredibly complex mental and social activities at play in the intra- and intersubjective dynamics of projective identification, I engage with a section of a literary work. The dynamics of social conflict plaguing two "fictional" sisters with warring stances on humanity are depicted in J.M. Coetzee's short story "The Humanities in Africa". I pinpoint moments of affective bond and antagonism between the sisters as giving way to their opposing interpretations of the significant and dangerous role humanistic endeavor plays in the colonizing history of humanity. Their argument culminates through a projection onto the lived reality of Joseph, an African convert who makes a momentary appearance in the story. Coetzee's representation of the sisters' warring interpretations in relation to each other and upon Joseph exposes the human tendency to fall back to self-preserving and violating methods and means of knowledge production with which to name, represent and explain the lives of others.

Wild readings of the lives of others in "The Humanities in Africa"

Elizabeth Costello, a main protagonist appearing in a number of J.M. Coetzee's literary works, is an aging mother, novelist, scholar, and animal-rights activist. As she grows older she finds herself entrenched in her ethical and political mission to find salvation for herself and her fellow human beings from the immense suffering she witnesses in and of the world. Her mission is enacted through a series of pseudo "lectures" uncontrollably steered by Costello's relentless imposition of her desires and ideas on others. As a result, Costello has difficulty convincing anyone to take seriously her intellectual positions on animal or human rights.

Coetzee's short story "The Humanities in Africa" finds Costello once again projecting her interpretations of human good and folly onto others. The story highlights Costello's perpetual problems defending her royal road to human salvation, this time with her sister, Blanche. Also known as Sister Bridget, Blanche is a missionary nun serving others on the ground in an "African" nation. The siblings' lifelong rivalry, their methods of knowledge production and rationalization, and their adult relationship come to a head in their conflict over the contested role the humanities play in a history of antagonistic human relations.

I use scenes of the novel[4] to demonstrate how wild reading on the part of each sister projects outwardly onto each other but also inadvertently onto their interpretations of the life of Joseph, an "African" convert the sisters encounter in a mission station run by Sister Bridget. I analyze the sisters' dispute on the humanities through the psychical dynamics of projective identification where familial bonds and past experiences steer their present interpretations of the humanities. I follow the transfer of the sisters' entrenched interpretations of the humanities on the life of Joseph as an effect of their unchecked, yet, colonially haunted, readings of the "human."

The reader finds the sisters bitterly embroiled in a debate on the humanities. The event occasioning their conflict is a lecture given by Blanche and attended by Costello. In the lecture, Blanche is invited to discuss the humanities and its central role in determining Western life and the lives of others in Africa. During the lecture, Blanche accuses the humanities of diminishing the spiritual aspects of human life. In a dramatic fashion Blanche predicts rather ominously: "The *studia humanitatis* have taken a long time to die, but now, at the end of the second millennium of our era, they are truly on their deathbed" (p. 123).

Costello's sister's thunderous claim greatly troubles her and the learned members of the audience. As humanists both Costello and the audience are sharply taken aback by the Sister's rigid stance that the humanities, with its emphasis on secular modes of deliberation and judgment, has banished the passion and suffering of human beings resultant of modern life. The death of the humanities signals for Sister Bridget a much needed catalyst to return to religious life and to an embodied existence that suffers rather than progresses to a higher state of being via Western tales of enlightenment and reason.

Blanche's argument stuns Costello. Rather than unwinding the strands of intellectual labor comprising Blanche's argument, Costello is personally attacked by her sister's harsh condemnation of the humanities, causing her to regress to a somewhat infantile state of feeling "put upon" by her sister. Costello somewhat narcissistically suspects that the lecture is aimed at her and, in particular, at her chosen humanistic vocations as an academic and writer of literature and wonders: "why this hostility on Blanche's part towards the humanities? *I do not need to consult novels*, said Blanche. Is this hostility, in some tangled way, aimed at her?" (p. 131).

Through the rapidly deteriorating reasonable discussions on the humanities, the narrative exposes their deep sibling rift and rivalry. Blanche's hostility targeting her sister through a scholarly argument on how best to live, Costello notes with some insight, is longstanding and tied up in the unfathomable dynamics of "mother," "blood," and the inability to let go of familial bonds (p. 134). Each woman's ontological justification for the human is entangled in the sisters' difficult relationship with the other: these enduring libidinal conflicts are worked out in each sister's existential philosophy, epistemological attachments, and chosen way of life. We too as researchers might believe that our positions are unencumbered by the constraints of our own frames of reference or that we are absolved from bias through the mere recognition or articulation of these frames. Yet our findings of the world and others are deeply tied to past life experiences and our chosen aesthetic and vocation for living. As in the case of the sisters, each of us is similarly constrained to interpret the world through our previous lived experiences, habits of living, and schooled understandings. Some aspects of our experience, as is demonstrated in this account, are also unconscious and not knowable. Our representations of knowledge bear the traces of our desire for knowledge as well as knowledge itself.

The unconscious dynamics of projective identification circulating between the sisters are rendered visible by Coetzee's narrative and can be, rather humorously, recognizable to the reader when benignly at play in their one-on-one debate. However, their reasoned and, at times, entertaining interpretations of the humanities take an unseen, dangerous, and wilder turn for the worse when the sisters begin projecting their deeply subjective views of humanity on others outside of their libidinal bond. When Sister Bridget takes Costello to visit the mission station on Marionhill where she spends her time administering an AIDS hospice for sick and dying children, Costello becomes viscerally aware that her sister brings her to the mission to "bring home" her argument on the human sacrifice required to bring about human salvation through one's care of and service to "the wretched of the earth." At first, Costello is reluctant to study the human subjects bolstering Blanche's claim: "She has seen it all on television, too often, till she cannot bear to look any more: The stick limbs, the bloated bellies, the great impassive eyes of children wasting away, beyond cure, beyond care" (p. 133). However, once at the mission station, Costello is surprised to encounter the vitality of the dying children, marveling at their resilience and at how "gay even a dying child can be" (p. 134).

This seemingly insignificant moment of "queer" misrecognition and gross misinterpretation of the lived realities of the children's lives exposes Costello's pre-conceptions of the lives of "Africans." The defaced images are significantly brought to bear on Costello's interaction with the "real" face she encounters in her "tour" of the mission when she accidently stumbles upon Joseph, an African Christian-convert who dedicates his daily existence and artistic ability to carving for tourists exact wood replications of Jesus depicting "our Savior's agony" on the cross

(p. 135). Curious about his artwork, Costello sets about interviewing Joseph on his profession. Horrified, she finds that Joseph's artistic talent is wasted on his efforts at "mindless" reproduction. Taken aback by Costello's interpretation, Blanche advances her own: Joseph's effort is an exemplar of spiritual life as one who chooses to suffer like Jesus rather than use his talent in service of a vain and hubristic humanity. Costello is unimpressed with the reasoning behind Blanche's interpretation:

> She does not like it when her sister gets on her high horse and preaches. It happened in her speech in Johannesburg and it is happening again. All that is most intolerant in Blanche's character emerges at such times: intolerant and rigid and bullying. (p. 138)

Ironically, Costello is oblivious to her equally rigid and negating stance on religious pursuits that triggers Sister Bridget's "tyrannical" responses to her. The sisters' warring interpretations on the significance of Joseph's life gain and lose traction until they spiral back to their initial debate on the role that the humanities has played in the diminishment of the lives of human beings. Frustrated with Costello's view that Joseph's talent would be better put to humanistic rather than religious use, Sister Bridget finally goads her sister into "asking Joseph" for his interpretation of his reality:

> Do you think, Elizabeth, that the Greeks are utterly foreign to Zululand? I tell you again, if you will not listen to me, at least have the decency to listen to Joseph. Do you think that Joseph carves suffering Jesus because he does not know better, that if you took Joseph on a tour around the Louvre his eyes would be opened and he would set about carving, for the benefit of his people, naked women preening themselves, or men flexing their muscles? [...] Joseph has *chosen* Jesus as his model. Speak to him. He will tell you. (p. 140)

Throughout their heated conversation and despite Sister Bridget's impassioned claims on his behalf, Joseph is silent. In Coetzee's narrative he is silenced, uninvited, unable or refusing to offer to either sister his thoughts or feeling on their misappropriations of his existence. Through his silence, his presence is felt rather than spoken in the text while the sisters' continuation of their debate rages on having lost the façade of reasonable dialog. Completely oblivious to Joseph's presence, the sisters turn on each other under his silence and continue to disparage and destroy each other's thoughts, ideas, and lived profession. Costello finds the Christian mission at fault for converting Joseph's gift and talent for artistic endeavors into blind faith in Jesus, a "mere man" while Sister Bridget finds that because they suffer the "Zulus knew better" for choosing Jesus over "those young fellows from Oxford and Cambridge and St Cyr" offering "their new barbarian subjects a false ideal" (p. 141). Frustrated, Sister Blanche leaves their debate and her intention of hearing from Joseph, to put an end to their fight for the human with one final, interpretive blow:

> This is *reality*: the reality of Zululand, the reality of Africa. It is the reality now and the reality of the future as far as we can see it. Which is why African people come to church to kneel before Jesus on the cross, African women above all, who have to bear the brunt of reality. Because they suffer and he suffers with them. (p. 141, italics added)

Still, Joseph does not speak. And in Sister Bridget's allusion to the improbable situation of the suffering women of Africa fortifying her case, "the women of Africa" are also terribly silenced. Coetzee's deliberate muting of Joseph at this precise moment in the narrative strongly brings home this point: In the war of interpretation over the colonial effect of Western humanistic endeavor in Africa, the African is radically subaltern. The African cannot speak subject to misinformed and distorting projections onto his humanity that, in the first place, deny his existence (Spivak, 1988). Without an interpretive context outside those of the sisters' qualifying the intricacies of his existence, Joseph is denied recourse to representation.

Kelly Oliver (2002) insists oppression is ultimately the act of denying one the capacity for one's psychical life to find symbolization, for one's interpretation of one's existence to find meaningful representation. Subject to the sisters' wild, unconscious, desire-filled interpretations, Joseph becomes a figment of the sisters' imagination, a mere shadow of humanity, without a reality represented according to his lived frames of intelligibility and reference. As Spivak (1988) points out, "If, in the context of colonial production, the subaltern has no history and cannot speak, the subaltern as female is even more deeply in shadow" (p. 287). In the confused desires steering the sisters' debate, Joseph's existence is lost to reason, humanistic endeavor, salvation, and suffering. His silence alerts us of the folly of interpreting the life of someone without taking into consideration the histories and discourses shaping one's capacity for having a voice, mind of one's own, and unique social existence, without taking into consideration our own desires for, interests in, and relation to the life under examination.

A fictional self-other encounter, staged by Coetzee and guiding my argument in this paper, between two aging and antagonistic sisters, between two "lay researchers" in Africa, between the sisters and the inhabitants of "Africa," can yield much insight on the problematic of interpretive practice as ultimately shaping one's readings of the other's reality. The sisters' warring claims of what is best for the "human" render Joseph subaltern, captive to both a faith-based and reason-driven colonial project. Suspended in the sisters' colonially inflected discourses that ensure his silence, Joseph literally has "no say" on the matter of his own existence. The subaltern's existence is muted by the philosophical and theological representations held by the sisters and historically enacted by unthinkable methods of conversion of Africans in Africa's traumatic colonial histories (Fanon, 1967). Through identification with the precious gift of his craft, the sisters feel an affinity with and to the humanity of Joseph. However, those identifications are not about Joseph nor do they represent Joseph's sense of himself. Instead each interpretation of Joseph's lived reality is a violating projection of the sisters' passionate attachments to themselves, to each other, and to their scholarly commitments of Western thought. Through these projections both historically and personally enacted, Joseph is denied a chance to articulate his inner thoughts as a person with a story to tell from which they might learn. Instead, through the wildness of each sister's mistaken claim to Joseph's inner thoughts and body, we learn more about the sisters' capacity for epistemological violence wedded to colonial discourse than we do of Joseph's existence. And after our engagements with this fictional account, there remain grave implications for social science researchers of the dangers of denying the historical and psychical, complex and invisible inter and intrapersonal dynamics at play in our seemingly "objective" constructions of knowledge of the self and others.

Rereading humanity

Our inquiry into the lived experience of the other's body unconsciously holds self-serving desires that need to be checked in the moments before, during, and after encounter. Through the careful construction of fictional characters and dialog, we are offered a window into the strange and unfamiliar perspective of one's inner world. Through fiction, Coetzee demonstrates that we have the inventive and imaginative resources to forge a concerted and penetrating analysis of the discursive constructions we make of the world and others. One can examine the dynamics of sociality informing this fictional encounter and in doing so begin to alter conventional means of "doing" theory and research. As researchers, we can examine the all-too-real conflict of fictional sisters as a problem of interpretation steeped in projective identifications and played out in the passion play of one's ontological and epistemological commitments. Through this story, Coetzee gives those committed to justly documenting qualities of human-lived reality a chance to engage interpretive inner conflicts in motion. Through our reading of this story, we might recognize ourselves in the rivalry of sisters. We might gain insight into the wrongness of their conviction when making misinterpretations of Joseph's lived reality. We might learn from their compulsion to project self-interested versions of a redemptive humanity on each other's life and the life of Joseph. We might, in other words, recognize the limits of knowing others and what is best for others through our shaky interpretations of another's lived reality. And these limits to interpretation, representation, and knowledge posed by the unwieldy dynamics of projective identification might form the basis of our qualitative investigations into our lives in relation to the lives of others, into the precarious relationship between the researcher and the researched.

Along with interpretive insight, Coetzee's fiction offers an analytical resource by which we can train ourselves and our students to represent the fleeting madness lurking within our everyday means of attaching to others and the world. Perhaps we can only account for the affective material driving and unraveling our interpretations and representations through the imaginative space afforded to us by literature and other artistic forms of textual production. Coetzee's device of speculating upon and symbolizing the colonial discourses at play in the sisters' interpretation of Joseph, for example, offers us an inventive consideration of the interpretive frames at play in our representations of others. Left to our own unchecked interpretive devices and mythologies of objectivity, we might make the mistake, as each of these sisters do, of taking our subjective means for making "real" sense of the world for a world that also comprises the means and sense of others.

Jacques Derrida insists that we forge a creative attendance to the madness of our methods for writing the self, other, and the world as a means to repair the damage done through wild and potentially demeaning interpretations of the other's humanity:

> I must try to write in such a way that my language does not make the language of the other suffer [*souffrir*] [...] It must be invented at every moment, every sentence, with no guarantee, no absolute guard-rail [*garde-foul*]. This is equivalent to saying, madness, a certain "madness" *must* watch each and every step, and eventually must watch over thinking, just like reason also does. (1995, pp. 290–291)

Representation, in Derrida's view, offers us a belated opportunity to check our wild interpretations in a coherent form. Representation is not a one-to-one correspondence with reality but instead offers the researcher a "text" with which to qualify and cross-check her interpretations through historical, social, and personal frameworks that do justice to the uniqueness of the human subject. Through Derrida's postcolonial orientation of representation, we can no longer take the other at her word as the truth of an existence. We can no longer take our own words for that truth either. Derrida suggests that histories of colonization and violation of others require us to forge a close analysis of the all-too-human logics, desires, and interests lurking behind the word, the madness that "lies" within representation. He suggests that without guarantee and with an ethic of the other we concentrate our efforts on "the invention of a language that does not make the other suffer" and that undoes or deconstructs the folly of interpreting the other's existence through the very objective and scientific modes of thought that, in the first place, over-determine, subjugate, injure, and eviscerate her humanity. Couze Venn (1996) has described this kind of interpretive activity as forging an "imaginative" excavation of the desires and enactments embedded in the genealogy of colonial discourse with an attention to the unconscious.

Attending to this certain madness that watches over thinking compels an altered interpretive practice. What is required of qualitative researchers is the development of an affected interpretive practice that penetrates the dynamics of projective identification at play in our selection of research projects and participants, in our techniques of interviewing, and in the discourses we use to support our representations of the other's existence. The traces of affective material left behind in writing provide us with the resources to unravel carefully constructed positions on the right or best way to live. Rather than defending against or suppressing what is difficult about representing human relations and life, we might begin to develop interpretive resources that support our blocked abilities to sympathetically and justly imagine and consider the other's position and experience. And through these creative efforts an altered narrative of humanity might give way to symbolization from our infantile capacity to be vulnerable and affected by others.

Literature can allow for and open up a conceptual problem space for researchers to work through our difficulties with our learned methods of making sense of the world (Britzman, 2009a). Analytical encounters with the lives of fictional characters, as the one I have engaged in this paper, can pedagogically develop and support an affective capacity to engage with the unthinkable human desires and acts that reside within "certain" methods, performances, and productions of Western knowledge and representation. The development of affected reading practices can serve as a kind of "training" for qualitative researchers interested in interpreting and representing the more unfathomable of educational processes and lived realities testing the limits of the scientific or systemizing discourse. Britzman (2009a) suggests that an affective, inventive, and speculative reading practice alerts us to our interpretive problem when we realize our ontological and epistemological "constructs fail" and we are faced with a feeling that "language can betray its promise of communication" (p. 45).

Fiction affords us the space to be mistaken about our interpretations of others that we cannot afford to make in real-life encounters with research subjects. From literary engagements, researchers can develop an affected practice of interpreting and examining the lives of others in relation to our own. Being promiscuous and open to the weakness of any given method might support more just and less self-justifying representations of the lives of others. Working with feminist promiscuous methods, researchers in the human sciences diversely and collectively move towards the liberation of human bodies dehumanized by the concerted patriarchal denial of the silent, incoherent, and wild remains of an infantile, inner life grounding a sentient humanity (Lyotard, 1991).

Recently Lauren Berlant (in Davis & Sarlin, 2011) has spoken about the need to develop the scholarly capacity for:

> Training in one's own incoherence, training in the ways in which one's complexity and contradiction can never be resolved by the political, is a really important part of a political theory of non-sovereignty. But we still have to find a place for adjudication, or working out, or working for, or working over, which requires a pedagogy of attention, of paying attention to the different ways in which we engender different kinds of claims on the world, in our attachments or ways of moving or desires for habituation or aspirations. (p. 16, ll. 9–15)

Berlant's statement highlights the problem of interpretation in our representations of the world and others. She (Berlant, 2011) seems to be suggesting that our historical moment requires an unconventional study of the human and of humanism to forge a radically altered vision of humanity. This humanity acknowledges that our knowledge accounts are vulnerable to a desire for the self at the expense of others. This humanity affirms that our methods for understanding the world and others are limited by the limits of knowledge. This humanity admits that we might not ever be able to know everything we might want to know about this world we inhabit with sentient others. This humanity might begin to search for a mode of reparation with which to reread sentient existence and a traumatic human history of hateful projections that disparage and demean the lives of others (Mishra Tarc, 2011; Phillips, 2006).

Our methods for representing human existence might begin to embrace the social fact that in some ways we are all promiscuous researchers as our birth plunges us into the world with few resources for navigating a foreign world. In infancy, we are able, through a mysterious intelligence, to forge together haphazardly and as a matter of survival an interpretive register. If our very survival forces us to contain and systematize our feelings through the interpretive gifts bestowed on us by our mother, the qualities of that system of interpretation remain unfaithful to any one form of knowing, mutable, and continually creatively adapting to whatever joy and suffering the world unexpectedly bestows (Lear, 2006).

Knowledge is produced through our relations with sentient and non-sentient others. The interpretive bases by which our knowledge accounts are created are already affected by a history of the world in which we are born and through prior attachments to and experiences with significant others. Rethinking our learned means of reading and writing our shared, fragile, and fleeting sentient existence can greatly affect how researchers represent the lives of others. Our present attempts for writing the world silence "the wild horse in us" and privilege methods that promote a seamless, logical, orthodox view of knowledge rather than reveal gaping holes in our coherent narratives of thinking and being. Training in one's incoherence requires an attendance to what cannot be articulated directly in words and only in feeling. Engagement with literature that attempts to convey an unspeakable felt knowledge of human existence can give social science researchers insight into the less rational processes driving human thought, representation, and epistemology. Through readings that attend to the wild desires driving our true attempts to know anything at all about the world, scholars might begin to reread and represent humanity as profoundly dependent on our felt response to others and objects – a humanity that acknowledges its debt to "this madness" that guides our deeply affected thinking and being with others in the world.

Notes

1. My use of the words "we" or "our" in this work refers to "we" (learners, thinkers, educators). By using this word, I do not wish to universalize singularities. Instead, as with Lyotard (1991), I use "we" to signal that modern processes of subject formation happen not only to me; "I am not the only one, which is why I write 'us'" (p. 4). My use of "we" or "our" also follows the convention of psychoanalysis that operates through the power of suggestion to supplement truth claims. The reader is invited to identify with or recognize the suggestion of truth according to her own circumstance rather than as a universal claim. The strategy intends to provoke and open the reader's mind toward the possibility of thinking with or against the underlying (wild) motivations for constructing the paper.
2. In my paper maternal does not refer solely to the relationship between the actual mother and the infant. The maternal relation refers to the processes of identification, care, and symbolization by which the infant gains a sense of herself in relation to others. In my paper, I present these processes of becoming someone as essential to human existence without reservation. If the social context in which the baby becomes a person matters, the fact remains that all human beings are born to a mother and through the care of a (m)other will develop into a person. The maternal relation need not be essentially feminine although historically and somewhat universally social practices of child-raising are gendered. I use "(m)other" to refer to the maternal environment, which may or may not consist of females; and "mother" to refer to a "real" mother, the historically and socially constructed, female and gendered and actual figure of mother. Similarly I use other in its general sense as other than one's self; and "Other" to signal the foreign and/or hated other of Western philosophy.
3. Winnicott (1995) did not subscribe to the biological determination of mother but to a role that a real person or persons played in the life and care of the child. Real mothers can be any gender but are maternal. The real mother is responsible for the child's becoming a person and also for the stability of herself – both of these responsibilities are highly dependent on the mother's personally and socially determined understandings and representations of motherhood, selfhood, and well-being.
4. Along with supporting the article's argument, this section provides a model of interpretive engagement with fictional lives that I engage with my graduate students in a decolonizing methods course that explicitly takes up the problem of studying the lives of others. I consider the development of this pedagogical mode of reading as a form of research "training" through which my students learn to engage the humanist concerns embedded in social science method and findings that "close and not (so) deep" literary reading unearths (Love, 2010, p. 375). Social scientific engagements with late modernist and/or postcolonial fictional texts depicting fraught human relations inevitably surface complicated discussions on a myriad of themes of interest to researchers. Our primary and secondary readings of fictional self-other encounter offer my students an opportunity to test out and reflect upon the defensive processes by which they attempt to make identification to the lives of unfamiliar others as a way to develop the capacity for a deepened regard for the other's unknowable life. Our discussions of social science methods are both philosophical and practical, involving the problems of subjectivity, ethics, history, colonial relations, injury, harm, desire, design, violence, and interpretation amongst other crises that arise when examining and representing the other's life.

References

Attwood, F. (2007). Sluts and riot grrrls: Female identity and sexual agency. *Journal of Gender Studies, 16*, 231–245.
Bhabha, H. K. (1994). *The location of culture*. London: Routledge.
Britzman, D. P. (1995). The question of belief. Writing "post-structural" ethnography. *International Journal of Qualitative Studies in Education, 3*, 229–238.
Britzman, D. P. (2009a). Reading. In *The very thought of education. Psychoanalysis and the helping professions* (pp. 45–60). New York, NY: SUNY Press.
Britzman, D. P. (2009b). Love's impression. A psychoanalytic contribution. *British Journal of Sociology of Education, 30*, 773–787.
Butler, J. (2005). *Giving an account of oneself*. Bronx, NY: Fordham University Press.
Cameron, P. (2012). Curriculum vitae: Embodied ethics at the seams of intelligibility. *Hypatia: A Journal of Feminist Philosophy, 27*, 423–439.
Coetzee, J. M. (2003). The humanities in Africa. In *Elizabeth Costello* (pp. 116–155). New York, NY: Viking.
Davis, H., & Sarlin, P. (2011). No one is sovereign in love: A conversation between Lauren Berlant and Michael Hardt. *No More Potlucks, 18*, electronic version. Retrieved December 12, 2011, from http://www.nomorepotlucks.org/article/amour-no-18/no-one-sovereign-love-conversation-between-lauren-berlant-and-michael-hardt
Denzin, N. K. (1994). Evaluating qualitative research in the poststructural moment: The lessons James Joyce teaches us. *International Journal of Qualitative Studies in Education, 7*, 295–308.
Derrida, J. (1998). *Monolingualism of the other, or, the prosthesis of origin*. (P. Menash, Trans.). Stanford, CA: Stanford University Press.
Derrida, J. (1995). A certain madness must watch over thinking. (D. Egae-Kuehne, Trans.). *Educational Theory, 45*, 273–291.
Fanon, F. (1967). *Black skins. White masks*. New York, NY: Grove Press.
Freud, S. (1930/1989). *Civilization and its discontents* (Standard ed.). (J. Strachey, Ed. and Trans.). New York: W.W. Norton.
Freud, S. (1938). Splitting of the ego in the process of defence. In *The standard edition of the complete psychological works of Sigmund Freud, volume XXIII (1937–1939)* (J. Strachey, Ed. and Trans., pp. 271–278). London: Hogarth Press.
Haraway, D. (1991). *Simians, cyborgs, women: The reinvention of nature*. London: Free Press.
Irigaray, L. (1993). *Sexes and genealogies*. New York, NY: Columbia University Press.
Klein, M. (1930/1984). The importance of symbol-formation in the development of the ego. In Roger Money-Kyrle (Ed.), *Love, guilt, and reparation, and other works, 1921–1945* (pp. 219–232). New York, NY: The Free Press.
Klein, M. (1946/1975). Notes on some schizoid mechanisms. In Roger Money-Kyrle (Ed.), *Envy and gratitude and other works, 1946–1963* (pp. 1–24). New York, NY: The Free Press.
Kristeva, J. (2001). *Melanie Klein*. New York, NY: Columbia University Press.
Lather, P. (2004). This *is* your father's paradigm: Government intrusion and the case of qualitative research in education. *Qualitative Inquiry, 10*, 15–34.
Lather, P. (2006). Paradigm proliferation as a good thing to think with: Teaching research in education as a wild profusion. *International Journal of Qualitative Studies in Education, 19*, 35–57.
Lear, J. (2006). *Radical hope. Ethics in the face of cultural devastation*. Boston, MA: University of Harvard Press.
Love, H. (2010). Close but not deep. Literary ethics and the descriptive turn. *New Literary History, 41*, 371–391.
Lyotard, J. (1991). *The inhuman. Reflections on time*. (G. Bennington & R. Bowlby, Trans.). Stanford, CA: Stanford University Press.
Mehan, H. (2012). Reducing inequities by linking basic research and political action. *Anthropology and Education Quarterly, 43*, 20–23.
Mishra Tarc, A. (2011). Reparative curriculum. *Curriculum Inquiry, 41*, 350–372.

Oliver, K. (2002). Psychic space and social melancholy. In K. Oliver & S. Edwin (Eds.), *Between the psyche and the social: Psychoanalytic social theory* (pp. 49–65). Lanham, MD: Rowman & Littlefield.

Phillips, A. (2006). *Side effects*. London: Hamish Hamilton.

Ringrose, J. (2012). Slut-shaming, girl power and "sexualisation": Thinking through the politics of international SlutWalks with teen girls. *Gender and Education, 24*, 333–343.

Segal, H. (1973). *Introduction to the work of Melanie Klein*. London: Karnac Books.

Spivak, G. (1988). Can the subaltern speak? In C. Nelson & L. Grossberg (Eds.), *Marxism and the interpretation of culture* (pp. 271–313). Basingstoke: Macmillan Education.

Spivak, G. (1999). *A critique of postcolonial reason: Toward a history of the vanishing present*. Cambridge, MA: Harvard University Press.

Venn, C. (1996). History lessons: Formation of subjects, (post)colonialism, an Other project. In B. Schwartz (Ed.), *The expansion of England: Race, ethnicity and cultural history* (pp. 32–60). London: Routledge.

Winnicott, D. W. (1995). *The family and individual development*. New York, NY: Routledge.

Woolf, V. (1922/1992). *Jacob's room*. New York, NY: Penguin Classics.

Wright, H. K. (2006). Are we (t)here yet? Qualitative research in education's profuse and contested present. *International Journal of Qualitative Studies in Education, 19*, 793–802.

Working on a failed research: promiscuity of wanting and doing both ways

Jeong-eun Rhee

College of Education, Information and Technology, Long Island University, Post, Brookville, NY, USA

> By mixing up various writing genres, the author interweaves a hybrid narrative of a fable, her postcolonial feminist subjectivity, and her research. The narrative begins with Aesop's fable, "the Bat, the Bird, and the Beast." In the fable, a bat wants to be both a bird and a beast, but being neither, s/he is refused by both. Connecting her postcolonial feminist subjectivity with the positioning of the bat in the fable, the author re-engages with the moral of the story that instructs exclusive loyalty, and highlights the promiscuous potential of the bat. Through this re-engagement, she examines how feminist researcher subjectivity, epistemology, and methodology can function both as the demand of exclusive loyalty and as the transgressive desire and move (of the bat). Then, how can she both refuse and take refuge in feminist research? The promiscuity of wanting and doing both is a contradiction that enables the author to re-visit her research with Korean working class parents in New York City schools, which she thought she had failed two years ago. Through three accounts of failure that involve (1) the divide between the condition of researcher employment and the needs of the field; (2) the divide between usable and unusable data; and (3) the divide between theoretical complexity and material simplicity, the author discusses how she promiscuously – persistently and patiently – re-engages with these divides in her failed research.

> If those who *stay* tend to meet such an inability to speak with great disappointment – as a loss, a lack to be filled, a deficiency in need of rehabilitation and (re)integration – those who leave and risk in multiplicity often tend to go on cold for a while, living life as it comes, fasting verbally and linguistically, before learning how to speak again, anew. (Trinh, 2011, p. 2, emphasis mine)

The wall that keeps out/in

Aesop's fable "the Bat, the Bird and the Beast" is one of the stories from my childhood, that I still vividly remember. I used to think that this was a traditional Korean folktale. While there were various versions, the main story was well known and shared by parents, grandparents, teachers as well as in school textbooks, children's books, and even cartoons. The version I remember is most similar with Joseph Jacobs' (1894) English translation:

> A great conflict was about to come off between the Birds and the Beasts. When the two armies were collected together the Bat hesitated which to join. The Birds that passed his perch said: "Come with us"; but he said: "I am a Beast." Later on, some Beasts who were passing underneath him looked up and said: "Come with us"; but he said: "I am a Bird." Luckily at the last moment peace was made, and no battle took place, so the Bat came to the Birds and wished to join in the rejoicings, but they all turned against him and he had to fly away. He then went to the Beasts, but soon had to beat a retreat, or else they would have torn him to pieces. "Ah," said the Bat, "I see now, He that is neither one thing nor the other has no friends." (http://www.myth-folklore.net/aesopica/jacobs/24.htm)

As the tale concludes, the moral is "He that is neither one thing nor the other has no friends." *It was explained* to me that this is why the bat *stays*, with shame, in dark hiding places like a cave during the day and comes out only at night.

In Korean colloquialism, indeed, a bat refers to a (opportunistic) traitor; that "You are/act like a bat" is a common expression used to condemn a person "who is neither one thing nor the other," who therefore *wants (to have) it both ways*. When a fable reaches this level of collective/cultural narrative, it becomes a tradition, does it not? When it is considered that I grew up in the postcolonial and postwar social context of South Korea in which citizens were dealing with the continuing aftermath of Japanese colonization and the Korean War staged as part of the Cold War, I can now see how this fable gathered such cultural resonance as a tale of exclusive loyalty. So, is this story an Aesop's fable or a Korean folktale? If I claim that the story is both Korean and Aesop's tale, does the story itself become the bat of the fable?

After two decades of living in the cultural borderlands between Korea and the US and the borderlands of gender, race, class, sexuality, language, and religion, I now find myself relating to the story quite differently. Perhaps because I see myself in the position of the "bat"; neither Korean nor American, neither feminist nor not feminist, something in between, neither bird nor beast, neither black nor white, a gray/yellow bat subjectivity that always carries the stigma of being a traitor (see Rhee, 2008; Subreenduth & Rhee, 2010); *You are/act like a bat*.

A traitor, I am not a "woman," not a bearer of any tradition/nation, instead I speak, write, and conduct my (yellow) body in English accented by Korean[1] (Kim & Choi, 1998; Rhee, 2009). I am neither a woman subject about/with/to/for whom white/western feminists are talking, nor am I a woman object who is hailed, "hey, you" (see Althusser, 1971; Fanon, 1952/1991) as woman/the other, victimized and essentialized (Mohanty, 2004; Narayan, 1997). I listen to the tales of various (postcolonial) writers of color, which illuminate the borderland subjectivity in many versions and traditions (Cha, 1982; Hull, Scott, & Smith, 1982; Morga & Anzaldúa, 1983): double consciousness (Du Bois, 1903/2003), mestizo consciousness (Anzaldúa, 1987), and hybridity and third space (Bhabha, 1994). These various versions of borderland subjectivity are representations of bat subjectivity. This fable, with its multiple readings, doubled origins, and shifting boundaries, can re-present the tale of the bat anew, within different contexts and traditions. I choose to focus on the promiscuous potential of the bat, of *wanting it both ways*, rather than reading this fable as a lesson in loyalty, exclusion, and shame; *You are/act like a bat.*

PROMISCUOUS FEMINIST METHODOLOGIES IN EDUCATION

The promiscuous desire of the bat subjectivity *wanting it both ways* transgresses the wall; "the high wall that keeps out is the same wall that keeps in" (Trinh, 2011, p. 3). The wall divides birds and beasts, these women and those women, those who research and those who are researched, "natives who belong here by our birth and natives who belong to exotic, primitive culture by their inferior/non-European being" (Trinh, 1989, p. 52) and the list continues. What happens when this promiscuous desire to transgress the wall seeps into the field of research methodology? Specifically, what can we learn about the boundary of academic research that walls in successful, loyal, and legitimate practice and walls out Othered failures?

Through the promiscuity generated by re-engaging with the fable, in this paper, I examine how feminist subjectivity, epistemology, and research methodology can function both as the moral demand of the fable – "He that is neither one thing nor the other has no friends" – and as the transgressive move of the bat; *You are/act like a bat*. To contextualize my discussion, I narrate how the promiscuity of *wanting it both ways* enabled me to re-member and thus speak again about a research project that (I thought) I had failed (under the demand) two years ago. By analyzing both material and discursive conditions of my particular bat subjectivity, academic life, and research, I work with three aspects of research failure that highlight certain subjective, epistemological and methodological divides. The first vignette of failure involves the divide between the materiality and conditions of my employment as a non-tenured faculty and the needs of the field that I faced as a researcher. The second vignette of failure deals with the divide between legible/intelligible/usable data and illegible/unintelligible/unusable data, especially in relation to the academic demand of research productivity and legitimacy. The last one is about the divide between the theoretical complexity of research and the material simplicity of life that raises a question about the boundary of research itself.

Rather than *staying* in the moral of the bat story, through these re-engagements, I am learning how to speak the bat subjectivity. Rather than *staying* within the boundary of academic research that differentiates successful research from failure, I am speaking again, anew, neither fluently nor flawlessly but trying hard, patiently, and persistently to describe and use the new grammar of a tongue/language that I have been learning from the research I thought I had failed. Therefore, it is through the promiscuity of *wanting and doing it both ways* that I join feminist methodologies and transgress those divides.

You are/act like a bat; both taking refuge in and refusing the feminist universe

I knew a feminism before, long before I found myself in this location of neither these women nor those women. While not refusing outright the western feminists' persistent claim of feminism as a Western social movement, I also insist that feminism is one of the speaking/mother tongues I had acquired in Korea as a daughter watching my mother, who must have been her mother's daughter, but was (heard) only (as) a dutiful mother, wife, and daughter in-law. *It was explained*; to be a dutiful daughter is to be a daughter-in-law who must *forget* that she is the daughter of her mother (Shin, 2008); *forget, a lost connection.* Like a Bird is a Bird, a Beast is a Beast and a Bat is a Bat. A Bat is no more a Bird or a Beast, but a traitor who *stays* in the dark, with shame, if she wants it both ways. How this simple explanation ripped up her heart, dismembered her memory, and tore her experience apart into pieces, countless pieces, illegible, shapeless, invisible tears that evaporate: *airy existence or no existence*.

Be a dutiful and loyal Bird.[2] My dutiful and loyal mother's terrible, searing longing for what she *forgot* swallowed her mother's daughter; *forget, a lost connection*. Growing up, I only saw my dutiful mother, who must have been her mother's daughter. And my loyal mother raised me with her beastly longing, tears, and fire for/from what she dutifully forgot. Yet, *it was still explained*, to be a dutiful daughter was to be a daughter-in-law who must *forget* that she was the daughter of her mother. Do not become the Bat who wants it both ways, *it was explained*. And my feminist/speaking/mother tongue wiggled to ask, "why, why mother?"

Feminism is one of my mother tongues; a critical, political, epistemological legacy of my mother's lost connection, exclusive loyalty, and airy/no existence that has provided me with ways of knowing, a different sense of agency, a language to talk back and a transgressive journey of no return. That feminist fire in my belly was the fuel of my travel to the USA. During that strenuous traveling in living or living in traveling (Rhee, 2008, 2009), I had to rely on that beastly fire to keep walking. But then, alas, *it was explained* that I am a Bat to this Beast called feminism here.

The absence of color/race made white feminist epistemology and methodology much less useful, quite irrelevant, and often destructive to "research" racialized and nationalized realities (Collins, 1990; Mohanty, 2004; Trinh, 1989; Tuhiwai Smith, 1999). As numerous feminists of color have had to repeat (Asher, 2003; Dillard, 2000; Villenas, 1996), due to the missing and neglected component of race, my research approaches did not fit neatly in what I read as feminist methodology. Feminist methodology emphasizes a specific focus on women's experiences through a narrowly defined category of gender/sexuality, often as women versus men only (Chow, 1991, p. 83).

Chow (1991) was asked by a feminist, right after the Tiananmen Square massacre: "*How should we read* what is going on in China *in terms of gender?*" (emphasis mine). Her response was/is, "We do not, because at the moment of shock Chinese people are degendered and become simply 'Chinese'" (p. 81). She writes:

> To ask how we can use gender to "read" a political crisis such as the present one is to insist on the universal and timeless sufficiency of an analytical category, and to forget the historicity that accompanies all categorical explanatory power. (p. 82)

Chow questions our desire, belief, and myth-building practice in the ontological and epistemological assurance of feminism through the words of Spivak:

> The will to explain was the symptom of a desire to have a self and a world ... the possibility of explanation carries the presupposition of an explainable (even if not fully) universe and an explaining (even if imperfectly) subject. These presuppositions assure our being. Explaining, we exclude the possibility of the *radically* heterogeneous. (Cited in p. 82; emphasis in original)

I plug this with Bove's (1990) questions: "How does it (feminism, research, and/or feminist research) function? Where is it to be found? How does it get produced and regulated? What are its social effects? How does it exist?" (St. Pierre & Pillow, 2000, p. 8).

It was explained that a Bat is neither the Beast nor the Bird, never both Beast and Bird. The Beast and the Bird are defined through each other. Their boundary is regulated by their rejection of the Bat. A new category is born, who stays in the dark, supposedly with shame; that is how *it was explained*. All must be explainable as a feminist researcher presupposes an explaining (even if imperfectly) researcher subject.

How should we read ... in terms of gender?

"Explaining, we exclude the possibility of the radically heterogeneous." (Spivak, 1987, p. 105 cited in Chow, 1991, p. 82)

What if all are not explainable? They do not belong to the universe; whether it is the feminists' universe, Marxists' universe, critical Race theorists' universe or nationalists' universe. Either you are with us, belong here or you are with them, go away/back. The tradition of the Bat, the Beast, and the Bird – whether it is Aesop's fable or Korean folktale – prevails.

Be a dutiful and loyal Beast. As researchers, dutifully following rituals, we randomly (or selectively) sample data, analyze (some of) them, privilege rich, valid data over others, and construct partial truths out of our scientific, academic, and research work from data (MacLure, 2011). There must be empirical ways to research anything and everything (Tuhiwai Smith, 1999). That ontological and epistemological assurance bestows a researcher with a methodological crown. When a researcher subject collects data that is not explainable within her universe, what does she do? What can a feminist researcher do when she recognizes, for example, that the Tiananmen Square massacre should not be read, *explained*, understood in terms of gender? How do you "re/search" such existence that your universe fails to recognize?; *forget, a lost connection.* For qualitative researchers, what happens when data exceed your intelligence, theoretical understanding, and will to explain? What happens when you face your inability to read, hear, speak, understand, and theorize data? You have speaking voices coming out from your recorder and telling texts on your transcripts but they are syntactically ambiguous and semantically incoherent (to you) (Watson, 2006). What happens when data presents such disturbing experiences that you do not know how to proffer explanations in your universe and in an ethical way (Lather & Smithies, 1997; Marker, 2003; Selby, 2004)?

I quit. I walked away. I abandoned the project. I forgot that I am the daughter of my mother to be a dutiful loyal Beast; *forget, a lost connection.*

A project (I thought) I had failed

Without any funding or institutional support, two years ago, I started an autoethnographic action research project on Korean working class parents' experiences in urban schools, which another researcher and I had decided to develop as a way to (re)connect with our own ethnic community. As non-tenured faculty, both of us were overwhelmed with the responsibilities and requirements of publications, teaching, and service. Yet, we had this longing that we needed to carve out time to get involved with our ethnic community. Despite and because of the increasingly intensified stereotype of the model minority in education discourse, we wanted to specify certain challenges, struggles, and issues that working class Korean parents and students face, some of which we were aware of through personal anecdotes, Korean local newspapers, and a few scholarly works (Lew, 2006, 2010). We were interested in the stories Korean working class parents would tell us about their experiences with schools. We also wanted to open up a space for local educational researchers, practitioners and community members to learn, discuss and work with the issues, concerns, and needs of local working class parents through our research. We were hoping and planning to write a grant proposal, although we later found that there were few opportunities for a grant project on Asian Americans as they were not typically recognized as an underrepresented minority group in the field of education. Still, at the time, grant writing was less valued than a publication for the tenure process in my institution.

Before we could move on to a funded or publishing project like "successful" researchers do, we first decided that we needed to immerse ourselves in the field. We agreed that this would be a long-term project while we recognized a need to find ways to sustain the project. We had diligently worked together for about two years before we came to a conclusion that our collaboration on this project was not really working out due to our different priorities and urgencies in life as well as different philosophical and methodological approaches. Each of us had to find a different and separate way to continue (the spirit of) this project.

At this point, we had visited four schools, met with school principals, city education department administrators, parent coordinators, teachers and community organizers, and participated in community events to collect data on the needs and experiences of Korean immigrant working class parents in urban schools. We had two sets of data gathered from preliminary surveys collected from Korean teachers and parents. Both from the surveys and from fieldwork with community organizers, we were able to identify and recruit a number of parent participants for interviews. When my research partner and I decided to terminate our collaborative efforts, we had completed five individual interviews. Despite my two years of fieldwork, in 2010, I ran away from the project; *forget, a lost connection.*

Failure 1: the divide between the conditions of untenured faculty employment and the needs of the field

During two years of conducting the project, I was quite frustrated with the unbearably slow process of building a pool of participants. I was tried and tired by various suspicions about the real intention behind the project and occasional rejections from community members about any consideration of working or meeting with me. However, I acknowledge that the nature of this fieldwork was not too different from what had already been discussed regarding the process of getting an entry to the field as well as building collaborative relationships with participants (Subedi & Rhee, 2008).

What really hampered my will to continue the project were the materiality and "conditions of employment and research funding" (MacLure, 2011, p. 998) that I experienced as an untenured faculty member. Without institutional support and recognition, pursuing research like this was scary. I had to spend a great deal of time in the field conducting research without knowing if this time spent would contribute to writing the articles that would secure my tenure. Sometimes, I felt I was engaging with some kind of illegitimate work and making a wrong professional decision; *you are/act like a Bat*. When I had to face that the needs of the field and community and the demands of academy and my professional life were clashing in my work, this time, I did not want to become a Bat: I took a side and gave up the fieldwork.

For a while I wondered if and how this failed project was different from other projects I had completed such as my dissertation research, evaluation research for a grant, and partially funded ethnographic research in Korea. About two years later, in 2012, I was watching a TV news show where a young journalist was defending the integrity of her work against the inquiry of how her seven-figure contract had affected it. She said:

> First of all, you never do your work as a reporter based on for how much you are being paid or whether you are being paid a lot or a little. You always try to ascertain the same standard of the fairness and accuracy. (Up With Christ Hayes, 2012, http://www.msnbc.msn.com/id/21134540/Vp/46264099#46264099)

Her certainty and assurance ironically prompted me to realize that all my other research projects were stamped with their own institutional legitimacy like a doctoral degree or a grant. In discussing who studies what in which circumstances, bell hooks notes "white women are given grant money to do research on black women but I can find no instances where black women have received funds to research white women's history." Then she wonders if "scholars are motivated by a sincere interest in the history of black women or are merely responding to an available market" (cited in Reinharz, 1992, p. 257). In light of this materiality, even if one begins research with a sincere interest, how does one sustain the project if the academic institution devalues it? In other words, can I be a productive – dutiful, loyal – feminist researcher without institutional legitimacy (e.g. tenure, publications, or grants) in this commodified, hierarchal US academic structure? What kind of research will be completed, by whom, and who will exert its impact through their research on educational practices including policy? Asking these questions prompted by the weekend TV news show, I started to revisit the project that I thought I had left and thus failed, transgressing the boundary of (failure and success in) research practice and completion.

Failure 2: facing the boundary of (il)legibile, (un)intelligible, and (un)usable data

Drawing from Said (1978), Britzman (2000) brings educational researchers/ethnographers' attention to issues of both the structure of the narration and what it is that structures its mode of intelligibility. What structure does an ethnographic researcher use to narrate (and thus explain) her research? How does it affect the significance, validity, reliability, and legitimacy of the narration? Britzman problematizes the attractive and mythic notion of how, "ethnography is both a process and a product; there are methods for how to go about narrating culture, and these social strategies promise a text" (p. 27). Apparently, I was walled in that mythic land of ethnography – feeling secure about the procedure of my research. I had gone through the Institutional Review Board (IRB) process, worked to gain access to "the field" through multiple venues, knew the language, culture, and people, and produced hundreds of data texts, following the guidelines of "methods for how to go about narrating culture" (p. 27).

When I consulted other colleagues about how I felt that this project was not really going anywhere in terms of both getting institutional support and making effective progress in recruiting participants and collecting data, some suggested I write about my partial experience in the fieldwork instead of aborting the project. Even if I did not think that the fieldwork was saturated with data yet, I should be able to write a partial tale of the field or a reflective piece on the process. Two years of fieldwork was supposedly enough to employ these social or discipline strategies that promise a text, *it was explained*.

However, I was not able to write. It is a lie if I claim I could not understand or explain any part of the data. Yet it is another lie if I claim that I could make sense of all the stories without omitting a large part of them, patching rough details, and streamlining/fictionalizing elements of the story. Due to so many gaps, inconsistencies, ambiguities, and temporal disorders I encountered, both during the interviews and working with transcripts, I was constantly asking clarifications of names, a sequence of events, chronological ordering of their stories, more detailed elements of their experiences – why, how, what, who, whom, where, when. At several points of various interviews, I even jotted down, "listen to this part of the response" after I had failed in following their stories even with several clarification questions.

I wondered if a participant did not feel comfortable talking about some of her experience or if she did not want to reveal certain parts of her story. I assumed that another participant was also struggling to make sense of her own experiences. I imagined, conjectured, and speculated about the causes of this discomfort, such as immigration status or child neglect. At what point should I analyze, make a statement about it, argue, and conclude? I was experiencing my inability and participants' "inability to speak with great disappointment – as a loss, a lack to be filled, a deficiency in need of rehabilitation and (re)integration" (Trinh, 2011, p. 2).

Absent are parts of the storyline. Are they silence, loss, failure, ruin, refusal, resistance, or crisis? As researcher, what do I do with them? Ignore, skip, omit, problematize, criticize, comment, or follow up? Trinh (2011, p. 109) invokes a dream to re-engage with our demand/desire for usable stories/data:

> Strange is the way language and memory operate, but stranger still is the pervasive need of ours to track the words for fear of going off the rails of access and communication. In trying to relate the dream and to write it down, we tend to focus on the storyline, thereby threatening the dream to disappear quickly into illegibility. Accounts and analyses (of a work or of someone's life hi-story) built on storylines heavily (if not exclusively) based on chronology and on external retrievable facts (the one privileged path to the gate of Approval) prove to be limiting and at times, despairingly inadequate.

When the researcher works with and presents understandable and explainable storylines only, what politics of knowledge is she engaging with and which universe is she prescribing? All must be explainable as a feminist researcher presupposes an explaining (even if imperfectly) researcher subject. *It was explained* how to be a dutiful daughter of her mother and why not to be a bat. How this simple explanation ripped up her/my mother/my heart, dismembered her memory, and tore her experience apart into pieces, countless pieces, illegible, shapeless, invisible tears that evaporate: *airy existence or no existence; forget, a lost connection.* How do you "re/search" such airy existence or no existence and write intelligently?

Have we, feminist researchers, learned anything from Spivak's (1988) seminal piece, "Can the subaltern speak?" As long as researchers, who are walled in, fail to (learn to) learn from the possibility of the radically heterogeneous, researchers will never know that the subaltern, who are walled out, can speak. What if the researcher takes in Marguerite Dura's wisdom (cited in Trinh, 2011, p. 42): "one can only gain insight by letting oneself go blind as one gropes one's way through the oversaid and the all-too-clear of one's language." She goes on: "The theoretical sphere is losing influence... it should lose itself in a reawakening of the senses, blind itself, and be still," and warns how theory works to break the silence when:

> silence is precisely the sum of the voices of everyone, the equivalent of the sum of our collective breathing ... And this collective silence was necessary because it would have been through this silence that a new mode of being would have been fostered. (p. 42)

What does it mean to "go blind and be still" to get in touch with the silence and a new mode of being? Will "going blind" become "a loss, a lack to be filled, [or] a deficiency in need of rehabilitation and (re)integration" (Trinh, 2011, p. 2) for the researcher's (explaining) theoretical impulse? Or will it allow a researcher to awaken other senses after being still? Unfortunately, I do not have answers yet for these questions. By asking these questions and groping for answers through engaging with the unintelligible part of data, a researcher may vaguely sense the promiscuous possibility of transgressing the boundary of (il)legibility and (un)intelligibility in silence.

Failure 3: the divide between the theoretical complexity of research and the material simplicity of life

I still tried to continue the project. This might be another moment of research in ruin. I could write about that stuck place where the reality exceeded my intelligence, theories, and will to explain. I was re-reading Patti Lather's poststructural feminist methodology of getting lost:

> The task becomes to throw ourselves against the stubborn materiality of others, willing to risk loss, relishing the power of others to constrain our interpretive "will to power," saving us from narcissism and its melancholy through the very otherness that cannot be exhausted by us, the otherness that always exceeds us. To situate inquiry as a ruin/rune is to foreground the limits and necessary misfiring of a project, problematizing the researcher as "the one who knows." Placed outside of master and victory narratives, inquiry becomes a kind of self-wounding laboratory for discovering the rules by which truth is produced. (2007, p. 11)

These words, all the wor(l)ds I thought I had learned evaporated; *forget, a lost connection.*

On 5 March 2009, my colleague and I scheduled a couple of appointments. Depending on the traffic, it took between 40 and 90 minutes for us to go to that part of the city. We wanted to meet as many participants as possible whenever we were in the field. Besides, we did not think it was appropriate for us to take more than two hours of our participants' time. So we scheduled these meetings accordingly. What we did not realize was that at least for Jun Hee's mom who has three children, this was a rare occasion for her to talk about herself, her life, and her story. She introduced herself as Jun Hee's mom as it is a customary practice of Korean culture that a parent, particularly a mother, is called by the name of her eldest child. She said that she usually worked seven days a week. It was not clear if she took the day off for this meeting. She also said it was her birthday so her daughter who now lives apart would come to eat dinner with her but she had not eaten lunch when we met around one o'clock. I was not sure if she was eating properly these days after I heard her life story.

For two hours, she was busy talking and could not finish her lunch. And we were getting late for our next appointment. I felt terrible. This was the outcome of being efficient. We left Jun Hee's mom behind so that she could finish her meal by herself. She probably would have walked back home as she did not have a car. We reaped her story and moved to another site for our productivity. This particular ruinous moment of this research was not about a crisis of representation, all-knowing researcher self, or victory narrative. The productive and efficient researcher role I had assumed and taken for myself ruined the reciprocal, and thus (culturally) respectful interactions and relations between the researcher and the participant in this physical setting.

Jun Hee's mother was narrating the details of her 12–14 hours of work over six days, sometimes seven days a week for the last 25 years, which required her to leave home in the dark before dawn and come home in the dark after dusk. She added "It almost feels like I am in a labor camp in North Korea. You know we used to say people in North Korea leave home watching morning stars and come home watching evening stars." I nodded, desperately trying to ease the weight of each word coming out of her mouth. She recollected, "They [her daughter's high school] were charging $2 for water and $3.80 for pizza. It was $1.25 in my neighborhood. Her school was in another town. My goodness, even with $5, you could not eat much." Her high school-aged daughter who had gone to school at seven am and worked as a private tutor for younger students until seven pm usually had a slice of pizza all day and would come home always so hungry. As the mother of a teenaged girl myself, I could not stomach another mother's acute awareness of her own daughter's everyday hunger. What changes would my study bring to this material condition?

Once an encouraging challenge of epistemological-methodological engagement with the complexity of interpretation, representation and explanation became irrelevant. The task was not about working the ruins through the failure of the Enlightenment or a discursive discussion on human agency. Nor was the task about using the text as a site of the failures of representation. The task was to face squarely every day structural-physical hunger, pain, and exhaustion of other immigrants and admit the complete inability of science and research as a discursive practice. The task was to work on ways in which the research can have at least some impacts on material conditions of schooling that she poignantly pinpointed.

Attempting to be accountable to the complexity of representation, I was not prepared to face a North Korean labor camp like life in my research. One might ask "*How should we read* Jun Hee's hunger *in terms of gender*, or for that matter, working the ruins of feminism?" *It was explained,* to be a dutiful researcher, work the issues of representation and discover the rules by which the truth is produced; *forget* the materiality of the others that is walled out by the boundary of fieldwork, *a lost connection.* Or stay in the dark, with shame, *it was explained.* So, I left the field. The terrible, searing longing swallowed my mother's daughter as I tried to forget that I am the daughter of my mother. I did not write my partial experience, partial data analysis, or partial reflective piece. The divide between the research as a discursive practice and the field as the material conditions of life completely silenced me. I called the project failed and lost; *forget, a lost connection.* Yet, a transgressive journey of no return goes on even in silence, in the dark. *You are/act like a bat.*

Wanting and doing promiscuous research/work

In "Righting wrongs," Spivak (2004) problematizes a sacred notion of human right; the history, politics and ethics of human rights have been fraught with the agenda of "a kind of" social Darwinism – the fittest must shoulder the burden of righting the wrongs of the unfit – and the possibility of an alibi for the fittest. Therefore, as she aptly writes, the white (wo)man's burden, undertaking to civilize and develop, which became an alibi for economic, military, and political intervention, was only "a kind of" oppression. In order to disrupt this permanent sanction of the social Darwinism etched in the idea and practice of human rights, Spivak argues for suturing a responsibility-based system into the episteme of human rights through which one must *learn to learn* from below, instead of *staying* in the divide between those who right wrongs and those who are wronged. To learn to learn from below is "to enter ritual practice transgressively, as a hacker enters software" (p. 559), writes Spivak. She declares, however, much to readers' dismay, "I will not be able to produce anthropologically satisfying general descriptions here (of ritual-hacking below) because no trainer can provide satisfactory descriptions of the grammar of a language that s/he is learning painfully" (p. 559).

To my dismay, this paper is "a kind of" reiteration of Spivak's point on how no researcher can provide anthropologically satisfactory descriptions of how to learn to learn from below that s/he is learning painfully in her research/work. Like human rights work, feminist research involves the divide between those who right wrongs/ research and those who are wronged/researched. Like human rights work, feminism and research work is "a corrupt ruin of the colonial model" that gives the possibility of an alibi for researchers (Spivak, 2004, p. 563; see also Tuhiwai Smith, 1999). I repeat what Spivak has argued for: suturing a responsibility-based system into the episteme of research through which one must learn to learn from below not only discursively but also materially, instead of residing in the divide between those who research and those who are researched.

As Visweswaran (1994, p. 100) writes:

> Failure is not just a sign of epistemological crisis (for it is indeed also that), but also, I would argue, an epistemological construct. Failure signals a project that may no longer be attempted, or at least not on the same terms.

My three accounts of failure signal a research project that may no longer be attempted, at least not on the same terms; research is and needs to be more than a discursive practice. Complicating, transgressing, and working through feminist subjectivity, epistemology, and methodology is an inevitable theoretical work that the bird, the beast, and the bat feminist subjects will continue to do. However, when these ever increasingly complex discursive theorizing works evade the materiality of research, life, and our particular historical context, feminist researchers will continuously participate in the violence of "righting wrongs" without realizing we are in fact walling ourselves in and limiting our ability to work with a responsibility-based system.

"Refuge, Refugee, Refuse ..." (Trinh, 2011, p. 47). What happens when one refuses to take refuge within camps/boundaries/walls that promise security, assistance, and placement? Trinh writes that the story of refugees is the story of people refused; like the bat who stays in the dark. Therefore, "refugeeism differs from voluntary immigration in that it does not have a future orientation – the utopia of material, social or religious betterment" (p. 47). For this no-return journey between refuse and refuge, I have not collected "data" for the last two years. But, I have become more regularly and deeply involved with grassroots organizers and other interested educators, parents, and members of the Korean immigrant community, many of whom I met through the research. Is this work research or not? Is my previous research failed or not? At the same time, note that I have more flexibility with the condition of my employment as a tenured professor.

Any of my attempts to produce an *explainable* narrative of promiscuous feminist research/work would be unsatisfactory because I am still grappling not to get completely lost in my engagements with learning to learn below. In addition, for an explanation to work, it must be linked with structural arrangements so that these social structures and everyday experiences can be organized and accounted for. If there were such social structures, I might not have (felt that I) failed the research.

Yet, I am willing to write that promiscuity insists persistence and patience rather than efficiency, productivity, and effectiveness. Also, wanting and doing both ways – to write for peer researchers and to learn to learn below – is a promiscuous desire and act. It brings together violent, apartheid epistemic structures, where the demands of (academic) productivity, ethnographic intelligibility, proliferating rituals of complexity in research, and good intention miserably fail to access or enter the multiplicity of subaltern materiality, languages, and experiences, and vice versa. In this research/work, anointed researchers may need to leave (their research) and risk in multiplicity, living life as it comes, fasting verbally and linguistically for a while (Trinh, 2011) to do a "necessary and impossible responsibility" (Spivak, 2004, p. 559) to learn to learn below so that our research/work *becomes* promiscuous affiliations of the Bat, the Bird, and the Beast, both discursively and materially. And, I still want to write as "words and images can be starting points for actions; together they form memory and history" (Trinh, 2011, p. 52). *You are/act like a Bat.*

Acknowledgements

The author expresses her appreciation for the reviewers, Sara Childers, and Stephanie Daza for their careful reading and feedback on various versions of this article.

Notes

1. In this paper, I intentionally utilize a hybrid of writing genres, literary conventions, and cultural narratives. In this, I am writing in US English accented by Korean. Rather than trying to contain the "promiscuity" of the bat subjectivity in westernized English and academic writing, I experiment to write a research tale that crosses the boundaries of personal, cultural, and academic language. This is another promiscuous attempt of a bat that *wants it both ways*.
2. Throughout the paper, I apply an analogy of the Bird, the Beast, and the Bat to my own experience, relationship, and research work. What I attempt to highlight is not necessarily who can be a bird or beast. Instead, both represent what keeps the boundary. In fact, these identities can be shifting in different contexts. While I identify with a bat in this paper, I can also perform a bird or a beast in other situations, contexts, and relationships.

References

Althusser, L. (1971). Ideology and ideological state apparatuses. In *Lenin and philosophy and other essays* (pp. 127–186). New York, NY: Monthly Review Press.

Anzaldúa, G. (1987). *Borderlands: La frontera*. San Francisco, CA: Aunt Lute.

Asher, N. (2003). At the intersections: A postcolonialist woman of color considers Western feminism. *Social Education, 67*, 47–50.

Bhabha, H. (1994). *The location of culture*. New York, NY: Routledge.

Britzman, D. P. (2000). "The question of belief": Writing poststructural ethnography. In E. St. Pierre & W. S. Pillow (Eds.), *Working the ruins: Feminist poststructural theory and methods in education* (pp. 27–40). London: Routledge.

Cha, T. H. K. (1982/2001). *Dictee*. Berkeley, CA: University of California Press.

Chow, R. (1991). Violence in other countries: China as crisis, spectacle and women. In C. T. Mohanty, A. Russo, & L. Torres (Eds.), *Third world women and the politics of feminism* (pp. 81–100). Bloomington, IN: Indiana University Press.

Collins, P. H. (1990). *Black feminist thought: Knowledge, consciousness, and the politics of empowerment*. New York, NY: Routledge.

Dillard, C. B. (2000). The substance of things hoped for, the evidence of things not seen: Examining endarkened feminist epistemology in educational research and leadership. *International Journal of Qualitative Studies in Education, 13*, 661–681.

Du Bois, W. E. B. (1903/2003). *The souls of Black folks*. New York, NY: Barnes & Noble Classics.

Fanon, F. (1952/1991). *Black skin white masks*. New York, NY: Grove.

Hull, G., Scott, P. B., & Smith, B. (1982/1993). *But some of us are brave: All the women are white, all the blacks are men: Black women's studies*. New York: The Feminist Press at the City University of New York.

Kim, E. H., & Chungmoo, C. (1998). *Dangerous women: Gender and Korean nationalism*. New York, NY: Routledge.

Lather, P. (2007). *Getting lost: Feminist efforts toward a double(d) science*. Albany, NY: State University of New York.

Lather, P., & Smithies, C. S. (1997). *Troubling the angels: Women living with HIV/AIDS*. Boulder, CO: Westview Press.

Lew, J. (2006). *Asian Americans in class: Charting the achievement gap among Korean American youth*. New York, NY: Teachers College Press.

Lew, J. (2010). Asian American youth in poverty: Benefits and limitations of ethnic networks in postsecondary and labor force options. *Journal of Education for Students Placed at Risk, 15*, 127–143.

MacLure, M. (2011). Qualitative inquiry: Where are the ruins? *Qualitative Inquiry, 17*, 997–1005.

Marker, M. (2003). Indigenous voice, community, and epistemic violence: The ethnographer's "interests" and what "interests" the ethnographer. *International Journal of Qualitative Studies in Education, 16*, 361–375.

Mohanty, C. T. (2004). *Feminism without borders: Decolonizing theory, practicing solidarity*. Durham, NC: Duke University Press.

Morga, C., & Anzaldúa, G. (1983). *This bridge called my back: Writings by radical women of color* (2nd ed.). Latham, NY: Kitchen Table: Women of Color Press.

Narayan, U. (1997). *Dislocating cultures: Identities, traditions, and third world feminism*. New York, NY: Routledge.

Reinharz, S. (1992). *Feminist methods in social research*. New York, NY: Oxford University Press.

Rhee, J.-E. (2008). Risking to be wounded again: Performing open eye/I. *Race Ethnicity and Education, 11*, 29–40.

Rhee, J.-E. (2009). Dislocating oriental citizen-subject makings: A postcolonial reading of Korean/Asian American women's narratives. In R. S. Coloma (Ed.), *Postcolonial challenges in education* (pp. 249–267). New York, NY: Peter Lang.

Said, E. (1978). *Orientalism*. New York, NY: Random House.

Selby, J. (2004). Working divides between indigenous and non-indigenous: Disruptions of identity. *International Journal of Qualitative Studies in Education, 17*, 143–156.

Shin, K.-S. (2008). 엄마를 부탁해 [Please look after mom]. Kyung Gi Do: Changbi.

Spivak, G. (1988). Can the subaltern speak? In P. Williams & L. Chrisman (Eds.), *Colonial discourse and post-colonial theory: A reader* (pp. 66–111). New York, NY: Columbia University Press.

Spivak, G. (2004). Righting wrongs. *The South Atlantic Quarterly, 103*, 523–581.

St. Pierre, E., & Pillow, W. S. (Eds.). (2000). *Working the ruins: Feminist poststructural theory and methods in education*. London: Routledge.

Subedi, B., & Rhee, J.-E. (2008). Negotiating collaboration across differences. *Qualitative Inquiry, 14*, 1070–1092.

Subreenduth, S., & Rhee, J.-E. (2010). A porous, morphing, and circulatory mode of self-other: Decolonizing identity politics by engaging transnational reflexivity. *International Journal of Qualitative Studies in Education, 23*, 331–346.

Trinh, T. M.-h. (1989). *Woman, native, other: Writing postcoloniality and feminism*. Bloomington, IN: Indiana University Press.

Trinh, T. M.-h. (2011). *Elsewhere, within here: Immigration, refugeeism and the boundary event*. New York, NY: Routledge.

Tuhiwai Smith, L. (1999). *Decolonizing methodologies: Research and indigenous peoples*. New York: Zed Books.

Up With Christ Hayes. (2012, February 4). *MSNBC*. Retrieved from http://www.msnbc.msn.com/id/21134540/vp/46264099#46264099.

Villenas, S. (1996). The colonizer/colonized Chicana ethnographer: Identity, marginalization, and co-optation in the field. *Harvard Educational Review, 66*, 711–732.

Visweswaran, K. (1994). *Fictions of feminist ethnography*. Minneapolis, MN: University of Minnesota Press.

Watson, C. (2006). Unreliable narrators? 'Inconsistency' (and some inconstancy) in interviews. *Qualitative Research, 6*, 367–385.

Much more than power: the pedagogy of promiscuous black feminism

M. Francyne Huckaby

Center for Urban Education, College of Education, Texas Christian University, Fort Worth, TX, USA

> This paper explores promiscuous black feminism by juxtaposing the pedagogies of black feminism, Foucualt's poststructuralism, and my grandmother. The tensions created by these juxtapositions illuminate the ways black feminism and poststructuralism are resources and challenges to each other, and how both offer understandings of the relations at play that shape identities and lives. Making use of these theories and lessons from my grandmother, I explore the necessity and dangers of experience in theorizing power and vulnerability in theorizing experience. Focusing on experiences and feminist lessons from my grandmother, I propose that much more than power is at play.

Much more than power: the pedagogy of promiscuous black feminism

I use black feminism as well as feminism to study, theorize, and represent this twenty-first-century world. But I am not a promiscuous feminist scholar because I resist and push beyond the boundaries of roles, work, and scripts prescribed for and inscribed on the categorizations of woman and female. Nor is my feminist work promiscuous because it pushes feminist theory, research, and practice beyond the study of women, sex, and gender; pulls in non-feminist realms; or makes use of experiences and theory – instead of restraining feminist thought.

Might I dare suggest that limited social imaginations occupied with differently valued binaries produce the logic that relegates feminist scholarship to "woman" thus rendering other feminist work promiscuous? For those who do not yet understand the relevance of feminist scholarship and movements that push against and step over provincial notions of feminism, feminist attention beyond gender seems disconcerting if not absurd. Faced with scholarship that may seem like a hodgepodge, the indiscriminate reader may force expanding feminisms into categories limited to gender in general and female in particular. Thus feminist scholars, knowing the potentiality of our work, understand that we exist in a world not fully conscious of feminism even in its most provincial sense, let alone feminist scholarship that goes beyond womanhood and gender. Facing this situation, we claim the label *promiscuous* and its historical function to describe women who live outside prescribed boundaries in this *QSE* special issue. In this twenty-first century where the twentieth-century progress of women has regressed, we transgress.

The making of a promiscuous feminist

Feminist and feminism as signifiers are easily rejected. For example, recent chronicles of famous women's commentary on feminism include Beyoncé suggesting "Bootylicous" as a new name for feminism (Wright, 2011); Sandra Day O'Connor stating, "I don't call myself that" (Wright, 2011); Bjork resisting the label because, "it's more important to do positive stuff ... to be asking than complaining" (Wright, 2011); Marissa Mayer claiming, "I don't think that I would consider myself a feminist. I think I certainly believe in equal rights ... but I do think that feminism has become in many ways a more negative word" (Reinsberg, 2012); and Melissa Leo saying, "I don't think of myself as a feminist at all. As soon as we start labeling and categorizing ourselves and others, that's going to shut down the world" (Reinsberg, 2012). I also find that undergraduate students in my educational foundations classes sometimes struggle with openly feminist scholars. On one occasion, a student vehemently proclaimed that Jane Roland Martin could not be a feminist. When I pushed to understand her reasoning despite Martin's clarity on the subject, the student stated that her ideas were reasonable; implying that, as she understood it, feminism was unreasonable. Even when expressing views consistent with feminist theory and practice, women reject the label in fear of how the world will respond. Feminism is not widely understood within or outside academia and this lack of understanding narrowly genders and devalues it.

Zeilinger (2012, p. 113) acknowledges "that the word 'feminism' can be kind of alienating" as she compares feminism to a popular candy, explaining that the label is like the outer candy coating, while the movement, history, sentiments, truth, and power are like the chocolate center. I personally find the candy delicious even after the coating dissolves, but easier to handle with the shell. Similarly, feminism facilitates making sense of the messiness of the world without oversimplifying or tidying things up too much. Turning away from feminisms is dangerous at this time, when the conditions for women are becoming more like those of our ancestors, and the separation of our bodies from public discourse, policy, and law is wearing thin. In 2012 alone legitimate rape (Moore, 2012), g-d-willed pregnancies resulting from rape (Sorcha, 2012), and "binders full of women" (Noguchi, 2012) were viral discourses, and the laws to curtail the reproductive choices of women and families spread like contagions across the states (Gold & Nash, 2012). While such views may indeed be minority views, as I hope they are, our laws and discourses have curtailed women's progress. Furthermore, feminisms have made possible discourses that protested and countered these actions. Feminism is not just about the impact of policy on our lives as women; it is important for making sense of the world theoretically.

Even in academia, feminism faces challenges. In a grant application, for example, I sought support for research on public discourse and educational advocacy. In the proposal I stated:

> Drawing theoretically on the practices of the ancient Greek *parrhesiastes* [speaker of dangerous truth] and extending the theoretical and methodological work of the French philosopher, Michel Foucault, with feminist and womanist critiques, the

study explores the ways 21st century school teachers, community members, and academics engage *parrhesia* [truth telling] within popular and political discourses about education ... Given the ways the profession of education has become feminized and gender mediates public discourse within the United States, feminist/womanist critique of Foucault within the field of education is essential.

Part of the feedback I received from the reviewers questioned why my research only focused on women. Even though this reading of my proposal surprised me, in some ways I understand their question as I wrote of feminization, education, gender assumptions, and feminist/womanist critique. Nonetheless, such signifiers are not limited to female research participants. Education, public discourse, *parrhesia,* theory, method, and critique reach beyond the category of female in the binary conception of gender. Furthermore, the use of feminist theories for the purposes of criticisms does not and should not lead reviewers to assume that only female educators, community members, or academics would be interviewed.

The study of this grant proposal brings black feminism, poststructuralism, feminism, and postmodernism into the study of discourse, education, equity, advocacy, and activism: an area of study important for society as a whole, not just women. Central to my work is how education is discursively rendered in public discourse and how communities of citizens, educators, and teacher educators engage power and vulnerability as they advocate for education and equity. Because experience, power, and vulnerability are at the heart of the study, I make use of feminist theories, in particular, black feminism. Created at the junction of multiple oppressions, black feminism sheds light on power and vulnerability in a way that I find useful.

One way to think about this rendering of feminist scholarship, thought, and experience as promiscuous is as a working of power. As an academic and theorist, I have made and continue to make use of Foucault as I wrestle to understand and engage relations of power. However, the intimate curriculum of my pre/extra-academic life, like that of most people, is at work and mediates my interpretations and use of Foucault and now fuels my challenges to power as I am re-theorizing it through an attention to vulnerabilities (Huckaby, 2011). Feminism in and of itself is rendered promiscuous for theorizing our own lives and the existence of the world – as people (female, male, transgender, transsexual, intersexual) who claim feminism. But approaching the world with black feminism as theoretical and practical orientation is not an unnatural act for a black woman even as it challenges patriarchy.

The curriculum for a promiscuous black feminist

My grandmother approached the world through observation and conversation; encouraging me to do so as well. She introduced me to black feminism even though I did not learn to claim the ideas we explored as such until decades later and still wonder if she knew this body of work that began in the 1800s with black women abolitionists and suffragists. Black feminism attends to race, gender, class, education, labor/work, sexuality, and religion, because each of these is important to black women's experiences (Davidson, Gines, & Marcano, 2010). Gender, race, and class were central to my grandmother's questions.

In third grade, I transferred from an African American neighborhood school to a school diverse in terms of race, ethnicity, social class, and student age range, if not religion. With this transition, my grandmother's questions began to focus more directly on race and class, but gender remained present. At first I was quite comfortable making generalizations from a simple observation, but Grandma would push me to look more closely and broadly and ask a question to complicate my oversimplifications, "Can you think of an example when that is not so?" As I got older, I began to feel like the questions were not just for my own education, but were an opportunity for us to study the world together.

Black feminism as pedagogy and theory offers connections to experiences, not as *women*, but as *black women* on this planet across time and space. Black feminism moves beyond the earlier work of African American studies, women's studies, and feminism. Black women's commitment to the liberation of black people and women is profoundly rooted in lived experience (Guy-Sheftall, 2010). Thus black feminism – as practice, discourse, politics, and philosophy – comes from and responds to black women's experiences and complex social locations. Feminisms cannot be understood through one singular experience as black feminism illustrates. To use black feminism and other feminisms, from my perspective, is to attend to an ethic of equity and an expectation of justice that grows out of working to understand the experiences and relations that make the systematic production and reproduction of rather stable inequities possible.

> **Black feminism is pedagogy.**
> Because my mother worked and was my only active parent, I spent many hours with three elders of my extended family – my aunt, uncle, and grandmother. Magical things happened in their home and it became an important portal to my understanding the world.
> I was a quiet child, often content listening. I loved Grandma's fascinating stories, poetry recitations, and piano playing. Discontent with my quiet nature, she regularly requested, "Paint me a picture with words." I'd try to make my stories vivid and lively, like hers. With attention and gentle prodding, she encouraged more detail, occasionally offering a more aptly descriptive word I did not yet know.
> After I started preschool, my grandmother posed one deceptively simple after-school query, "How do you know if someone is a boy or a girl?" This uncharacteristically direct question surprised me. While always interested in what I had to say and how I saw the world, she was not usually so direct. I was perplexed – did my grandmother not know the differences between girls and boys? This was not the first time she came to me for information. Even though we never played with store-bought toys in her home, I answered her questions about how my plastic and battery operated toys worked. I understood these questions, after all born in the late 1800s, she'd never seen such toys. But she taught girls and boys, raised daughters and sons, and had male and female grandchildren. I took her question seriously and decided to start with obvious things like clothing and hair. I suspect I must have painted some troubling pictures about gender that led Grandma to this rather direct pedagogy.
> As her questions on gender continued to fuel our discussions, I found myself paying attention to the things girls and boys did, the ways we interacted, and how adults treated us. If I answered one of her questions insufficiently, I wanted to go back to her the next time more knowledgeable with something to share.
> As time passed, her questions expanded: What's different about your new school? What kinds of families do your friends have? What kinds of work do their mothers do, their fathers? How should you determine who your friends should be; by their race; whether they are wealthy or poor? Why do you think we have a society with poor people and wealthy people? Why is skin color important? Why does being a girl matter? Is it better to be rich or poor, a girl or boy, colored or white?
> **Pedagogy requires attention to the world.**

The syllabus for a promiscuous Foucauldian

Spivak's (2009) close analysis of Foucault's terminology and its French meanings is instructive. She points out how his naming *power* and *knowledge* are catachrestic, misuses of the words. Nonetheless, *pouvoir* gets close to naming "the condition of possibility of power is the condition of possibility of a viewpoint that renders intelligible its exercise" (p. 33), and *pouvoir/savoir* attempts to define the process. Power as *pouvoir* has a can-do essence to it as it means to be able to or possible (Spivak, 2009). *Savoir* is "implicit knowledge special to society," whereas *connaissance* is intellectual knowledge "that one can find in scientific books, philosophical theories, and religious justifications" (Foucault cited in Scheurich & McKenzie, 2005, p. 846). It is the *savoir*, Foucault continues, that "makes possible at a given moment the appearance of a theory ..." (p. 846). *Pouvoir/savoir* (power/knowledge) is "being able to do something – only as you are able to make sense of it" (Spivak, 2009, p. 38).

Black feminism also has this can-do-ness about it but instead of being knowledge that makes power possible, black feminism is at work in the impossibilities of relations that have as much to do with vulnerability as they do power. Yet, attention to vulnerability is consistently dismissed in the ever-present pursuit of power. Furthermore, when vulnerability does come into play, the focus tends to be on minimizing one's own vulnerability or using that of others for leverage.

My grandmother's lessons are instructive here as she stressed the importance of moving beyond my own experiences and questioning the world around me, particularly the dynamics at play in terms of race, class, and gender. For Guy-Sheftall (2010, p. ix) such a *feminist* orientation:

> capture[s] the emancipatory vision and acts of resistance among a diverse group of African American women who attempt in their writings to articulate their understanding of the complex nature of black womanhood, the interlocking nature of the oppressions black women suffer, and the necessity of sustained struggle in their quest for self-definition, the liberation of black people, and gender equality.

In her questioning and conversations, Grandma connected me to

---

Black Feminism is as old as Black Women.

After my first semester of college, I returned home for the winter holiday and spent a day with my grandmother. Her pedagogy was directive, planned, and choreographed. Our bodies sat at the dining room table for hours, but with her words we traveled through time. Grandma divulged the history of every woman she knew in our family. She started with her grandmother, who in the nineteenth century was the first freed woman in our family, and ended with my cousins who were a few years my senior.

I learned about their educations; who married, when and why; who did not; who had children, when and why; who did not; sacrifices made and responsibilities accepted; those not; limitations faced and creation of possibilities or not; miracles within means; unrealistic expectations that limited progress; their assertiveness and strategies for protection. Remembering lives of women – their love and grief

Coming to understand
Their vulnerabilities and powers
Like family history, black feminism is savoir.

---

the intersectionality of black feminism, challenging feminism and its fidelity to gender (Crenshaw, 1991). The theory behind her questioning and telling – along with Latina, Indigenous, Asian, and Womanist feminisms – reveals the polyvocality of women's experiences and the necessity of attending to women's complex identities and social locations (Villaverde, 2008) situated on the vulnerable side of too many binaries. Even though she challenged me to attend to categories of race, class, gender, I am not divided. Instead, I developed a lens through which I came to know myself as whole yet able to recognize without internalizing the segmentations the world imposes. Such attention to the complex interaction of identities, heavy with social significance and historical context, is important and necessary not because we compartmentalize ourselves, but because we were born into and live within socio-historical contexts that see race and gender as separate and distinct entities, and both as distinct markers of otherness. I understand myself as a singular entity and make use of theory that honors the inseparability of who I am even as I seemingly step away from feminism and toward Foucault.

Foucault's work explicitly attends to power and the ways power/knowledge constructs identifiable bodies and relegates some forms of knowledge to the margins and unintelligibility. While Foucault does not tell his readers what to do, he does offer theory that constructs power as relational, dynamic, totalizing, and dispersed. Not only is such work a resource to black feminism in "understanding issues of agency, subjectivity, the feminine, marginalization, and difference" (Davidson et al., 2010, p. 222), but black feminism is equally its resource. Black feminism informs by offering challenges (Davidson et al., 2010), exceptions, and contradictions. Despite the fact that poststructuralism often relies upon inaccessible language (hooks cited in Perpich, 2010) and may offer "no clear and significant implication for practice" (Collins in McKay, Collins, Henderson, & Jordon, 1991, p. 24), black feminists like myself draw upon it. After all, marginalized groups such as ourselves challenge the authority of Western normativity and create space to know previously silenced, muted, and ignored experiences. For Collins (in McKay et al., 1991) this focus on multiple histories, perspectives, and experiences in efforts to theorize is a strength of poststructuralism that functions to undermine a presumed norm that serves to define and measure deviance. While specific concerns and positions of individuals and groups may differ as do strategies to envision and actualize equity, the project of undoing the center is similar for black feminism, feminism, and poststructuralism.

The insufficiency of power

Foucault thinks of relations of power as sites for reversals and inversions; that the thing that may establish a relation in a configuration, say age as status, may be the thing to reverse it. Foucault states:

> I mean a relationship in which one person tries to control the conduct of the other ... these power relations are mobile, they can be modified, they are not fixed once and for all. For example, the fact that I may be older than you, and that you may initially have been intimidated, may be turned around during the course of our conversation, and I may end up being intimidated before someone precisely because he is younger than I am. These power relations are thus mobile, reversible, and unstable. (1997, p. 292)

Baudrillard claims that Foucault's "... power returns to its own identity again as a final principle: it is the last term, the irreducible web, the last tale that can be told ..." (Baudrillard, 1987, p. 40). What Foucault does with power is unmask "all the final or casual illusions concerning power ... Power is an irreversible principle of organization because it fabricates the real (always more and more of the real ...)" (Baudrillard, 1987, p. 40). "While exploiters and exploited do in fact exist, they are on different sides because there is no reversibility in production, which is precisely the point: nothing essential happens at that level," thus Foucault's relations of power offer "no antagonistic positions" (Baudrillard, 1987, p. 44). Baudrillard claims that "nowhere does [power] cancel itself out, become entangled in itself, or mingle with death" (1987, p. 40). Even when Foucault considers change in relations of power, he cannot release power and speaks of relations of power reversing, flipping, inverting themselves.

Foucault's relations of power, wherein one attempts to act upon the possible actions of others with intent to control or shape their future actions, counter more common and even feminist conceptions of power as held or invested in particular entities, institutions, or individuals – the powerful. Understanding power as an embodied quality or possession is consistent with Gilson's claim that invulnerability is a form of willful ignorance (2011). For Baudrillard (1987), power is an illusion sustained as simulacrum. Invulnerability is also a type of simulacrum that denies vulnerability for the self and projects it on others with whom one does not identify. Such a perspective assumes "that to be vulnerable is simply to be susceptible, exposed, at risk, and in danger. In short, it is to be somehow weaker, defenseless and dependent, open to harm and injury" (Gilson, 2011, p. 310). Power then is good and desirable; vulnerability negative and abominable. Within such illusions, "the powerful" can ignore their vulnerabilities and "the vulnerable" their powers.

Production makes things intelligible.
At first, my intellectual flirtation with Foucault was utilitarian as I wanted a particular theoretical perspective to study how people in subjugated positions engage relations of power. I read Foucault, made him my research companion, brought him into my dreams; eventually introducing him to friends and students and delighting in conversations about him. While Foucault thoughtfully theorized the constitution of the self within relations of power, creating space for reversals within these relations; his production over-protects power at the expense of rendering vulnerability intelligible. Production in what Baudrillard (1987) calls its original form – *pro-ducere* – means to cause to appear. Since such knowledge is "theoretico-active" (Foucault, 1998, p. 262), not simply explanatory, production renders things discursively and makes them visible. Power as productive or theoretico-active holds even with conceptions of power as repressive because making sense of power as repressive is a form of production. Furthermore, theoretico-active and productive functions of knowledge attract our consciousness to perceptible formations and away from other possibilities that fall into the unintelligible through seduction or *se-ducere*. Seduction counters production and "withdraws something from the visible order" (Baudrillard, 1987, p. 21), thus power, in order to be strong according to Foucault, must be effective on the levels of desire, knowledge, and production (Foucault, 1980).

One might think that such a poststructuralist is incommensurable with feminisms because continental philosophy typically excludes feminism. Foucault's work rarely attends to gender (Butler, 1990; McNeil, 1993) nor was he "a champion of feminism" (McNeil, 1993, p. 151). Ramazanoğlu suggests that his theory as it pertains to power, knowledge, the self, and sexuality, challenges feminist politics based on a conception of men having power over women (1993, p. 3). hooks (2000) points out that beyond feminism, "power is commonly equated with domination and control over people and things" (p. 84). Furthermore, Jordon disavows poststructuralism as "abject worshiping of European fathers at their worst" and irrelevant to her work (McKay et al., 1991, p. 24). Black feminists leverage other criticisms against poststructuralism, which include an inattention to the role of power and domination in the construction of difference. While an attention to difference and diversity may be promising, accommodating "too many 'others'" in a discourse without a center results in further ignorance of historically marginalized groups in the competition for knowledge claims (McKay et al., 1991). Collins suggests that the reliance on *diversity* as a buzzword is an illustration of this inattention to power. Furthermore, authority, subjectivity, and tradition were dismantled by poststructuralism at a time when marginalized groups were "asserting authorship, tradition, and subjectivity" (McKay et al., 1991, p. 24).

Nonetheless, Foucault offers possibilities.
Seduction renders things inconceivable.

While vulnerability may seem the opposite to notions of power as invested in certain bodies, positions, and institutions – the powerful – the contrary is true. Both conceptions of the powerful and the vulnerable as identifiable entities function by theoretically investing bodies with specific qualities. Thus, they are the same – reductionistic, static, and ill-advised. These are notions of the powerful and the vulnerable that could lead one to mistake impotence, an inability to act, one of power's antonyms, as its opposite. Even though certain relations of power may seek non-action at times for certain purposes, at other times actions are desirable and necessary. Furthermore, non-action may be appropriate action for a variety of purposes. My grandmother's lessons with their attention to how I was situated in the world and the ways my ancestors faced the realities of their lives were a resistance to conceptions of power and vulnerability as possessions embodied in identifiable beings. Furthermore, she made the inability to act inconceivable and responsive intentional actions, even those of standing down or stepping aside, highly valued.

Kipnis (2007) in her essay, *Vulnerability*, suggests that power "come[s] in more than one guise. There's the power of public shame, for instance, and the power of underlings to humiliate and humble their superiors ..." (pp. 1789–1790). While such actions show changes in relative positions and offer challenges to conceptions of power as invested in specific entities, no reversal in the dynamics of the relations takes place. These reversals of power that Foucault acknowledges are more like rotations on a fulcrum that continue to reify power. To offer a simplistic metaphor, it is as if relations of power invert or reverse much like the teetering of a seesaw.

Reversals within certain kinds of relations of power, however, can become exponentially burdensome for some. Kipnis' work on the vulnerability of the female body acknowledges the symbolic and monetary value of vaginas, writing:

> Pricey dinners, diamond rings ... – in what other system of exchange can you trade exclusive access to an orifice for a suburban split-level and a lifetime of monetary support? Not such a bad deal, considering the backbreaking and alienated things a lot of people end up doing for money. (p. 1485)

While Kipnis is instructive, she attends to the anatomy of women as a seemingly unified category without consideration of the ways race and class exponentially change the scenario. Indeed her description relies on middle, if not upper-middle-class assumptions. She continues, "overvalued things so often provoke that mischievous human urge to demote them: as we know, vaginas aren't only revered, they're also continually denigrated (along with those who possess one, of course)" (pp. 1504–1506). Kipnis illustrates how reversals within relations of power can work to further disadvantage people in marginalized positions. Given women's histories and the social productions at play, some women have access to particularly valuable benefits and risks – powers and vulnerabilities. But the relations of power have not reversed to favor women (or people of color) as they have favored men (or white people).

This dynamic of relations was clear to me in the family history my grandmother shared, and may be why I cannot imagine a theory of power sans experience, nor experience without theorizing vulnerability. At no point did my female ancestors have an upper hand in relations of power. Always responding to the world and the society that imagined and reified them in particular ways, they acted. Sometimes they extended beyond and other times they succumbed to the limitations constructed for women like them in their times and places. Even though they existed within relations of power, those relations did not flip, invert, or reverse to their advantage, and when reversals did occur, they did so person-to-person and not on the macro or ideological levels that made their race and gender such significant characteristics around which to justify oppression, discrimination, and marginalization. Attention to power renders unintelligible other relations at work, mainly, *relations of vulnerability* (Huckaby, 2011).

Such denial of vulnerability is problematic, for vulnerability is a common phenomenon, not something that only those lacking power experience. As Butler (2003) states, "This means that each of us is constituted politically in part by virtue of the social vulnerability of our bodies – as a site of desire and physical vulnerability, as a site of publicity at once assertive and exposed" (p. 10). As a common condition, vulnerability is not a condition for some; it is our shared corporeal, physical, social, political, public, and essentially a primary human condition (Butler, 2003). Vulnerability is an openness to being affected by others and also

Refusals may indeed be possible.
Not only did my grandmother tell stories about other women in our family that day at the dinner table, she also shared her own stories. I was not surprised with her lingering sadness at the loss of her first husband which too quickly followed that of her second daughter. But that she remained, into her mid-90s, besotted with him took me by surprise. I don't think I had seen her smile as deeply as she did while she remembered him. She was quite clear on three points about her second husband – her gratefulness for the life they shared, her love for him, and the necessity of the marriage since she was a young woman with a toddler at the turn of the twentieth century.

I immediately realized how one of her choices rippled down the generations of her family. My mother is Grandma's youngest child – by the time she came, her older siblings had left home and started their adult lives. Mom is just a few years younger than Grandma's oldest grandchildren, and when she was young, Grandma refused to expose her children or grandchildren to segregated experiences. She avoided public buses, choosing to walk or ride with family. This meant daily activities outside her home required more physical effort, time, and planning. Similarly, she boycotted segregated movie theatres, shopped in stores where they could walk through the front door, and took family trips that minimized if not eliminated such marginalizing experiences. If I remember correctly, she traveled to Mexico with my mom and her grandchildren one summer instead of staying in Texas. She ensured she traveled with enough food so purchasing food from a back window was not necessary. My grandmother was a proud and self-sufficient woman, but I believe part of her decision here had much to do with who her family is. Our skin colors, facial characteristics, and hair textures vary, and her decision limited the ability of the larger society to impose its biases on her family. While she possessed the power to control to some degree what her family experienced, she could not change the relations at play in society, the rule of public busing, or the discrimination that might let one grandchild slip through the front door and relegate another one to the theatre balcony.

Escaping the relations at play is impossible.

affecting others in ways that are not simply negative, but also positive. Unfortunately, the quest for power and more power only produces (*pro-ducere*) a negative, undesirable understanding of vulnerability. But as a condition of potential, other conditions are possible because of vulnerability – suffering, harm, love, pleasure. These are conditions that both limit and enable (Gilson, 2011, p. 310). Despite the commonness of vulnerability for embodied beings, "we live, experience, and are affected by it differently, thus we need to understand it through our particular embodied, social experiences" (Gilson, 2011, p. 311).

The necessity and dangers of experience

The emergence of academic feminism (Spivak, 2009) and black feminism (McKay et al., 1991) in the USA focused on discovering and revealing experience, practice, and accomplishments. Through the narrating of stories and recovering stories, we now know more about the lives, experiences, and contexts of the women who came before and share the world with us now. While grateful for this knowledge, it is a place to start, not the conclusion.

Perpich (2010) warns against the uncritical use of experience by drawing on Scott's claim that "[i]t is not individuals who have experience, but subjects who are constituted through experience" (cited in Perpich, 2010, pp. 473–478). In this sense, experience explains nothing and offers no evidence on which to base truth. Instead experience is "that which we seek to explain, that about which knowledge is produced" (Scott cited in Perpich, 2010). Thus, experience discursively produces identities, and both experiences and the identities they produce are historical. Defaulting to experience as evidence of truth or as explanation, however, is dangerous, particularly for marginalized groups. Distinguishable groups are not natural occurrences; they are historical, created discursively through multiple forms of discrimination, marginalization, and oppression. In other words, turning to experience as evidence for knowledge can function to the disadvantage of oppressed groups and the advantage of privileged groups.

For Gilson (2011), such a "refusal to recognize historical context constitutes ignorance about race [and gender] and facilitates an ignorant preservation of white [gendered] privilege" (p. 320). Claims of truth based on experience can make differences seem natural, including privilege and its role in history. Within such naturalization, the assumptions, practices, ideologies, premises, and representations at work are rendered invisible and the resulting experiences of an identifiable marginalized group natural. Thus marginalized peoples are discursively more vulnerable to and privileged groups likely unaware of the processes at work. Such a state is an "[i]njustice, which can be understood as the unjust distribution of vulnerability" (Gilson, 2011, p. 309). To be vulnerable is to understand "the self as being shaped through its relationships to others, its world, and environs" (Gilson, 2011, p. 319).

My last lesson in black feminism from my grandmother occurred during the winter break of my freshman year in college. As my grandmother divulged the history of women in our family, I came to understand their vulnerabilities and powers as they related to the social contexts of their existences. Similarly, Scott seeks to understand how more vulnerable identities are "ascribed, resisted, or embraced" but also to discover the means by which such processes remain unremarkable, achieving their effect precisely because they go unnoticed (Perpich, 2010, p. 491). Relying on experiences to build claims to truth or even to challenge dominant forms of knowledge can reify the perspectives that function to privilege dominant groups and disadvantage marginalized groups. Stories, histories, research, and other forms of knowledge creation have a heavy hand in creating taken-for-granted notions that function to exacerbate discrimination, oppression, and domination while also concealing how they work.

Cannella and Manuelito (2008) argue that scholars, consistently repeating the "Eurocentric error" (Jaimes cited in Cannella & Manuelito, 2008), quite possibly unconsciously, impose upon marginalized peoples constructions and interpretations that distort their lives and histories. An uncritical reliance on experiences that do not address and challenge the constructions, strategies, and tactics at work further marginalizes. Even experiences that challenge or show exceptions to dominant assumptions as black feminism does are dangerous (Perpich, 2010) as they reify the conditions of marginalization not just for dominant and privileged groups,

> **Mixing savoir and connaissance is critical.**
> My writing where I foreground experiences in my theoretical offerings or use theory to make sense of experiences pleases me most and receives more insightful commentary from students, scholars, family and friends. These pieces invite readers to think about the experiences I share with them and to bring their own into the reading. This mixing is important to me even though the common criticism reviewers offer is either that my writing is too practical or too theoretical. Despite these critiques, I continue to bring both to my writing and try to do so with some thought, skill, and craft. I believe I am better able to reveal the dynamics at play when both *savoir* and *connaissance* are present.
>
> I am often unable to conceptualize my writing until I know what experience(s) and which aspects of a theory will become the catalyst. Even when I think I am certain about theory or analysis, juxtaposing experience and theory changes theory, complicates experiences, and makes analysis possible. This article, for example, began to crystalize as I remembered one of my grandmother's poems – Oh, Sun Flower! I began writing:
>
> > One summer we visited the sunflower patch we planted as the sun lowered each evening. At first we watered the soil. As the seedlings grew, we weeded the tiniest ones and watched the others grow. Just after the flowers had bloomed, Grandma began one evening, "Oh, Sun Flower …" I was in awe as she seemed to both capture and command the flowers' movement toward the sun with words. I listened to her recitation and eventually joined in.
> >
> > The last tête-à-tête with my grandmother was her final lesson in black feminism as she passed away during the finals week that ended my freshman year. I soon realized our visits to the sunflower patch are of my most cherished memories, but after her death I was disappointed that I could not remember the experience more fully. In the mood for poetry years later, I purchased Blake's *Songs of Innocence and Songs of Experience* (1992) from the sale table for one dollar. I noticed *Ah! Sun-Flower* in the table of contents (p. 39). After reading the first line silently – Ah, Sun-Flower! weary of time – I was delighted.
> >
> > While written by a white, European male, Ah, Sun-Flower was useful for my grandmother and me. His words added a layer of significance to our sunflower patch – an experience we created. The combination of such a loving pedagogy and a stranger's words in my grandmother's voice tethered me to the world. Finding Blake's book of poems in my mid-twenties returned my grandmother and our sunflowers to me and me to them.
>
> **Promiscuous black feminism is not new.**

but also for marginalized people. Spivak (2009) claims that such forms of judgment "may become auto-immune" (p. xiv) and requests "the opportunity to step out of confinement" and to "take a position on [said confinement]" (p. xiv).

Feminist, Native, and womanist scholars Cannella and Manuelito argue for research that would focus on the "underlying assumptions, the will to power, that creates such constructs in the first place" (2008, p. 50). Being a promiscuous black feminist is one of my answers to their challenge. By releasing feminisms and black feminism from the confines of gender and race I am able to make use of them to understand, theorize, and make visible relations of power and relations of vulnerability at work.

My claim that vulnerability, not just power, is important feminist work is promiscuous. Like hooks (2000) I believe that waiting for a time when we have power or working to sufficiently possess enough power to exercise it is ill-advised and instead suggest that an attention to relations of power and relations of vulnerability opens the possibility of "power that is creative and life affirming" (p. 85). Black feminism with its attention to the lives and experiences of black working-class women, hooks argues, offers a conception "that equates power with the ability to act, with strength and ability, or with action that brings a sense of accomplishment" (p. 90). Such a power is not a possession, but an ability with an understanding that all beings are within relations of vulnerability and power even when some of us unjustly face more vulnerabilities.

Black feminist scholars, my grandmother, and poststructuralists help in the exploration of the contexts that make the experiences of women of color knowable. Such insights are instructive and offer both theoretical and practical ways to understand and to act even as the label "feminism" and the identity "feminist" are resisted as Bjork does: "Because" she stated, "I think it would isolate me" (Reinsberg, 2012). Feminism is necessary and not only in its traditional use to theorize and improve the lives of women. Much more than power is at play for maybe too quietly for some to notice and too obvious for some to ignore is a vulnerability that we share. Just as women's roles and jobs have expanded in unimaginable ways since the eighteenth and nineteenth centuries, feminism promiscuously draws on knowledge from outside feminism and puts feminism – a "dirty" word and essential constellation of theories, philosophies, practices, politics, histories, and ideologies – to work. Instead of stepping up to a seesaw teetering around power and hoping to reverse a relation around an already identified fulcrum, promiscuous feminisms work to reveal such teetering as a simulacrum so we may turn our attention to the dynamics at play in shaping our experiences.

References

Baudrillard, J. (1987). *Forget Foucault/forget Baudrillard*. New York, NY: Seemiotext(e).
Blake, W. (1992). *Songs of innocence and songs of experience*. New York, NY: Dover Publications.

Butler, J. (1990). *Gender trouble: Feminism and the subversion of identity*. New York, NY: Routledge.
Butler, J. (2003). Violence, mourning, politics. *Studies in Gender and Sexuality, 4*, 9–37.
Cannella, G. S., & Manuelito, K. D. (2008). Feminism from unthought locations: Indigenous worldviews, marginalized feminisms, and revisioning an anticolonial social science. In N. K. Denzin, Y. S. Lincoln, & L. T. Smith (Eds.), *Handbook of critical and indigenous methodologies* (pp. 45–59). Los Angeles, CA: Sage.
Crenshaw, K. W. (1991). Mapping the margins: Intersectionality, identity politics, and violence against women of color. *Stanford Law Review, 43*, 1241–1299.
Davidson, M. G., Gines, K. T., & Marcano, D.-D. L. (2010). *Convergences: Black feminism and continental philosophy*. New York, NY: SUNY Press.
Foucault, M. (1980). Truth and power. In C. Gordon (Ed.), *Power/knowledge: Selected interviews and other writings 1972–1977* (pp. 109–133). New York, NY: Pantheon Books.
Foucault, M. (1997). The ethics of the concern for self as practice of freedom. In P. Rabinow (Ed.), *Michel Foucault: Ethics: Subjectivity and truth* (pp. 281–302). New York, NY: The New Press.
Foucault, M. (1998). The order of things. In J. D. Faubion (Ed.), *Michel Foucault: Aesthetics, method and epistemology* (pp. 261–267). New York, NY: The New Press.
Gilson, E. (2011). Vulnerability, ignorance, and oppression. *Hypatia, 26*, 308–332.
Gold, R. B., & Nash, E. (2012). Troubling trend: More states hostile to abortion rights as middle ground shrinks. *Guttmacher Policy Review, 15*, 15–19.
Guy-Sheftall, B. (2010). Forward. In M. G. Davidson, K. T. Gines, & D.-D. L. Marcano (Eds.), *Convergences: Black feminism and continental philosophy* (pp. x–xii). New York, NY: SUNY Press.
hooks, b. (2000). *Feminist theory: From margin to center*. Cambridge, MA: South End.
Huckaby, M. F. (2011). Researcher/researched: Relations of vulnerability/relations of power. *International Journal of Qualitative Studies in Education, 24*, 165–183.
Kipnis, L. (2007). Vulnerability. In L. Kipnis (Ed.), *The female thing: Dirt, sex, envy, vulnerability* (Kindle Ed., pp. 1485–1970). New York, NY: Vintage.
McKay, N., Collins, P. H., Henderson, M., & Jordon, J. (1991). The state of the art. *The Women's Review of Books, 8*, 23–26.
McNeil, M. (1993). Dancing with Foucault: Feminism and power-knowledge. In C. Ramazanoğlu (Ed.), *Up against Foucault: Explorations of some tensions between Foucault and feminism* (pp. 147–175). New York, NY: Routledge.
Moore, L. (2012, August 21). The statement and the reaction. *New York Times*, p. A13.
Noguchi, Y. (2012, October 17). 'Binders of women' becomes viral sensation. *All Things Considered*. Retrieved January 17, 2013, from http://www.npr.org/2012/10/17/163109387/binders-of-women-becomes-viral-sensation
Perpich, D. (2010). Black feminism, poststructuralism, and the contested character of experience. In M. G. Davidson, K. T. Gines, & D.-D. L. Marcano (Eds.), *Convergences: Black feminism and continental philosophy* (pp. 3–37). New York, NY: SUNY Press.
Pollak, S. (2012, October 24). Fallout continues from Richard Mourdock's 'gift from god' rape comment. *Times NewsFeed*. Retrieved January 17, 2013, from http://newsfeed.time.com/2012/10/24/indiana-republican-rep-another-rape-gaffe/
Ramazanoğlu, C. (Ed.). (1993). *Up against Foucault: Explorations of some tensions between Foucault and feminism*. New York, NY: Routledge.
Reinsberg, H. (2012, August 21). 6 famous women who say they're not feminists. *BuzzFeed*. Retrieved from www.buzzfeed.com/hillaryreinsberg/6-famous-women-who-say-theyre-not-feminists
Scheurich, J. J., & McKenzie, K. B. (2005). Foucault's methodologies: Archaeology and genealogy. In N. K. Denzin & Y. S. Lincoln (Eds.), *Handbook of qualitative research* (3rd ed., pp. 841–868). Thousand Oaks, CA: Sage.
Spivak, G. C. (2009). *Outside in the teaching machine*. New York, NY: Routledge.
Villaverde, L. E. (2008). *Feminist theories and education*. New York, NY: Peter Lang.
Wright, J. (2011, September 23). Celebrities who want you to know they aren't feminists. *The Gloss*. Retrieved from http://thegloss.com/culture/celebrities-who-want-you-to-know-they-arent-feminists-396/
Zeilinger, J. (2012). *A little f'd up: Why feminism is not a dirty word*. Berkley, CA: Seal Press.

A promiscuous (feminist) look at grant-science: how colliding imaginaries shape the practice of NSF policy

Stephanie L. Daza

Education and Social Research Institute, Manchester Metropolitan University, Manchester, UK

There is nothing new about a federal focus on investing in science in US higher education (often through contracts and grants), but there is a new intimacy between grants and science. Increasingly, what happens and is valued in the name of research and knowledge production in universities is *grant-science*. In this article, I provide insight into grant-science by analyzing aspects of the proposal writing process on one of my own National Science Foundation (NSF) grants. This article provides a context-specific look at how broader impacts criteria (BIC) and ethics are re/produced through relations of power and consequently mis/interpreted and mitigated in the proposal writing process. Grant work may not seem explicitly feminist, but as a woman of color who is part of a generation of research/ers trained in feminist methodology by second- and third-wave feminist research/ers, I approach research with a feminist of color imaginary. I take up promiscuous feminism through the theoretical perspectives of Spivak to discuss how my feminist of color imaginary shapes my take on research and grant work. This analytical lens helps make visible how my interpretation and practice of NSF policies of BIC and ethics collide with the more technical ways that some other investigators on the grant projects interpret them.

Introduction

Increasingly, what happens and is valued in the name of research and knowledge production in universities is *grant-science*. *Grant-science* is the mediation of science by a culture of grants under *neoliberal scientism*. As I have written about previously (Daza, 2012), *neoliberal scientism* is my term for the worldwide, but uneven convergence of the discourses of business and pre-Kuhnian (positivist) views of science shaping our lives and institutions (Kuhn, 1962; Moss, Phillips, & Erickson, 2009). *Neoliberal scientism* together with grants culture is colonizing[1] research through its material and ideological demands for accounting, efficiency, austerity, utility, and measured effectiveness (Eisenhart, 2005), and its innocent, logical empiricist view of knowledge production that rests on White, patriarchal, heterosexual, North/West imperialist norms (Tuhiwai Smith, 1999, 2005).

There is nothing new about a federal focus on investing in science in US higher education (often through contracts and grants), but there is a new intimacy between grants and science that is retooling higher education institutions, its researchers, and consequently, inquiry (Baez & Boyles, 2009). Research in institutions of US higher education is becoming inseparable from "grant culture," and the "(ab)-use"[2] of grants and science that has emerged from the relationship between "the power of science as a profession [and its intricate ties] to the capitalist forces reshaping the economy and restructuring social institutions accordingly" (Baez & Boyles, 2009, p. 177). It is not only that funding priorities, calls for proposals, and criteria for evaluation are set by funding agencies but also how the increased press for grants by institutions of higher education is shaping knowledge production and knowledge producers. According to Bozeman and Boardman (2009), research is needed to better understand how science policy is negotiated and who is involved in shaping it.

In this article, I provide insight into grant-science by analyzing aspects of the proposal writing process on one of my own NSF grants. Since NSF's development as an organization in 1950, it has been an arbitrator of science policy, albeit sometimes reluctantly (The National Science Foundation Bill May 22, 1950). From the beginning, questions have been raised about the challenge of measuring the broader social impacts of science which "contains a strong element of faith that goes beyond what can be measured," as well as the problem that practical projects with obvious applications are easier "for administrators to justify to Congress" (Murphy, 1950, p. 1265). The shift to grant-science is connected to this challenge of evaluation and accountability in order to justify and obtain funding. Funded research shifted from a process based on the grant seekers' personal qualifications and networks in the 1950s to a more regulated one emerging since the 1970s into the professionalization of grant-science that emphasizes "a heightened ability to judge, oversee, and evaluate grant requests" in the name of accountability (Lagemann, 2000, p. 93). According to Holbrook (2009a, p. 178), "the increasing demand for demonstrable results has led to the widespread introduction of considerations of societal impact (SI) into the peer review process of public S&T [Science and Technology] funding agencies worldwide."

In the last 20 years, NSF policies and practices, including its criteria to evaluate grant proposals and make award decisions, have shifted from primarily using intellectual merit to including broader impacts, ethics, a data management plan, and (on some grants) qualitative and quantitative program evaluation. Proposals are reviewed and ranked by a panel of peers and project directors make award decisions (Holbrook, 2009b; NSB MR-11-22, 2011). Currently, there are two major criteria – intellectual merit and broader impacts – and the NSF also requires proposals to include an ethics component as a way of complying with Section 7009 of the Responsible Conduct of Research of the America Competes Act (US Public Law 110-69, 2009). Broader impacts criteria (BIC) and ethics components do not emerge from nowhere; that the NSF includes these kinds of policy practice is a reflection of historical, political, and sociocultural shifts (see Slaton, 2010). The NSF, an arbiter of these shifts, is also shaped by broader forces.

This article provides a context-specific look at how BIC and ethics are re/produced through relations of power and consequently mis/interpreted and mitigated in the proposal writing process. The use of the slash, "/", in the preceding sentence and throughout is to suggest more than one reading of the word and text. For example, as the article will bear out, whether or not these policies are interpreted or misinterpreted depends on one's perspective and imaginary. In other words, the context-specific policy practice of individuals emerges from larger power dynamics. While this article analyzes the micro-context of practice – how individuals practice grant policy in a specific context matters – the article especially seeks to connect this micro-analysis to the macro-analysis of power and policy – of neoliberal scientism – producing grant-science.

Over the last six years, I have collaborated with 11 faculty members in Engineering to co-write four NSF grant proposals, totaling more than $5 million US. To date, we have been awarded over $800,000.00 worth of funding (NSF 09-598, 2011; NSF 11-509, 2011). As co-principal investigator (Co-PI), I serve as the research methodologist and diversity education specialist on these grant projects that provide research experiences in engineering for undergraduates and high school teachers and are aimed at diversifying Science, Technology, Engineering, and Math education and careers. (STEM will be used from here on to refer to Science, Technology, Engineering, and Math education and careers.)

Elsewhere, I have written about how I – a qualitative researcher, trained in feminist post-structural theories (Lather, 2010) and critical ethnography (Foley & Valenzuela, 2005) – ended up infiltrating the logical empiricist, positivist world of grant-science (Daza, 2012). I describe my infiltration as "going rogue" and draw on Spivak, (1993) to explain how I am "outside" but also complicit within grant-science so that my decolonizing struggle continues but in different ways. Rather than setting up a straight dichotomy between the center and an outside other's resistance, Spivak describes this position as a Marxist outsider's impatient but respectful position in the bosom of the establishment; she deconstructs either/or positioning into "an impure, contaminating, negotiated, bastard and violent ... filiation ..." (1993, pp. ix–x; citing Derrida, 1990, p. 1035). What this means is that while grant-science drives science, presses researchers like me into (unlikely) collaborations, and re/shapes research and researcher imaginaries, I simultaneously infiltrate grants culture as a post-critical feminist ethnographer of color.

This position takes seriously the researcher as an instrument of inquiry and understands culture as an ongoing negotiation. As a critical ethnographer of educational policy, I "attempt to unpack the complex social, political, and historical relationships that undergird policy outcomes" (Dixon, Borman, & Cotner, 2009, p. 84). As the research methodologist on the awarded grants, I take a critical ethnographic approach to program evaluation; meaning that assessment is not designed to be simply a value-neutral measurement of the project's effectiveness, but rather to understand the culture of the grant project and the experiences of the researchers and participants.[3]

Grant work may not seem explicitly feminist, but as a woman of color who is part of a generation of research/ers trained in feminist methodology by second- and third-wave feminist research/ers, I cannot help but approach research with a feminist of color imaginary. By "feminist of color" imaginary, I mean that my identities (e.g. race, ethnicity, gender, etc.), experiences (e.g. border-crosser, female born in 1970), and trainings (e.g. in feminist methodology and critical ethnography) inform the way I see and make sense of the world. In this way, I am of a generation of feminist researchers – perhaps we might call ourselves fourth-wave (feminist) researchers – that has always already been colonized by feminisms.[4] My generation of researchers came of age after Roe v Wade; we saw females as professors, astronauts, supreme court judges, and presidential and vice presidential candidates; and we studied with feminist methodologists who imparted a particular world view to us through their syllabi, readings, lectures, and supervision of our research.

While Women's Studies Departments, feminist ways of knowing, and the widespread influx of women into the academy have not eliminated patriarchy and sexism, such results of past feminisms have done some work in disabusing the illusion of patriarchal hegemony and shaping knowledge production and producers like me.

Promiscuous feminism(s) is not the denial or death of feminism but rather setting its legacy to work (Spivak, 2008, pp. 14, 263, n. 2; 1993, p. 144).[5] Therefore, researchers of my generation, who have been shaped by feminisms in various ways, may do (feminist) research differently – in promiscuous ways – often beyond the boundaries of women, gender, sexuality, and the issues traditionally considered by feminist researchers and methodologists. How my feminist of color imaginary is working to shape my research is even more visible to me when I am being promiscuous – when my object of inquiry is grant-science and not explicitly related to equity issues of women of color, for instance. In this article, I take up promiscuous feminism through the theoretical perspectives of Spivak to discuss how my feminist of color imaginary shapes my take on research and grant work. In particular, it provides an analytical lens for seeing how my interpretation and practice of NSF policies of BIC and ethics are different and in tension with a more technical approach exhibited by some of the other investigators on the project.

In the next section, I further discuss the theoretical perspectives of my promiscuous (feminist) science. In particular, I draw on Spivak's (1985) concept of "worlding" to further describe the way in which imaginaries are colonized and why this is important for knowledge production. Then, in a section discussing NSF's BIC and ethics policies for grants, I provide some context for a vignette that provides an example of my perspectives on promiscuous (feminist) science. The vignette is a realist tale (Van Maanen, 1988) about the proposal writing process on one of my own grants. A window into grant-science, the vignette will illustrate how the collision of imaginaries (e.g. feminist of color and positivist/technical) shapes the mis/interpretation and implementation of grant policies. Finally, the conclusion will discuss some of the implications for a promiscuous (feminist) theoretical approach to critical ethnography and for making sense of policy practice within grant-science.

Promiscuous (feminist) science: theoretical perspectives of analysis

Promiscuity, as haphazard mixing (see Voithofer, this issue), is relative to containment – the arbitrary norms of power, albeit historically and socioculturally engrained, that produce meaning, subjects, identity, truths, etc. So that what is, and who is being, promiscuous is context- and subject-specific – based on their relative containments. Promiscuity, then, is an often ironic contamination or infiltration (Daza, 2012) of containment. By drawing on Spivak, my approach is to map the contours of containment – to provide enough insight into power relations, contexts, and subject-imaginaries – so that the ironies of how and why a phenomenon mixes and emerges within (and sometimes contaminates and infiltrates) power's containment can be noticed and tracked. Thus, promiscuous (feminist) science is to make visible the contours – material and discursive – of containment and its contaminations.

In this article, I draw on Spivak's ideas – particularly, her concept of "worlding" – to inform my promiscuous feminist approach. By "worlding," Spivak means that the imagination is always already contaminated and contained by what is already understood; so, desires, understanding, and thinking – and consequently knowledge production – are always already complicit and constrained by past and present contaminations (Spivak, 1985, 2008). For instance, (1) feminisms of the past shape how we view and research in the present and the future. (2) Diagnosis of what is reform may appear confident given the worlding of one's imaginary (Spivak, 1985, p. 269). (3) What can be thought – even what appears to be alternative – is often "consolidated by the desire of the dominant to have it so" (Spivak, 2008, p. 3).

Promiscuous science "engender[s] possibilities that are not necessarily contained in … dominant versions, radical or conservative" (Spivak, 2008, p. 4). In this light, promiscuous science – as a way of decolonizing worlding and one's imaginary – is the responsibility of research, and the responsibility of researchers who seek to know and represent empirical reality as less certain and full of possibility. Promiscuity here is the possibility of knowledge production rattling containment, rather than using containment to justify itself as knowledge and consequently reproduce containment. Promiscuity is, as Spivak (2008, p. 3) states, the possibility that "… thought may become a textual blank for others to suture" in the cracks and contaminations of containment. Part of research/ers' responsibility, then, is to track and crack knowledge containment – worlding – in such a way that knowledge production's complicities with it are not lost, hidden, or ignored.

To be promiscuous is to reveal the contours of imaginaries, especially our own, and what we consider liberating, including feminisms' imaginaries. In this way, a promiscuous feminist approach can make visible containment – the relations of power within the worlding – of grant-science. For instance, to be a qualitative researcher and scholar of color on an NSF engineering grant is in some ways to be both complicit with and contaminating containment.

The remainder of this article is an example of promiscuous (feminist) science. First, in the next section, a discussion of NSF's BIC and ethics policies provides a context for analyzing a vignette from my own grant projects. This analysis attempts to make visible how the competing imaginaries of a feminist of color lens and a technocratic lens collide to shape grant proposal writing, but that this particular context-specific collision is the result of larger power dynamics and policy practice. And, in complying with NSF's grant policies, BIC and ethics may be mis/interpreted.

BIC and ethics: NSF grant policy practice

In order to contextualize the analysis of the narrative in the following section, this section provides a brief outline of the emergence of BIC and ethics in NSF policies. These policies drive and reflect needs articulated by the academy, industry, government, and society.[6] What BIC are and how they might be articulated in grants have been an ongoing negotiation of competing ideas about what is the purpose of science and tensions among the needs of scientists, the government, and society. The challenge of interpreting BIC policy practice also was the subject of a special issue of *Social Epistemology* in December 2009 (Holbrook, 2009b). Merit and BIC criteria emerged in 1996 and NSF implemented the change in review criteria in 1997. According to NSF historian Rothenberg (2010, p. 297), the 1996 changes were in part an attempt to remediate "the Reagan administration attack on NSF funding of education that resulted in a cut of some 81% of the NSFY FY 1982 budget for education, including all of the funds for precollegiate programs." In Chapter 2: The Policy Context for the NSF's Programs for Broadening Participation of NSF's

Framework for Evaluating Impacts of Broadening Participation Projects (Clewell & Fortenberry, 2009, pp. 22–32), Fortenberry traces the emergence of BIC policy from the Science and Engineering Equal Opportunity Act of 1980. Although BIC has become part of the culture of NSF grant-science, the policy continues to be capricious and contested (American Physical Society, 2007; Holbrook, 2009b; Lok, 2010; NSB MR-11-22, 2011). The NSB admits it "was aware of persistent anecdotal reports about confusion related to the Broader Impacts criterion, and inconsistency in how the criterion was being applied" (NSB MR-11-22, 2011, p. 4).

NSF has continued to struggle to better explicate what it means by BIC. NSF has provided a laundry list of possible ways to address its review policies and it has conducted workshops for investigators (Clewell & Fortenberry, 2009; NSB MR-96-15, 1996; NSB-04-72, 2003). In 2007, NSF provided the following list, but stated that "the list is not intended to be exhaustive, nor is any particular example relevant to all proposals" (July 2007, p. 1; emphasis original):

> The components of the broader impacts criterion as defined by the National Science Board are listed below …
>
> **Broader Impacts Criterion: What are the broader impacts of the proposed activity?**
>
> - How well does the activity advance discovery and understanding while promoting teaching, training and learning?
> - How well does the proposed activity broaden the participation of underrepresented groups (e.g. gender, ethnicity, disability, geographic, etc.)?
> - To what extent will it enhance the infrastructure for research and education, such as facilities, instrumentation, networks, and partnerships?
> - Will the results be disseminated broadly to enhance scientific and technological understanding?
> - What may be the benefits of the proposed activity to society?

Peter March (2007), the Director of the Division of Mathematical Sciences, provided a letter of clarification, stating that:

> The following list is neither prescriptive nor exhaustive and should not be read in ways that constrain the creativity of researchers in proposing activities with broader impact. However, in all instances a proposal must be specific in how it addresses the Broader Impacts criterion.

Several examples of clarification offered in the letter are as follows (emphasis original):

> **Advance discovery and understanding while promoting teaching, training, and learning,** for example, by training graduate students, mentoring postdoctoral researchers and junior faculty, involving undergraduates in research experiences, and participating in the recruitment, training, and professional development of K-12 mathematics and science teachers.
>
> **Broaden participation of under-represented groups,** for example, by establishing collaborations with students and faculty from institutions and organizations serving women, minorities, and other groups under-represented in the mathematical sciences …

Benefits to society may occur, for example, when results of research and education projects are applied to other fields of science and technology to create startup companies, to improve commercial technology, to inform public policy, and to enhance national security.

Most recently, the NSF conducted a review of its evaluation criteria and draft revisions have been made available (NSB MR-11-22, 2011). The proposed criteria include a set of goals reminiscent of the previous BIC, but there is a new focus on economics (4 of 9 goals) that is not surprising in the age of neoliberal scientism. My intention in this paper is not to analyze these changes and clarification attempts per se, but rather use them as context – to illustrate the way in which policy is not simply a document or a directive but a living practice of ongoing interpretation (see Sutton & Levinson, 2001), often of needs. To further illustrate this, one of the NSF project directors interpreted the BIC policy as meeting the need of diversifying the field. At the NSF Education awardees conference that I attended in February 2009, an NSF project director stated, "We don't want to hear excuses; other universities are finding ways to recruit teachers from diverse backgrounds and anything else is unacceptable," in response to a PI who expressed difficulty in recruiting women, minorities of color, and differently abled people into his program.

This approach of interpreting BIC can fall short in the sense that it focuses on recruiting individuals from specific groups into STEM and not on changing a technocratic culture of STEM that reproduces inequities. First, individuals' group affiliation does not necessarily reflect similarities among group members or ensure that diverse perspectives will be brought, included, or valued (Daza, 2008). For instance, the diversity present in our grant team certainly matters, but white male privilege in a technocratic imaginary also continues to matter. Secondly, keeping broader impacts at the level of individuals compartmentalizes difference (Slaton, 2010) and ignores more systemic and epistemic shifts towards social justice that NSF's ongoing focus on BIC policy suggests (Intemann, 2009, p. 252). In general, a technocratic STEM community continues to subordinate women and other minority groups by allowing, "white, upper-class men [to] define engineering and engineering institutions … where their own values are equated with power and prestige" and "by failing to recognize the context of the supposed value-free, neutral science" (Goodman Research Group, Inc., 2002, p. 13; citing Rosser, 1995; Tonso, 1998). Again, if the NSF's policies have implications for social justice and are intended to create a change in "core values" and "personnel" that some research on the engineering profession has called for (Chubin, May, & Babco, 2005), the irony is not lost that an engineer on my grant writing team dismisses them (discussed below in the vignette).

To be clear, diversifying higher education and STEM is a relatively recent goal marked by the US Civil Rights Act of 1964, the 1957 launch of Sputnik,[7] and US involvement in World War II. According to Slaton (2010, p. 2), "the understandings of race among engineering educators and policy makers in the United States since the 1940s [can be described as] a landscape of reformist ambitions playing out amid episodes of social stasis." The presumption that broadening the participation in STEM education and careers is desirable has its own history; waxing and waning in popularity, justifications (e.g. legal, economic, workforce talent, national security, and social justice) have shifted over time and contexts (Slaton, 2010).

While debates in part focus on the purpose and definition of BIC, much of the concern is on how to meet needs defined by BIC and mis/interpreted by investigators and reviewers. At the crux of these debates, and widely unaddressed, is who defines needs for whom and how needs are defined. For instance, diversification needs may be "met" at the level of individuals, who can satisfy needs-driven policies, but individuals will be pressed to conform once they gain access.[8]

The ethics component is an even newer policy than BIC for NSF grants, but it has a precursor. In 2004, the NSF Directorates for Biological Sciences, Computer and Information Science and Engineering, Education and Human Resources, Engineering, and Social, Behavioral and Economic Sciences joined together to initiate the Ethics Education in Science and Engineering (EESE) grant program (NSF 11-514, 2011). The current policy is a response to Public Law 110-69 America Competes Act Section 7009 on Responsible Conduct of Research. NSF moved from encouraging grant writers to include an ethics component in their project to a required ethics policy in 2010 (Grant, 2009). Specifically, NSF's (2009, p. 42126) implementation plan states:

> Effective January 4, 2010, NSF will require that, at the time of proposal submission to NSF, a proposing institution's Authorized Organizational Representative certify that the institution has a plan to provide appropriate training and oversight in the responsible and ethical conduct of research to undergraduates, graduate students, and postdoctoral researchers who will be supported by NSF to conduct research. While training plans are not required to be included in proposals submitted to NSF, institutions are advised that they are subject to review upon request.

Like the BIC policy, the ethics component is a need being framed in individual and technocratic ways. According to Grant (2009), the new ethics policy is a response to researchers' misconduct and may help researchers learn how to deal with ethical challenges. John Galland, NSF's director of the division of education and integrity at the Office of Research Integrity (ORI), is quoted as stating: "As you're making an investment in research, it's wise to also make an investment in the researchers who are performing that research" (Grant, 2009). Moreover, the ethics component is described by John Dahlberg, the director of ORI's oversight, as needed to address the ethical misconduct of a few "bad actors" so that "there may be fewer allegations of research misconduct" (Grant, 2009). In my view, this is again a technocratic interpretation of policy at the level of individuals. More research is needed to understand how ethics policy will play out in grant-science (see Daza, 2013).

Below, I present an analysis of a narrative vignette to describe how relations of power played out in the proposal writing process on one of my own NSF grants. I particularly examine how approaches to NSF's BIC and ethics policies from different imaginaries led to the mis/interpretations of these policies in the grant proposal and consequently the project.

"Social justice crap?": the power and politics of grant proposal writing

"We don't want any of that social justice crap" said one White male – an associate professor, engineer, and Co-PI – to another White male, who was at the time an assistant professor of educational policy and the Co-PI in charge of the grant's ethics component.[9] In a conversation with the ethics Co-PI, I wondered, "How are we supposed to actually get an NSF grant to diversify STEM if we don't include 'any of that social justice crap?'" I thought, "Wow! ... What a comment, given the diversity of our grant team."

In addition to these two White males, our project team included another White male and three males of color, two from "home" countries beyond the USA. One of these two males also served as PI and was a Department Chair in the College of Engineering. Our team also had five female faculty members. There were three White women – one was an assistant professor who has since been promoted to associate professor, one was an associate professor to start, and another was an assistant dean and senior lecturer. Including me, there were two female faculty of color. I am a light-brown assistant professor, who also identifies as queer; I have written more extensively about my own identity in previous articles (Daza, 2008, 2009). The other woman of color was in a senior lecturer position and has since been promoted to an Associate Chair position. She self-identifies as an African-American woman with a disability. Arguably, our proposal writing team could be considered diverse in several ways. It included five people of color and six Whites; six males and five females; two education faculty and nine engineers; as well as three tenured professors, six tenure-track professors, and two lecturers. That all of the team members besides the ethics Co-PI and me were engineers may be significant. Although I have become an integral partner of our grant collaborations over the last six years, at first, the educator evaluator and ethics Co-PI were considered add-ons to what was an engineering project; I address this and some of the limits and possibilities of collaborating across disciplines in a previous article (Daza, 2012).

As a female assistant professor of color committed to social justice and critical ethnography, I am no stranger to gender, race/ethnic, and ideological biases in the academy. So at first, I was encouraged because it seemed to me that social justice was not crap to the NSF or to most of the members of this grant writing team. After all, we had read and discussed NSF's call for RET proposals, the ethics component, and especially, the BIC as social justice imperatives. By the time of this "social justice crap" comment, we had been meeting weekly in various conference rooms of one of the university's engineering buildings and the proposal was well developed. What became clear to me over the course of writing the proposal and analyzing the experience is that we did not all interpret NSF's policies as a charge (need) for social justice or if NSF's policies were interpreted as a social justice imperative, then investigators who disagreed with this could find ways to resist it.

I joined the grant writing process in late September of 2007, much earlier than the ethics Co-PI but after the nine engineers had begun developing the proposal at the beginning of the semester. One idea that I brought to the grant writing team was to utilize *Teaching the Levees: A Curriculum for Democratic Dialogue and Civic Engagement,* developed by Teachers College at Columbia University in partnership with The Rockefeller Foundation, HBO Films, and others (www.teachingthelevees.org). Until the "crap" comment, most of the other Co-PIs, including the ethics Co-PI when he came on board, seemed to either support the idea of using the *Teaching the Levees* curriculum (*TLC*) or not have an opinion about it. I argued that using the curriculum would be a useful vehicle for meeting NSF's BIC and ethics policies because it would allow us to examine social justice and ethical issues of privilege, difference, access, (in)equity, and responsibility in light of the engineering challenges revealed by Katrina, the 2005 hurricane that flooded New

Orleans. I stated that Katrina and the *TLC* would raise questions about the racial and socioeconomic aspects of the effects of Katrina, as well as the response and recovery efforts following it, which would likely have implications for engineering ethics. Perhaps, most compelling, *TLC* and Katrina fit for our theme of Hazard Mitigation perfectly.

From the same engineer who uttered the "crap" comment, I heard: "None of that matters for engineering." He dismissed the notion that there were racial and class dimensions to Katrina and engineering. From his technocratic imaginary, I have come to see his reading of Katrina as a technocratic approach. In this way, Katrina was purely a technical event, devoid of sociocultural aspects. For me, this is a quintessential example of the technocratic worlding of lived experience. Additionally, this technocratic imaginary is reproducing, and reproduced by, traditional perceptions and practices of STEM culture and by neoliberal scientism's positivists and managerial ways of organizing academic and social life. Grant-science counts on research/ers to ignore, simplify, manage, and eliminate all the messy stuff – "Values and politics, human volition and program variability, cultural diversity, multiple disciplinary perspectives, the import of partnerships with practitioners, even the ethical considerations of random designs" – that gets in the way of a technocratic approach (Lather, 2010, p. 25; see also Daza, forthcoming). In contrast, NSF policies seem to be trying to shift norms and perceptions of STEM to recognize and promote the social dimensions and impacts of STEM. However, the technocratic imaginary of this engineer works to appropriate the NSF policy. This is how worlding works and is reproduced through our colonized imaginaries. Likewise, my feminist of color imaginary works to appropriate my interpretation of the policy. A Spivakian approach to promiscuous feminism works the tensions of colliding imaginaries and emerging needs.

During the proposal writing, I suggested that there were several additional benefits to using the *TLC*. It was free; it included the Spike Lee film *When the Levees Broke: A Requiem in Four Acts*; teachers in our project would have free access to the curriculum for their own classes if they wanted it; and importantly, the curriculum was already designed to explore multiple perspectives and interpretations. Yet, the same engineer expressed his concern that the film, which he had not seen, was by the "controversial and one-sided" director Spike Lee.

An analysis of Spike Lee and his work is beyond the scope of this article. However, readers might consider that this engineer and others label Lee and his work as "controversial" and "one-sided" to legitimate the notion that a neutral and objective view exists, and then, if that exists, competing views can be politicized as a way of dismissing them (Kumashiro, 2008, 2010). In the technocratic imaginary, STEM, events, and films are not always already value-laden cultural productions. The possibility of being/appearing race, gender, and class neutral is a presupposed advantage in the age of neoliberal scientism that seeks to ignore and dismiss privilege and the politics of power. Dismissing the social dimensions of STEM and Katrina and using neutralizing language like "controversial" and "one-sided" may replace blatantly biased language but nonetheless reflects deficit perspectives of marginal positions and is still about maintaining the status quo of the center, all the while denying that privilege exists. In this way, "controversial" and "one-sided" is code for Black-centric or even so-called "reverse racism."

In short, Lee's work is not color-blind or muted (Pollock, 2004). Much of Lee's work unapologetically demystifies and humanizes the experiences and contexts of people of color from their own perspectives. In my view, it has a decolonizing effect of making visible the frameworks through which stories are told and disrupts the worlding of whitestream forces. Lee tells stories on film from his Black imaginary, not from a White point of view or necessarily for the consumption of a whitestream audience. For this, Lee's work may make some whitestream viewers uncomfortable. The *TLC* website (www.teachingthelevees.org) ameliorates this potential discomfort in a kind of disclaimer entitled Spike Lee's Views that states the following:

> We acknowledge that Spike Lee has his own strong views about racism. Readers should be aware that ... director's commentary provid[es] insights into Lee's perspective on individuals featured in the film and the ways in which his perspective shaped the film. As any director does, Spike Lee uses a variety of techniques to get his point across. Discussion leaders should discuss these techniques with students and other users of this curriculum in order to reveal how the subject of Katrina and the levees gets "framed" by Spike Lee in the film ...
>
> As citizens, we all have a perspective about why events unfolded as they did, about who should be held responsible for what occurred, about what needs to be done to remedy the situation, and about how citizens might be better prepared for times of crisis. The great contribution of Spike Lee's film lies in raising issues which must not be avoided – in schools and colleges, libraries, churches, and community groups: the meaning of racism, the increasing social class stratification of American society, personal, communal, and governmental responsibility for social welfare. Encouraging democratic dialogue about these matters and responding to this deliberation with civic engagement is the central purpose of this curriculum.

As the above alludes, Lee's film and the *TLC* raise important issues about public policy and investments in engineering that often work to the advantage of some neighborhoods and peoples and the disadvantage of others, disproportionately impacting different populations. The Performance Evaluation of the New Orleans and Southeast Louisiana Hurricane Protection System Final Report of the Interagency Performance Evaluation Task Force stated: "Over 70% of the fatalities were people over age 70. The poor, elderly, and disabled, the groups least likely to be able to evacuate without assistance, were disproportionately impacted" (2009, p. I-3). Moreover, the American Communities Project of the Spatial Structures in the Social Sciences at Brown University reported in *The Impact of Katrina: Race and Class in Storm-Damaged Neighborhoods* that while "suffering from the storm partly cut across racial and class lines," Blacks, renters, and poor people were disproportionately impacted and had "fewer resources for returning and rebuilding" (Logan, 2006, p. 7). Based on the analysis in their report, New Orleans risked losing more than 80% of its Black population. Tellingly, the end of the report asks, "Whose city will be rebuilt?" (p. 16).

The US Army Corps of Engineers took responsibility for the flooding of New Orleans in their 2009 report "and said the levees failed because they were built in a disjointed fashion using outdated data" (CBS News, 2009). In November of 2009, a federal court ruled that the Army Corps of Engineers failed to maintain the Mississippi River Gulf Outlet (MRGO), a shipping channel linking New Orleans, Louisiana, to the Gulf of Mexico, and that the Reach II Levee protecting the Chalmette and the Lower Ninth Ward would be compromised by the continued deterioration of the MRGO (Hayes, 2009). Finally, this decision was upheld by a federal appeals court in March 2012 (Schleifstein, 2012). In retrospect, it seems hard to deny that Katrina invoked a societal debate of the sociocultural, political, economic, and ethical dilemmas of engineering. Perhaps this is only relevant if you do not think social justice is crap. From my feminist of color imaginary, Katrina and *TLC* would have allowed us to meet NSF's grant policies of BIC and engineering ethics in a better and more meaningful way. It is important to note that using Katrina to teach engineering ethics and explore the SIs of engineering is a debate in engineering and among engineers and not all engineers operate out of a purely technocratic imaginary (Newberry, 2009; Schleifstein, 2009). According to The Goodman Research Group, Inc. (2002, p. 13), some STEM scholars say that "the characterization of science (and, by extension, engineering) as value-neutral truth is preposterous; our knowledge about the world cannot be stripped from the context in which we live (i.e. our race, class, and gender) (Hubbard, 1989)."

Notably, the ethics Co-PI and the author of the "crap" comment left the grant project early, and neither one contributed much labor to the grant writing process. The engineer left the grant team before we submitted our proposal to NSF and to my knowledge, did not actually write any parts of the proposal. I cannot help but wonder if he was just too uncomfortable to continue working with a grant team led by three people of color, including two females. From a technocratic imaginary, we probably produced a lot of crap that complicated rather than simplified research; and of course, an imperative of neoliberal scientism is to reduce all the messy stuff that gets in its way.

The ethics Co-PI joined the grant writing team after most of the grant was already written; he wrote a small section related to the ethics component; and left the project after the first year. In a meeting unrelated to the grant, he was upfront about his minimal involvement and announced that he was a "late addition" and not very involved in the larger project. I do not believe the ethics Co-PI agreed that social justice is crap. I continue to ponder why the engineer shared his comment in an aside with the ethics Co-PI, rather than with the whole group where it might have been better countered and/or dismissed. Did the engineer assume an affiliation with the ethics Co-PI because they were both White males? I also wonder if this manner of making his view known, without saying it aloud publicly, somehow allowed the message – that social justice is crap – to operate almost clandestinely.

At the end of the day, what happened in the proposal writing process and policy practice is that BIC and ethics are included per NSF's policy directives, but *TLC* was not included. The way that BIC and ethics are included in the proposal and project is more piecemeal and not as well integrated with engineering and real world events as they might have been had we included the *TLC*. For example, although we include information on culturally relevant pedagogy (Richards, Brown, & Forde, 2006), our BICs are more about recruiting individual minorities into STEM than about retooling engineering and society to be more socially just and culturally relevant. Managing diversity and containing so-called social justice initiatives, especially by limiting this work to the level of individuals, is a strategy of the center to contain the periphery. How needs are defined and met fortify containment. By inhibiting epistemic and systemic change in STEM, STEM and its white, male privilege "as purveyors of absolute truth" (Goodman Research Group, Inc., 2002, p. 13) are also maintained.

This also shows that the peripheral involvement of individual PIs does matter, but also that our behaviors and investments are symptomatic of larger dynamics at work, whether technocracy of neoliberal scientism or promiscuous feminism. Some investigators from the first project have not been involved in our subsequent grant projects. The engineer of the "crap" line neither had any involvement in the six-week program that we ultimately implemented for high school STEM teachers for three summers nor any interaction with the teachers or high school students over the course of the last six years. Plus, even though we did not include the *TLC* in the proposal, I was able to share it with teachers in our grant project as an example of how they might integrate culture-relevant pedagogy and ethics into their own curriculum. Teachers expressed an interest in the curriculum and its interdisciplinary focus. Some of them acquired the free curriculum on the website. One teacher confessed that it was "a bit of a letdown" that we were not using it. She indicated she might "have partnered with a teacher in social studies on it" as she reportedly was "interested in making connections between physics and other subjects." Her expressed interest is in line with research on STEM that finds women often prefer to view STEM as having social dimensions and altruistic value in helping society and people (see Goodman Research Group, Inc., 2002).

Over the last six years, I have continued thinking about the negotiation of NSF policy in our proposal writing process. Utilizing a promiscuous feminist lens has helped me to see how collaborators on this grant, including me, mis/interpret grant policies through different imaginaries and emerging needs. The female of color Co-PIs on our grant writing team interpreted NSF's policies of BIC and ethics through a feminist of color imaginary – and as social justice goals related to in/equities based on race, class, gender, (dis)ability, and other differences. One tenured, White male engineer did not interpret NSF policies in the same way; I argue his interpretations emerge from a more technocratic imaginary. This example is not meant to implicate this individual, or the females of color as simply individuals, but rather to show the insidious, and unequal, power dynamics of different imaginaries at work within neoliberal scientism. Perhaps our position, not only as females of color, but also as untenured faculty (and in my case as a methodologist and educator, not an engineer), allowed his more technocratic imaginary to shape the proposal even though the individual himself ended up not participating in the project. At the same time, his technocratic imaginary likely succeeds because it fits well within the press of grant-science overall for a more technocratic approach that is being positioned as neutral, objective, and legitimate. In this way, both local and global power dynamics shape policy practice. Indeed, the worlding of the mainstream imaginary works by establishing itself as neutral and, therefore, legitimate, while at the same time politicizing a competing view as, in this case, "crap." Perhaps this guise of neutrality and legitimacy makes it easier for the other collaborators to appear to go along.

Below in the final section, I discuss some of the implications of utilizing a promiscuous (feminist) theoretical approach to critical ethnography of policy practice. This theoretical approach makes visible competing interpretations of policy made possible through two colliding imaginaries – feminist of color and technocratic. By showing the messiness of policy practice within grant-science, this case study provides insight into the workings of grant-science. It shows how the press for social justice is contested by the technocracy of neoliberal scientism and technocratic mis/interpretations of NSF's BIC and ethics policies.

Implications: promiscuity in policy practice and methodology

Within the context of grant-science, collaborative work is encouraged and often required to obtain funding. In my experience, a team is required to meet the labor and infrastructure involved in implementing a large grant project. The NSF grants of which I am a part are structured in a way that requires STEM faculty to partner across disciplines and schooling contexts. In other words, the NSF largely defines needs and how they are to be met. In our case, engineers partnered with a methodologist and an ethics Co-PI from the field of education. As the above analysis shows, in such collaborations of strange bedfellows, different imaginaries may collide. As I tell it, our policy practice emerges from the collision between a feminist of color imaginary and a technocratic imaginary. From my feminist of color imaginary, I interpret NSF's BIC and ethics policies for grants as impetuses to retool the culture of STEM to be more than technical content; to be more socially just and less biased; and to make more clear the relationship between STEM and society. This is not a technocratic, surface-level interpretation of social justice that addresses inequity and equality at the level of individuals and fails to shift the culture of STEM in systemic and epistemic ways. From my imaginary, social justice is an imperative and not just a means to satisfy needs-driven policy criteria, defined by technocrats, in a technical way. A technocratic approach to the criteria could result in getting and implementing the grant but still failing to impact the culture and practice of STEM.

The STEM culture and engineers that the BIC and ethics policies set out to (re)form are not docile subjects but active participants in interpreting (and resisting) policies during the process of grant proposal writing. Neoliberal scientism's press for positivist and technocratic approaches to science also influences the context of grant-science within which NSF grant policies are produced and practiced. Not only are the socio-ethical dimensions of STEM contained, but also who can participate and how they may be limited by these norms. When NSF policies are mis/interpreted technocratically, it follows that the technocratic worlding of grant-science and STEM's culture of neoliberal scientism may persist in spite of NSF's social justice policies that may contradict or at least complicate them.

Promiscuous feminism through a Spivakian lens allows for this more complicated, nuanced, and open-ended analysis of the emergence of needs from within colliding imaginaries. It helps to make visible how the competing interests and imaginaries of grant collaborators collide to produce grant policy practice that is continuously being negotiated and reappropriated. Being promiscuous is concerned with how to incite what Spivak (1999, p. 428) calls an "experience of the impossible," where the contours of imaginaries through which policy is mis/interpreted are made visible but without fully formulating, determining, or justifying policy practice. In this way, irony (complicities, contaminations, contradictions) and uncertainty give way to the possibility of being otherwise that more chaste approaches to knowledge production – those that would avoid and deny uncertainty – do not. For Spivak, this is the task of the humanities – rearranging desires towards a decolonizing of the imagination that does not bypass our own imaginaries. Drawing on Spivak (2008, p. 4), the consequence of this promiscuous use of feminism is "the ability to think absent things." In other words, policy practice even in today's grant-science, under the press of neoliberal scientism, through the prism of a feminist imaginary also has the potential to be promiscuous.

Promiscuous (feminist) ethnography maps the contours of worlding in such a way that both containment and uncertainty are revealed.

Acknowledgements
The author wishes to thank her reviewers, as well as Sara Childers, Jeong-eun Rhee, Fran Huckaby, and Doug Foley, for their helpful feedback on drafts of this article. Special appreciation goes to the NSF, her grant colleagues, and participants.

Notes
1. Colonization is the self-establishment of an outside ruler (e.g. nation-state; ideology) and/or rule that impresses its own agenda (e.g. laws and systems of education; truths) and rearranges "the mode of production for its own ... benefit" – often in ways that are taken-for-granted and supported internally (Spivak, 2008). According to Spivak (2008), "using the colonizer-colonized model creatively" can provide an interesting model for analysis; and "'colonizer' and 'colonized' can be fairly elastic if you define scrupulously." Thus, colonization is violence resulting from colonizer–colonized relations of power. It implies a nearly inescapable (mis)appropriation – forced, coerced, and in part voluntary – of bodies, minds, ideas, and places (Daza, 2006; see also Puiggrós, 1999, p. 176). Colonization infringes on what it means to be free, self-determined, and sovereign. One of Spivak's primary contributions to understanding these power dynamics is to show that resistance to power – forms of what becomes sanctioned as liberation – can also be colonizing (e.g. a violent infringement inseparable from the production of subjects), and thus determine, as well as limit, agency (Spivak, 1985, 2008, 2012). An example in the field of education is Ellsworth's (1994/1989) problematizing of the limits of critical pedagogy and the "reaction-formations" that followed (Spivak, 2012; see also Lather, 1991).
2. "(Ab)-use" is a term employed by Spivak (1999, p. 142, note 43) that roughly translates "to use from below" but not be outside of; it is meant to convey more than simply "abuse" and to be distinct from other attempts to use the Enlightenment critically. According to Spivak (2012, pp. 3–4), "the Latin prefix 'ab' says much more than 'below.' Indicating both 'motion away' and 'agency, point of origin,' 'supporting,' as well as 'the duties of slaves,' [the (*ab*)-use of European Enlightenment] nicely captures the double bind of the postcolonial and the metropolitan migrant ... the public sphere gains and the private sphere constraints of the Enlightenment."
3. At the same time, the evaluation must fulfill NSF's requirement of reporting the results of the grant project's effectiveness both qualitatively and quantitatively. As Guba and Lincoln have made clear (1989, p. 18), methods of gathering data are often confused with methodologies; methodology is the overall paradigm – the theoretical strategy or framework of analysis – that governs the research process. Methodological differences are matters of ontology and are much bigger than those between quantitative and qualitative methods in empirical research (Erickson, 2009, in Moss et al., 2009). Thus, methods (tools and techniques), while perhaps associated with certain methodologies, do not define methodology alone; and quantitative or qualitative methods might be used within different methodological frameworks.
4. The "wave metaphor" is widely used to describe the shifts and trajectory of feminism over time with the current period of feminism often known as the "third wave;" recently, in trying to imagine futures of feminism – born from, but not bound by, feminisms of previous waves – some feminists, who themselves emerged from these waves, are problematizing and questioning feminism and a generational account of it (Gillis, Howie, Munford, & Spencer, 2004). Thus, some (feminist) researchers and activists of this generation are not dismissing the "legacy of feminism," but rather taking it seriously by using it and pushing its boundaries, despite reaction-formations (see note 1) and strategies of containment (Bhabha, 1994, p. 31; see also Spivak, 1994). According to Spivak (1999), the imagination is always already contaminated and contained by what is already understood, including feminisms; likewise, desires, understanding, thinking, and doing – and research – are always already complicit and constrained by past and present contaminations (see Daza, forthcoming). So, everything being exceeded comes into

being through existing logics and available discourses – everything becomes what it is, and what can be, through what is already contaminated, understood, and contained. Here, an ab-use of feminisms is to take seriously the trace of feminisms – to honor feminisms' legacy from below (see also note 2). This means that "what is becoming (the future) and the present cannot exist except through the past – what is already understood through relations of power (e.g. 'colonized by feminisms'). Yet, what happens and is continuously happening in deconstruction is that the present is always already being exceeded, which is what Spivak (1999) means by 'a history of the vanishing present.' The future, in becoming present, is at once not just the future or even the present, but emerging from pasts – through worlding" (Daza, forthcoming). For more about what is meant by "colonized by feminism," see notes 1 and 2.
5. See also note 4.
6. According to Spivak (2012), there is an important difference between needs, as articulated by others invested in center–margin binaries, and desires that come from below. In line with Spivak (2012), decolonizing needs-driven policies, practices, and grants rests on the rearrangement, and displacement, of desires that ultimately keep center–margin binaries salient.
7. Sputnik refers to a small orbiting radio satellite that was launched into space by the Soviet Union, 4 October 1957. The launch, often cited as the beginning of the Space Race, had an impact on the US national approach to science and technology and eventually led to an overhaul of science and math instruction in the USA.
8 See note 6.
9. Data in this article will be shared obscurely to keep identities anonymous, as well as to deter to the extent possible connections among characters, roles, and institutions, even though more details about the roles and statuses of the characters involved in a narrative might produce more specific levels of meaning (Erickson, 1985).

References

American Physical Society. (2007). NSF's "broader impacts" criterion gets mixed reviews. *APS News, 16*(6). Retrieved from http://www.aps.org/publications/apsnews/200706/nsf.cfm
Baez, B., & Boyles, D. (2009). *The politics of inquiry: Education research and the "culture of science"*. New York, NY: State University of New York Press.
Bhabha, H. K. (1994). *The location of culture*. London: Routledge.
Bozeman, B., & Boardman, C. (2009). Broad impacts and narrow perspectives: Passing the buck on science and social impacts. *Social Epistemology, 23*, 183–198.
CBS News. (2009). Katrina report blames levees. *CBS News*. Retrieved from http://www.cbsnews.com/2100-201_162-1675244.html
Chubin, D. E., May, G. S., & Babco, E. L. (2005). Diversifying the engineering workforce. *Journal of Engineering Education, 94*, 73–86.
Clewell, B. C., & Fortenberry, N. (Eds.). (2009). *Framework for evaluating impacts of broadening participation projects: Report from a National Science Foundation workshop*. Retrieved from http://www.nsf.gov/od/broadeningparticipation/framework-evaluating-impacts-broadening-participation-projects_1101.pdf
Daza, S. (2006). Local responses to globalizing trends: Student-produced materials at a Colombian public university. *International Journal of Qualitative Studies in Education, 19*, 553–571.
Daza, S. (2008). Decolonizing researcher authenticity. *Race Ethnicity and Education, 11*, 71–85.

Daza, S. (2009). The noninnocence of recognition: Subjects and agency in education. In R. S. Coloma (Ed.), *Postcolonial challenges in education* (pp. 326–343). New York, NY: Peter Lang.

Daza, S. L. (2012). Complicity as infiltration: The (im)possibilities of research with/in NSF engineering grants in the age of neoliberal scientism. *Qualitative Inquiry, 18*, 773–786. doi: 10.1177/1077800412453021

Daza, S. (2013). The challenge of STEM culture and grant-science for an aesthetic education. *Qualitative Inquiry*. Forthcoming special issue.

Daza, S. (Forthcoming). Putting Spivakian theorizing to work: Decolonizing neoliberal scientism in education. *Educational Theory*.

Dixon, M. L., Borman, K. M., & Cotner, B. A. (2009). Current approaches to research in anthropology and education. In G. Sykes, B. Schneider, & D. N. Plank (Eds.), *Handbook of education policy research* (pp. 83–92). New York, NY: American Educational Research Association by Routledge.

Eisenhart, M. (2005). Science plus: A response to the responses to scientific research in education. *The Teachers College Record, 107*, 52–58.

Ellsworth, E. (1994/1989). Why doesn't this feel empowering? Working through the repressive myths of critical pedagogy. In L. Stone & G. Masuchika Boldt (Eds.), *The education feminist reader* (pp. 300–327). New York: Routledge.

Erickson, F. (1985). *Qualitative methods in research on teaching*. Occasional paper no. 81. Washington, DC: National Institute of Education.

Foley, D. E., & Valenzuela, A. (2005). Critical ethnography: The politics of collaboration. In N. K. Denzin & Y. S. Lincoln (Eds.), *The Sage handbook of qualitative research* (3rd ed., pp. 217–234). Thousand Oaks, CA: Sage.

Goodman Research Group, Inc. (2002). *Final report of the women's experiences in college engineering (WECE) project*. Retrieved from http://www.grginc.com/WECE_FINAL_REPORT.pdf

Grant, B. (2009). NSF adopts new ethics rules. *The Scientist: Magazine of the Life Sciences*. Retrieved from http://classic.the-scientist.com/blog/display/55962/

Guba, E. G., & Lincoln, Y. S. (1989). *Fourth generation evaluation*. Thousand Oaks, CA: Sage.

Hayes, A. (2009). Court: Army Corps of Engineers liable for Katrina flooding. *CNN US*. Retrieved from http://articles.cnn.com/2009-11-18/us/louisiana.katrina.lawsuit_1_lower-ninth-ward-new-orleans-east-ruling?_s=PM:US

Holbrook, J. B. (2009a). Editor's introduction. *Social Epistemology, 23*, 177–181.

Holbrook, J. B. (Ed.). (2009b). Special issue: US National Science Foundation's broader impacts criterion. *Social Epistemology, 23* (3/4).

Hubbard, R. (1989). Science, facts, and feminism. In N. Tuana (Ed.), *Feminism and science* (pp. 119–131). Bloomington, IN: Indiana University Press.

Intemann, K. (2009). Why diversity matters: Understanding and applying the diversity component of the National Science Foundation's broader impacts criterion. *Social Epistemology, 23*, 249–266.

Kuhn, T. (1962). *The structure of scientific revolutions*. Chicago, IL: University of Chicago Press.

Kumashiro, K. K. (2008). *The seduction of common sense: How the right has framed the debate on America's schools*. Teaching for social justice series. New York, NY: Teachers College Press.

Kumashiro, K. K. (2010). Seeing the bigger picture: Troubling movements to end teacher education. *Journal of Teacher Education, 61*, 56–65.

Lagemann, E. C. (2000). *An elusive science: The troubling history of education research*. Chicago, IL: University of Chicago Press.

Lather, P. (1991). *Getting smart: Feminist research and pedagogy with/in the postmodern*. New York, NY: Routledge.

Lather, P. (2010). *Engaging science policy: From the side of the messy*. New York, NY: Peter Lang.

Logan, J. R. (2006). *The impact of Katrina: Race and class in storm-damaged neighborhoods*. Report by the American Communities Project, Brown University. Retrieved from http://www.s4.brown.edu/Katrina/report.pdf

Lok, C. (2010). Science for the masses. *Nature, 465*, 416–418.
March, P. (2007). *Broader impacts review criterion*. Retrieved from http://www.nsf.gov/pubs/2007/nsf07046/nsf07046.jsp
Moss, P. A., Phillips, D. C., Erickson, F. D., Floden, R. E., Lather, P. A., & Schneider, B. L. (2009). Learning from our differences: A dialogue across perspectives on quality in education research. *Educational Researcher, 38*, 501–517.
Murphy, W. J. (1950, July). How firm a foundation? I. The National Science Foundation and its scope. *Industrial and Engineering Chemistry, 42*, 1265.
Newberry, B. (2009). Katrina: Macro-ethical issues for engineers. *Science and Engineering Ethics, 16*, 535–571.
NSB-04-72. (2003). *Broadening participation in science and engineering research and education: Workshop proceedings*. Retrieved from http://www.nsf.gov/pubs/2004/nsb0472/nsb0472.pdf
NSB MR-11-22. (2011). *National Science Foundation's merit review criteria: Review and revisions*. Arlington, VA: NSF.
NSB MR-96-15. (1996). *National Science Board and National Science Foundation staff task force on merit review: Discussion report*. Retrieved from http://www.nsf.gov/nsb/documents/1996/nsbmr9615/nsbmr9615.htm
NSF. (2007, July). *Merit review broader impacts criterion: Representative activities*. Retrieved from http://www.nsf.gov/pubs/gpg/broaderimpacts.pdf
NSF. (2009). *NSF's implementation of Section 7009 of the America COMPETES Act*. Federal Register 74 (160). Retrieved from http://edocket.access.gpo.gov/2009/E9-19930.htm
NSF 09-598. (2011). *Research Experience for Undergrads (REU). National Science Foundation*. Original edition, NSF 09-598.
NSF 11-509. (2011). *Research Experiences for Teachers (RET) in engineering and computer science*. National Science Foundation. Original edition, NSF 07-557.
NSF 11-514. (2011). *Ethics education in science and engineering (EESE)*. National Science Foundation. Original edition, NSF 05-532.
Pollock, M. (2004). *Colormute: Race talk dilemmas in an American school*. Princeton, NJ: Princeton University Press.
Puiggrós, A. (1999). *Neoliberalism and education in the Americas*. Boulder, CO: Westview Press.
Richards, H. V., Brown, A. F., & Forde, T. B. (2006). *Addressing diversity in schools: Culturally responsive pedagogy*. Retrieved from http://www.nccrest.org/Briefs/Diversity_Brief.pdf
Rothenberg, M. (2010). Making judgments about grant proposals: A brief history of the merit review criteria at the National Science Foundation. *Technology and Innovation, 12*, 189–195.
Schleifstein, M. (2009). American Society of Civil engineers finds no ethical violations in its own Katrina levee review. *The Times-Picayune*. Retrieved from http://www.nola.com/news/index.ssf/2009/04/american_society_of_civil_engi.html
Schleifstein, M. (2012). Hurricane Katrina flood ruling upheld by federal appeals court. *The Times-Picayune*. Retrieved from http://www.nola.com/katrina/index.ssf/2012/03/hurricane_katrina_flood_ruling.html
Slaton, A. E. (2010). *Race, rigor, and selectivity in US engineering: The history of an occupational color line*. Cambridge, MA: Harvard University Press.
Spivak, G. C. (1985). Three women's texts and a critique of imperialism. *Critical Inquiry: Race, Writing, and Difference, 12*, 243–261.
Spivak, G. C. (1993). *Outside in the teaching machine*. New York, NY: Routledge.
Spivak, G. C. (1994). Responsibility. *Boundary 2, 21*, 19–64.
Spivak, G. C. (1999). *A critique of postcolonial reason: Toward a history of the vanishing present*. Cambridge, MA: Harvard University Press.
Spivak, G. C. (2008). *Other Asias*. Oxford: Blackwell.
Spivak, G. C. (2012). *An aesthetic education in the era of globalization*. Cambridge, MA: Harvard University Press.
Sutton, M., & Levinson, B. A. (Eds.). (2001). *Policy as practice: Toward a comparative sociocultural analysis of educational policy. Sociocultural studies in educational policy formation and appropriation* (Vol. 1). Westport, CT: Ablex.

The National Science Foundation Bill. (1950, May 22). *Chemical and Engineering News, 28*, 1729–1732.

Tuhiwai Smith, L. (1999). *Decolonizing methodologies: Research and indigenous peoples.* London; New York: Zed Books; University of Otago Press; distributed in the USA exclusively by St Martin's Press.

Tuhiwai Smith, L. (2005). On tricky ground: Researching the native in the age of uncertainty. In N. K. Denzin & Y. S. Lincoln (Eds.), *The Sage handbook of qualitative research* (pp. 85–107). Thousand Oaks, CA: Sage.

United States Public Law 110-69. (2009). *The responsible conduct of research of the America Competes Act.*

Van Maanen, J. (1988). *Tales of the field: On writing ethnography.* Chicago, IL: University of Chicago Press.

The materiality of fieldwork: an ontology of feminist becoming

Sara M. Childers

Educational Studies in Psychology, Research Methodology, and Counseling, University of Alabama, Tuscaloosa, AL, USA

> Through the materiality of fieldwork at a high-achieving high-poverty high school, I discuss how the collision between practices of feminist methodology and the materiality of fieldwork forced me to rethink the "feminist" in feminist research. Using the work of Karen Barad, this material–discursive account of methodology as ontology looks at feminist research as a constitutive intra-action between the materiality of the field and discursive representations of "what count" as feminist research. I discuss "the matter" of feminist research, or how representations of it in the literature rubbed up against its practice. I illustrate how "the matter" of inquiry – bodies, buildings, books, desks, policies, theories, and discourses – was agential and affective. "Doing" of feminist research is an ontological engagement where the force of the material was simultaneously (re)constitutive of feminist methodology, theory, and practice. By engaging with these entangled intra-actions, I hope to narrate an ontological event of feminist becoming.

This paper is concerned with two connected issues: (1) articulating an ontology of research where the "materiality" of the field, or the physical as well as the discursive, are viewed as equally constitutive forces that shape our ontological and therefore methodological engagements as constant, iterative processes; and (2) how such a process lends itself to feminist research as endless becoming, where the boundaries of feminist research are continuously pushed and disrupted by the materiality, and what it means then to come through such disruptions of feminism and (re)claim a position as a feminist researcher.

Through the materiality of fieldwork at a high-achieving high-poverty high school, my direct confrontation with racism in public schooling, and the intra-action with the students, parents, and teachers whose bodies bore the effects, I will attempt to delineate how the collision between practices of feminist methodology and the materiality of fieldwork forced me to rethink the "feminist" in feminist research. First I will discuss "the matter" of what counts as feminist research, or how representations of feminist research in the literature rubbed up against the materiality of fieldwork. Then I will illustrate how "the matter" of inquiry – material–discursive productions of bodies, buildings, books, desks, policies, theories, and discourses – was agential and affective in relation to "the doing" of feminist research, and how the force of the material was simultaneously constitutive of feminist methodology, theory, and practice. This material–discursive account of methodology as ontology looks at feminist research as a constitutive and compulsive intra-action between matter and discourse. By engaging with these entangled intra-actions, I hope to narrate an ontological event of feminist "becoming" (Deleuze, 1990).

I will briefly untie this entanglement to think about how the theory, methodology, fieldwork, and daily life of researchers and participants can all be thought of as material agents that are affective in the becoming of feminist research. What count as the empirical materials for this piece include not only "data" from the field study, but also narrative "data." My goal though is not to center myself or my experience, but to use it to narrate methodology as ontology, or as entangled practices that slip and slide against personal histories, ways of knowing, and the lived experiences that collide with and wreck preconceived notions of what counts as feminist research. I attempt then to present an "autoethnography of methodology" (Childers, 2008) and ontology, rather than an autoethnography of myself.

I argue that when the materiality of our engagements with the world is taken seriously, it becomes apparent that feminist theory and methodology move promiscuously through and beyond gender. What changed my vision regarding what counts as feminist research was the conflict and contradiction affected by the material, when faithful representations of the "feminist" fell apart against the "real" empirical materiality of doing research. Worded differently, what I thought feminist research was could not stand up against its becoming.

A "matter" of feminist research

Feminist research, be it qualitative or otherwise, is an engagement with the material, but material engagement tends to be downplayed in discussions of the development of methodology, the application of theory, or conducting a study. The materiality of fieldwork never really left, it always mattered, but in coming around the postmodern turn to the crisis of representation, the material also lost status in the name of other political projects – in the case of feminism, demonstrating how sex and gender are discursively determined constructions which have the potential to limit women's political subjectivity, and this is a critique that is still necessary. But at the same time representations of what counted as feminist research in the literature and in my training also set up a boundary. I found rather quickly that feminist research in practice exceeded any definition, and when working in this space outside the boundaries of what counted as feminist research, I felt like I was cheating on feminism.

Cheating on feminism

My base training in feminist theory began in a department of women's studies which integrated ways of doing research on/with/for women with theories of knowledge from multiple feminist perspectives that did not take for granted the distinctions imposed through ability, class, race, sexuality, or the intersectionality of differences. Feminist epistemological claims and women's ways of knowing were at the center of knowledge production. Women's bodies in all their complexity were the pivot point for a critique of sexual difference. Feminist research and theory therefore undoubtedly engaged at every turn women, gender, sexual subjectivity, and their intersectionality with other markers of difference.[1]

I was supported through my master's and doctoral degrees by many feminist mentors and was funded as a graduate assistant by a women's policy office on campus. Due to my political investments in feminism and my early training, women and gender were for me anticipated subjects of inquiry. As I began my doctoral study in an educational foundations program, I developed an intense interest in educational anthropology and sociocultural policy studies in education. Much in the same way that I was "turned on" by issues of gender and feminist/poststructural theory, I experienced a passionate engagement with school ethnographies and critical policy studies methodologies inside and outside of feminist research. The notion of "policy as practice" (Sutton & Levinson, 2001) constantly circulated in my work and became a new frame for my thinking about teaching and learning. I began to develop what I viewed as a very complementary package of cross-disciplinary frameworks – post-structural theory, critical feminist and critical race theories, feminist methodology, ethnography, policy analysis, queer theory, and qualitative inquiry. As I took a more defined interest in educational policy and not necessarily its gendered implications, I could not help but wonder: by shifting my scholarship away from an interrogation of gender was I cheating on feminism?

The slight but constant discomfort, like the beginnings of a headache that is easy to ignore, rested with representations of what counts as feminist in feminist research. If one reviews the literature in feminist curriculum studies, policy studies, or methodology (see editor's introduction, this issue), areas within which I work and feel solidarity, each is often clearly defined by the specific focus on issues of gender, women, girls, and/or sexuality. While applications of feminist theory and research might be viewed as diverse and multiple in practice, in the discourse they are most commonly bonded by these foci.

Proponents of each of these feminist subfields have taken great care to delineate what sets particular feminist ways of doing research and seeing the world apart from others, and I am in no way discrediting the need for such work to maintain its political goals. In the process of looking to these fields to define my methodological position, I realized that my investments, when not within the discursive representations of feminist research, directly missed the mark of what was defined by feminist researchers and theorists as a feminist methodology. While there were of course educational issues percolating at the surface of a local high school that could bring me back to a gendered representation of feminist research, these issues were tangential to other larger issues that emerged and demanded attention. As a result of the displacement of gender in my research, I started ambivalently bracketing the term [feminist] in reference to my own work.

The force of the collision between the discursive representations of feminist work and my own practice was unsettling. Though Elizabeth St. Pierre and Wanda Pillow (2000) in their edited collection *Working the Ruins: Feminist Poststructural Theory and Methods in Education* spoke against the need to "prove" one's work as educational research or feminist research, it was one text in a sea of others keen on articulating a feminist position. In spite of all the wiggle room, fluidity, and contextuality allotted by post-structural theory, I became stymied by the self-questioning of my own positionality within feminist research, its excesses, and by my desire to locate myself within these disciplinary boundaries. This desire was fed by the anticipated "real" consequences of assuming a position from which to speak, of claiming a subject position inside feminist research that potentially was illegible to the feminist mainstream. Could I call this work feminist when I clearly lived outside recognizable mainstream definitions of what it meant to do such work? Without the markers of gender/women/girls/sexual difference, if I wanted to publish in a feminist journal, would it be legible and accepted as such? The politics of academic location and identity were important. I presented an early iteration of these thoughts at a conference in 2008, and the trepidation I experienced as I justified claiming the feminist in my not-so-feminist research was strange and overwhelming.

While I struggled with what to call the work I was doing, I moved forward with the research. It was "the doing" of research, experiencing the ontological practices of methodology, that helped me to think through and move through this quandary. Post-research, reading more theory that I did not have in my grasp at the time, I have found that new feminist materialism, particularly the work of Karen Barad (2007), helps me to think beyond fixed definitions of what feminist research can *be* to its constant becoming. If feminist theory and methodology is always in excess of itself (Derrida, 1997), a fiction (Visweswaran, 1994), and a productive failure (Lather, 2007), then I am not interested in how discursive representations of feminism contain my work; rather I shift to thinking about the complex entanglements through which feminist research becomes.

Making the material mean more

Via what has come to be called "new feminist materialism"[2], the material is brought back into the equation, and its subtle shift allows me to bring into an account of feminist research the materiality of the field. I am not only interested in how feminist methodology and theory shape my approaches to fieldwork, but also how the materiality of the field acts back on feminist methodology to produce something other than what we think it to be. Barad implores a return to matter – to make matter "matter," and I am very interested in the implications of this for thinking about feminist research. Therefore, in this account, the materiality of the field includes such things as human bodies, buildings, desks, books, spaces, policies, theories, practices, and other animate and inanimate objects. These materials are granted agential nature and undeniable affectivity, or an undeniable force in shaping inquiry. The material then carries equal weight with discursive constructions of feminist research and together they mutually constitute the "matter" of fieldwork.

It is important to emphasize that neither matter nor discourse is prior or privileged in this new feminist materialism; matter and meaning are mutually articulated, and discourse itself is material. As Barad explains, "Matter is not a linguistic construction but a discursive production; discursive practices are themselves material reconfigurings of the world through which the determination of boundaries, properties, and meanings is differentially enacted" (2007, p. 151). Discourses become "material" or agential and provocative, not as mere constructions but as affective agents that have the capacity to reconfigure and to be reconfigured by feminist research and the feminist researcher.

My knowledge of feminist research and my practice of feminist research then are not separate, but as Barad argues, complex "intra-actions" of simultaneous co-constitution. This idea prompts then a move away from a notion of the feminist as tied to representation, to a notion of the feminist as what Barad refers to as onto-epistemological, "a knowing through being," (Barad, 2007, p. 185) or what I have been referring to as the all-encompassing "doing" of inquiry. It becomes less about the object of study – women, gender, or sexuality – and more about the ontological practices of knowledge production. This shift to a broad materiality that grants agential status to both matter and discourse, and positions them as simultaneously constitutive allows for a shift to feminist research as an ontological account of feminist becoming. Therefore, what structures my account of the materiality of fieldwork and the matter of feminist research is a constitutive relationality, or intra-action, between theory, methodology, the researcher, the participants, and the agential nature of the field site in which I work.

Feminist intra-actions: when bodies and theories collide

Most of my work has focused on how "urban" students form their subjectivity in relation to policy, curriculum, and instruction and how issues of race and class are implicated in marking students as "other." Thinking back to how I came to this work, it was a direct result of the materiality of fieldwork conducted during an 18-month ethnographic case study at Ohio Public High School (OPHS). Though initially I gravitated to this school because of my interest in policy analysis, the materiality and affectivity of coming to a research project through theory, training, and living in the world had a deeper impact on the trajectory of my research.

My training in qualitative inquiry, feminist, and otherwise, focused a great deal on the crisis of representation and the potential violences of my research. Authority, voice, empathy, emancipatory aims, consciousness, and agency all are at stake in doing work with/about/for folks different from ourselves. The complications of "writing culture" (Clifford & Marcus, 1986), "racing research and researching race" (Twine & Jonathon, 2000), and extremely complex critiques made by feminists of color such as Collins (1990), Anzaldúa (1999/1987), hooks (1981), and others about the necessity of non-white, non-heteronormative feminist standpoints asserted by non-white and queer Feminists, forced me to consider how my outsider status as a white woman raised in a small town in West Virginia affected my research. Insider/outsider status goes beyond racial identification, but I purposely decided to avoid research topics that focused on non-white racial inequality in education. With this in mind, I decided to focus on policy as practice not only because I found it provocative, but also with hopes that it would provide a neutral subject matter where my white positionality and privilege would have a less severe effect. I had also taken an interest in this high-profile local high school that appeared to be subverting the constraining effects of the US educational policy of No Child Left Behind (NCLB) to support the achievement of its students, and I thought this critical case could be palpably and richly documented ethnographically.

Ohio Public High School was a nationally recognized high-achieving, high-poverty lottery[3] school in Central Ohio that served a predominantly African-American population. The demographics of the student body at OPHS closely mimicked the demographics of the district; the high rate of academic achievement did not, which was why OPHS was often cited as an example of the success possible in urban schools. According to the Ohio Department of Education, 65.5% of the students at OPHS were identified as African-American, 2.5% as Hispanic, and 3% as of Asian or Pacific Islander backgrounds. About 98.5% of OPHS students graduated in 2007 as compared to 73.9% of students in the district. Of the 19 high schools in Columbus City Schools, six exhibited graduation rates at or below 67.9%, with a lowest graduation rate of 49.6%. OPHS had the highest rate of graduation in the district, and this rate was met by only one other school. According to the school website,

96% of its 2007 graduates attended two- or four-year colleges and earned nearly $7 million in scholarships to 50 schools, including top Ivy League institutions.

Because of its astounding success, it offered a critical case study of how one high school exceeded achievement standards in the climate of accountability and high-stakes testing when other district schools were struggling to meet minimum benchmarks. It also served as a rare case study of a school that interpreted and appropriated district and national education policy in unique ways that appeared to contribute to the academic success and achievement of its students and to avert the constraining effects of high-stakes testing and accountability. OPHS provided the opportunity to think about the possibilities public schooling might hold for creating a climate of success that allows students to become academically engaged with the exploration and construction of knowledge "on their own terms." I was interested in documenting how these radical curriculum and instruction practices were subversions of NCLB. In spite of the demographic make-up of the school, I thought policy analysis of *successful* practices would provide distance from the racial issues of US public schools.

My naïve attempt to neutralize my racial positioning quickly fell apart. The school's image of "success for all students" became more complicated during fieldwork as I learned of internal racial stratification across the curriculum where students of color were overrepresented in the basic level courses while Advanced Placement and International Baccalaureate courses were majority white. I recognized how this stratification was deeply intertwined with local policy decisions and practices. Racial tracking was also a policy practice, one that carried negative effects for students. In spite of my whiteness and what it meant for me as a white woman to represent the lived experiences of students, teachers, and parents different from myself in many ways, I found it ethically deplorable to not address the inequality that I witnessed.

This was not just an ethical move driven by a deep commitment to anti-racism, though that was part of it. I allowed the materiality of the field to heavily guide my emergent project. As OPHS was designated by the district as an "urban"[4] school, urban had material meaning – a school that was physically falling apart, located in an undesirable urban neighborhood, and filled with low-income students of color, mostly African-American, who also came from other undesirable neighborhoods in the city. "Urban" education has racial and socioeconomic meaning in the USA. Though the generic term "urban" education is most often used, race and class function in meaningful ways within and through the bodies of its students. Urban students, their raced and classed bodies have been historically and socially coded by the language of risk, disadvantage, and deprivation. The notion of urban capitalizes on and solidifies historic and racialized narratives of the always failing, culturally deprived student of color, and due to the historical context of segregation in the USA, more specifically the African-American student, it excludes the history of successful African-American education, the failures of integration, and the implications of these failures for urban education today.

Deficit discourses permeated talk about this school and mingled with its materiality. Newspaper articles rang with praise as the school received numerous awards for working with "urban" students, where the term urban capitalized on deficit notions of urban student identity. It was students', teachers', and parents' material engagements with school inequality and the material enactments of policy that produced and maintained such inequality that moved my practice. Their bodies mattered in the discursive constructions of urban identity, and the discursive-materiality of what it meant to be an urban student, parent, or teacher at an urban school had an ontological impact, or affectivity, on the becoming of my feminist work.

Elizabeth Wilson defines affectivity as "the capacity to move and be moved – a more general capacity, intensity, or virtuality that animates matter as such" (Kirby & Wilson, 2011, p. 228). Fieldwork is an affective event where the materiality of the field rises up to meet us, rubs up against us, pushes back on our interpretations. I am most surprised as I look back by the affective force of schooling that I had discounted, how the dilapidated school building intersected with my memories and emotions of schooling, intersected with my scholarly knowledge about schooling, intersected with my politics, intersected with my theoretical investments, intersected with feminist/post/critical methodologies that materialized in my ontological engagements with participants and the field site. It was not just how students' raced bodies were rocked by inequity, but also the agential human and non-human matter that bore this material–discursive connection with which I intra-acted that had the capacity to move my practice of research in multiple ways. "Matter" does matter in the ontology of our methodologies. And I want it to matter more.

The same deep feminist concern about the crisis of representation that drove me away from dealing with race, also held me accountable as I studied this urban school. In the process, feminist theory/methodology materialized as a feminist becoming that engaged what counted as feminist research differently.

Feminist theorizing as a material–discursive becoming

I reconceptualize feminist theory and methodology not just as static practices circumscribed by static discourses, but as mutually constituted material–discursive processes. Feminist research is dynamic; it is what happens when theory, methodology, and action intra-act in the world. "*Theorizing, like experimenting is a material practice*" (Barad, 2007, p. 55). Feminist theorizing, part and parcel of the practices of research, is an entangled material–discursive practice that expands the field of vision and intra-actions that count. I situate theory as agential "matter" that effects and is affected by its material engagements. Theory then is not just something I think or read about, already positioned and socially constructed. Feminist theory as matter might supersede any preconceived discursive boundaries, effect knowledge production outside its prescribed domains, and be changed in the process.

Theory as "matter," or the result of material–discursive practices, might be thought of as something with the capacity to affect me as researcher, not only affecting my thinking, but to have an affective relationship with my body as material; theory also as something that can be acted upon by the material. Theory as material then resituates this from a question of epistemology to a question of social ontology. I want to keep hold of how the material and discursive are co-constituted – feminist research is a material–discursive becoming, a knowing through being, an ontology of methodology.

Feminist theory and methodology have left an indelible mark on my work that is ontological; I respond to the world, to the field, and to participants differently because of that training. The very debates in feminist research that pushed me away from studying the effects of racial inequity in schools also became useful in bringing me back. Once the materiality of the field drove me back to confronting race and dealing with my outsider position, it was also feminist work that held my feet to the fire. I acknowledged a different privilege, one where white researchers use insider/outsider critiques to run from addressing racial inequality. White identity could serve as another easy way out, another privileged position where I could seek solace in the idea that my representations and interpretations would themselves be inaccurate and too vested with authority to be ethical. This sort of white privilege, relinquishing responsibility to address the inequity I witnessed, was equally damaging within the context of this study in that it perpetuated white supremacy by ignoring it.

The ontological work invested in written representations of research is a site to analyze the feminist becoming of theory and methodology in relation to a subject matter outside the discursive constraints of what counts as feminist work. Writing was an ontological practice that constituted the materiality of research. My writing was driven by ethical imperatives as well as that affective engagement where I talked to students whose stories bore the material effects of inequity, observed from old desks under a falling ceiling in an old school, and witnessed a great many moments of success and achievement.

I determined that there were at least three ways I could represent what I learned while at OPHS: (1) an uncritical representation of educational excellence that focused solely on the positive policy practices at OPHS and avoided any analysis of racial inequality; (2) a critical representation of racial inequity that took the school to task for the overrepresentation of African-American students in college preparation courses and the racialized practices at work in the school, but ignored the success that was also happening so that such success could not be used as a vehicle to elide or justify the inequality; or, (3) a post-critical engagement that struggled to adequately represent the complications of both equity and excellence, one that acknowledged both the successes and the failures, and the productive effects of race, history, policy, and practice. It was in the space of these anxieties and dilemmas about representation that feminist post-critical methodologies and theories intersected and guided a research project that had nothing to do with gender, women, or sexuality.

I engaged a feminist post-critical methodology (Lather, 2007). Post-critical methodologies serve as tools for moving through what Lather (1998) calls "stuck places" and what Spivak (1999) via Derrida refers to as "aporias," places of doubt, non-passage, and effacement. This allowed me to situate the issue of racial representation as an aporia, a methodological trouble spot where I wrestled with attempts at adequate and ethical representation. As an aporia, I took my whiteness and research authority seriously rather than resisting taking it on at all.

Feminist post-critical methodology also requires that researchers trouble voice, agency, and emancipatory goals to move beyond constructions of essentialized, romanticized subjects. Though it did not give me the tools to do this work, it held me accountable. It also critiques the imperialist notion of the liberatory researcher and problematizes emancipatory space and aims in research. Feminist post-critical methodologies required me to address head-on my complicity in the representations of racial inequality in my fieldwork. It held me accountable for directly addressing representations of urban students in ways that might resist essentialized or romanticized portrayals of their daily lives.

As an ontology, it hinged on self-reflexive "double(d) practices of representation" (Lather, 2007, p. 47) that engaged both doing the research and troubling it simultaneously. Getting out of stuck places of researching racial inequality as a white woman meant performing research as a double(d) move, moving forward with "the doing" of the research while wrestling with my own inadequacies to do such work. While the post-critical privileges loss and failure as a consequence of trying to tell other people's stories, those feminist debates around ethicality of voice and narrative constructions of research moved me beyond accepting loss and failure. Reflexive admission that my representations were partial, full of complications, and from an outsider location was not enough. The ethical engagement with the materiality of the field moved me to adapt other frameworks and try to do some justice in writing about this school.

I tapped into other theoretical frameworks and methodologies to continue to wrestle with my ethical accountability. I utilized Critical Race Theory/in Education (CRT) as a framework to define and bear witness to structural inequities and racialized experiences that marked the connections between identity and achievement at OPHS. CRT is a highly theorized and complexly articulated framework that I only briefly discuss here (see Crenshaw, Gotanda, Peller, & Thomas, 1995; Taylor, Gillborn, & Ladson-Billings, 2009). It explicitly names and defines practices of racism and white privilege, and as a framework held me accountable to analyzing racialized practices of schooling theoretically and substantively. Post-structural theories of deconstruction and discourse analysis were crucial to recognizing the power relations held within these material experiences. CRT and post-structural theory together, while not always thought of as compatible, worked to unhinge deficit notions, to unfix urban students from identity constructions, and to see the complicated ways they live and learn in schools.

Feminist theory, enmeshed in the entanglements of research, became a material–discursive practice. Theory was material, affective, and affected by material engagements. And this entanglement engaged feminist theory/methodology/research as becoming outside any artificial discursive boundaries of what might count as "the feminist" in feminist research.

Conclusion

Rather than cheating, I prefer to think of these feminist entanglements as promiscuous, loyally disloyal, and wonderfully infectious. The materiality of fieldwork pushed me to think differently about representational and discursive boundaries circumscribing what counts as feminist research to see the *force* of a material–discursive feminist inquiry and the agential potential for it beyond gender. I argue that my feminist training has significantly shaped not only the way I see the lives of women and girls, but how I engage the world in its complexity, and this way of knowing through being is feminist in its becoming. Feminist theory and its companions of epistemology and methodology are lenses that I "cannot not" think with. Feminist methodology, as an onto-epistemological practice, is a way of seeing the world that is "in my bones" and promiscuously infiltrates and complicates my analysis of everything, not just the subject matter most often attributed to feminism.

With the feminist material (re)turn to matter and a emphasis on the material–discursive entanglement, what feminist methodology becomes is open to other radical possibilities and unresolvable tensions. What are the political implications of (re)thinking feminist theory and methodology in relation to a willful displacement of its foundations when politically necessary? I recognize the danger here of diffusing the political aims and goals of feminist inquiry. How is feminism identifiable then if gender, women, and sexuality are not its center? Yet, I also recognize the political potentiality, when our politics is sometimes about displacing our center in the name of doing "different knowledge differently" (St. Pierre & Roulston, 2006); feminist research then as "nomadic and non-sedentary" (Deleuze, 1990, p. 60), or always moving, shifting, infiltrating, and changing in relation to the world both inside and outside of normalized contexts and explicitly articulated feminist positions, infiltrates new spaces. It becomes visible that feminist methodological training, theory, and research can have much broader impacts and be undeniably useful to multiple knowledge projects, as opposed to being peripheral to knowledge production, particularly in the academy, due to its specificity (for example see Tuana, 2008).

As illustrated amongst the contributions to this special issue, this sort of promiscuous, nomadic feminism never ceases to circulate, infiltrate, and reorganize boundaries. What counts as the feminist as it becomes with the materiality of the world offers the opportunity to see feminist theorizing and research as powerful, agential, and undeniably necessary for thinking about and changing the world in which we live.

Acknowledgements

The author would like to thank Becky Atkinson, Stephanie Daza, Susan Hekman, Patti Lather and Jeong-eun Rhee for their feedback and support of this article.

Notes

1. This is not to say that feminist research/ers have not been invested in other types of projects. I am suggesting that those projects are not typically recognized or explicitly articulated as feminist. They still construct an outside of mainstream feminist research. See Editors' Introduction, this issue, for further discussion.
2. For an overview of new feminist materialism see Hekman (2010) and Jackson and Mazzei (2012).
3. As part of the choice initiative under NCLB, Columbus City Schools created a lottery process. Students who completed an application were randomly "drawn out of a hat" for enrollment. OPHS typically had lottery applications for close to 1000 students each year vying for 150 freshman seats.
4. OPHS is designated by the Ohio Department of Education (ODE) as a high-achieving, high-poverty urban school located in a Major Urban District. It has been recognized each year as an Urban School of Promise by ODE since 2004.

References

Anzaldúa, Gloria. (1999/1987). *Borderlands/La Frontera: The new mestiza*. San Francisco, CA: Aunt Lute Press.

Barad, Karen. (2007). *Meeting the universe halfway: Quantum physics and the entanglement of matter and meaning*. Durham, NC: Duke University Press.

Childers, Sara. (2008). Methodology, praxis, and autoethnography: A review of getting lost. *Educational Researcher, 37*, 298–301.
Clifford, James, & Marcus, George. (Eds.). (1986). *Writing culture: The poetics and politics of ethnography*. Berkeley: University of California Press.
Collins, Patricia Hill. (1990). *Black feminist thought: Knowledge, consciousness, and the politics of empowerment*. Minneapolis: University of Minnesota Press.
Crenshaw, Kimberle, Gotanda, Neil, Peller, Gary, & Thomas, Kendall. (Eds.). (1995). *Critical race theory: The key writings that formed the movement*. New York, NY: The New Press.
Deleuze, Gilles. (1990). *The logic of sense*. New York, NY: Columbia University Press.
Derrida, Jacques. (1997). *De la grammatologie* [Of grammatology] (Correct ed.). Baltimore, MD: Johns Hopkins University Press.
Hekman, Susan. (2010). *The material of knowledge: Feminist disclosures*. Bloomington: Indiana University Press.
hooks, bell. (1981). *Ain't I a woman: Black women and feminism*. New York, NY: South End Press.
Jackson, Alecia Youngblood, & Mazzei, Lisa. (2012). *Thinking with theory in qualitative research: Using epistemological frameworks in the production of meaning*. London: Routledge.
Kirby, Vicki, & Wilson, Elizabeth A. (2011). Feminist conversations with Vicki Kirby and Elizabeth A. Wilson. *Feminist Theory, 12*, 227–234.
Lather, Patti. (1998). *Getting smart: Feminist research and pedagogy with/in the postmodern*. New York, NY: Routledge.
Lather, Patti. (2007). *Getting lost: Feminist efforts toward a doubled science*. Albany, NY: State University of New York Press.
Spivak, Gayatri Chakravorty. (1999). Appendix: The setting to work of deconstruction. In Gayatri Chakravorty Spivak (Ed.), *A critique of postcolonial reason: Toward a history of the vanishing present* (pp. 423–431). Cambridge, MA: Harvard University Press.
St. Pierre, Elizabeth, & Pillow, Wanda. (Eds.). (2000). *Working the ruins: Feminist poststructural theory and methods in education*. New York, NY: Routledge.
St. Pierre, Elizabeth, & Roulston, Kathryn. (2006). The state of qualitative inquiry: A contested science. *International Journal of Qualitative Studies in Education, 19*, 673–684.
Sutton, Margaret, & Levinson, Barry A. U. (Eds.). (2001). *Policy as practice: Toward a comparative sociocultural analysis of educational policy*. Westport, CT: Ablex.
Taylor, Edward, Gillborn, David, & Ladson-Billings, Gloria. (2009). *Foundations of critical race theory in education*. New York, NY: Routledge.
Tuana, Nancy. (2008). Viscous porosity: Witnessing Katrina. In Stacy Alaimo & Susan Hekman (Eds.), *Material feminisms* (pp. 188–213). Bloomington: Indiana University Press.
Twine, Francis Winddance, & Warren, Jonathon. (Eds.). (2000). *Racing research, researching race*. New York: New York University Press.
Visweswaran, Kamala. (1994). *Fictions of feminist ethnography*. Minneapolis: University of Minnesota Press.

Was Jane Addams a promiscuous pragmatist?

Becky Atkinson

Educational Leadership, Policy and Technology Studies, The University of Alabama, Tuscaloosa, AL, USA

> Contemporary pragmatist and feminist scholars have proposed the possibilities for "changing the theoretical analyses and concrete practices" of both feminism and classical American pragmatism offered by its recuperation through feminism. Particularly, scholarship on Jane Addams has reached back to retrieve her activism, ethics, and social theory as emblematic of what a feminist pragmatism can offer. Whereas most of this scholarship recuperates an almost seamless integration of these theoretical and philosophical orientations in Addams' work, in this paper, I trouble those efforts by offering a promiscuous reading of Addams' feminist pragmatism from two dimensions. First, I offer an analysis of Addams' promiscuous appropriation of pragmatism and feminism that interrupts and perplexes both orientations. Second, I read Addams promiscuously through the ontoepistemological framework of material feminism, specifically Karen Barad's "agential realism", and prompt reconsiderations of how Addams performed how "matter matters" in knowing through being in twentieth-century Chicago.

Called the "most dangerous woman in America" for her pacifist stand during World War I and her top place on the federal War Department Military Intelligence list of individuals with "dangerous, destructive, and anarchistic sentiments" (Davis, 2000/1973, p. 252), Jane Addams remains a compelling and enigmatic figure. As an activist for women's rights, and social reformer, ethicist, pioneer sociologist, and social critic in the early twentieth century, Addams is perhaps best known as a feminist social reformer in her work as the founder and director of the Hull House settlement in Chicago beginning in 1889, winner of the Nobel Peace Prize in 1931, and first president of the Women's International League for Peace and Freedom.

Despite the well-known possessiveness of US-centric historical and philosophical traditions[1], Addams' philosophical thought, social ethics, and social activism practice remain relevant for international qualitative researchers in education and the many other social sciences from cultural policy to peace education that evince influence of her theory and practice (Behrends, 2011; Bilton, 2006; Davis, 2000/1973; Knight, 2010). Addams' work in social reform, settlement negotiation, and coalition building particularly demonstrated what one of her biographers called a "genius" for working within a diverse community or conflicting group of stakeholders to arrive at a peaceful compromise on a range of issues from local garbage collection, to educational methods and to initiating and sustaining women's political networks (Davis, 2000/1973). This genius grew from her commitment to arrive at the compromise through the processes of reciprocal social relations and examination of the consequences of potential practical actions across a community to "be sure that it is worth having" (Addams, 2002/1902, p. 97); key features of her social and philosophical thought significant to many areas in social science.

The majority of the social problems Addams encountered – struggling schools burdened with inadequate resources and governmental policy pushing for efficiency and "scientific" management; women's exploitation and lack of the vote; rising poverty and intolerance of differences spurred by immigration with their consequences for education; after-effects of the US Civil War and racial unrest; not to mention ongoing international conflicts leading to two world wars – remain concerns internationally, although some of the players have changed. Specifically for educators and those who research their work, Addams' political activism in a time when US women did not even have the franchise marks a kind of energy and network building useful for a profession facing loss of autonomy and increasing standardization, and that still labors as a hierarchized and gendered profession. Reformers and scholars in related social sciences continue to explore implications and expansions of her practice and scholarship for today's problems (Behrends, 2011; Bilton, 2006; Hamington, 2004; Knight, 2010).

One area of study that has attended closely to claiming and renewing Addams' social philosophy for education and social science is the assemblage of philosophical thoughts identified as classical American pragmatism. Although it seems to have been marginalized by the hegemony of analytical philosophy in higher education, over the last 50 years, there have been efforts to recover it as a relevant, dynamic, and "living tradition" with potential to generate changed and deeper thinking about social relations in democratic community[2] (Brandom, 2011; Haack, 2006; Hamington, 2004, 2009; Rooney, 1993; Seigfried, 1996; Sullivan, 2001). Not only have these efforts attended to recuperating classical pragmatism itself, they have also explored ways in which it articulates critically and generatively with more contemporary philosophical and theoretical inquiries such as feminism, critical studies in education, and critical race theory (Sullivan, 2001, 2006).

Contemporary pragmatist and feminist scholars in the USA have proposed the possibilities for "changing the theoretical analyses and concrete practices" (Seigfried, 1996, p. 4) of both feminism and classical American pragmatism generated by its recuperation through feminism (Duran, 1993; Hamington, 2004, 2009; Rooney, 1993; Seigfried, 1996; Sullivan, 2001). Since feminism is claimed by scholars worldwide, this effort holds promise for expansions of both feminism and pragmatism. In issuing an invitation to further develop this trajectory, these scholars have suggested that Jane Addams and other women pragmatists of her era such as Charlotte Perkins Gilman, Ida Wells Barnett, Elsie Ripley Clapp, and Lucy Sprague Mitchell actually forged a feminist-informed pragmatism. Particularly, scholarship on Addams has reached back to retrieve her activism, ethics, and social theory as emblematic and informative of what a feminist pragmatism can offer to these fields of inquiry.

Whereas most feminist pragmatist scholarship recuperates an almost seamless integration of these theoretical and philosophical orientations in Addams' work, in this paper, I aim to trouble those claims through a promiscuous reading of two selections from what may be her most well-known book, *Twenty Years at Hull*

House (1961/1912), an autobiographical account of the development of Addams' social thought and work through the Hull House settlement. This approach entails reading across theoretical boundaries to challenge some of the existing feminist pragmatist claims on Addams' work to suggest that her appropriation of feminist pragmatism complicated and perplexed both of the theoretical orientations with which her work associated. Loosening this theoretical hold on her work brings into relief contradictions that indicate Addams' restlessness with both philosophies as she knew them, and a reaching for something different. This unmoors her work for new questions and directions of inquiry from more contemporary theoretical frames to see how Addams may have been, like some of her fellow pragmatist colleagues, ahead of her time in forging social theory and practice for an emerging philosophy and methodology.

For this purpose, I bring the feminist materialist theoretical framework of Karen Barad's "agential realism" to bear on Addams' work because of the attention to the relationship between ontology and epistemology shared by feminist pragmatism as well as agential realism. Considered broadly, both theoretical frameworks insist on the importance of the realities of existence and physical conditions in accounts of meaning. However, in Addams' writing, I see possibilities that she was reaching for something akin to feminist pragmatism that was more attentive to materiality but that exceeded her theoretical grasp. I bring in Barad not randomly but in a way pragmatically, as a continued and more extensively theorized development of feminist materialism presaged in Addams' thinking. Barad enables us to loosen Addams from feminist pragmatism to see her more clearly.

To begin, I offer a brief overview of feminist pragmatism followed by a somewhat lengthier explanation of Barad's agential realism. Then, I explain what promiscuous reading is by contextualizing it within the theoretical tensions between Butler's post structuralism and Barad's agential realism. I follow that with promiscuous readings, of two of Addams' vignettes excerpted from *Twenty Years at Hull House* (1961/1912). Through those promiscuous readings, I first show how Addams troubled the feminist pragmatist concepts of reciprocity and perspectivism, and then how moving Addams' appropriations of reciprocity and perspectivism through Barad's framework evidences her recognition and insistence on the ontoepistemological entanglements that constitute knowing through being. Finally, I offer some final thoughts on how this promiscuous reading helps us unsettle Addams from the firm claim of feminist pragmatism and see her better, as one who reached to know and understand the excesses around her through being in them.

Feminist pragmatism

Two major threads run through much of the scholarship supporting a feminist pragmatist alliance. One is the claim that both feminism and pragmatism emphasize challenging and destabilizing the foundational assumptions and bases on which Enlightenment traditional philosophy forwarded claims of transcendence, the unitary subject, the universal and the normative, as well as the authority of abstract truth claims. Like the pragmatists, feminist pragmatists asserted the importance of "lived experience," but ground philosophical reflection in women's experience as the transaction of subject and object, "of organism and environment" in transactive processes of mutual constitutiveness (Seigfried, 1996, p. 18). Addams' work demonstrates feminist pragmatists' inclusion of not just women's experiences as knowledge-generating transactions within community context, but those of Chicago's poor and the immigrant working men and women in the Hull House community.

The second thread appears in the shifting of epistemic priorities that remaps the relationship between epistemology and ontology through an emphasis on philosophical inquiry, epistemology, ontology, and all meaning-making as accountable to and irreducibly mediated by the historical, physical, experiential, and epistemological consequences of their propositions (Rooney, 1993; Seigfried, 1996). The feminist pragmatist work of "undoing" uncovers how hegemonic male-centered epistemology asserts gender-inscribed hierarchical epistemic categories of knowledge and experience that discount ontology, and position women and their experiences as subordinate and marginal to universal male experience.

This shifting of epistemic priorities acknowledges contingency, the materiality of what pragmatists called "environment," cultural practices referred to as habits, and inquiries as social and relational, mutually and dialectically constitutive. It grounds the emergence and positioning of identity, epistemology, and ontology in reciprocity and relationality always within community and political relation, and always in relation to the historical context and the context of power relations. Finally, feminist pragmatists, like feminists then and now, anticipate their work as an ameliorative project aimed towards improvement of social conditions for the oppressed and marginalized in community, especially women.

In selecting Barad's ontoepistemological frame for this promiscuous reading, I considered how both feminist pragmatism and agential realism share concerns about the participation of the real world of materiality and practice in meaning-making processes. Both have been offered as correctives to preceding philosophical thought that discounted the impact and force of matter, nature, physical, social, and cultural contexts on how we know and make sense of existence. Clearly, more differences separate the two approaches than bring them together, but I think that Addams' writings from her books informing this project, *Twenty Years at Hull House* (1961/1912), and *Democracy and Social Ethics* (2002/1902), hint at what Barad more fully realizes in agential realism (2007, 2008).

Agential realism

Barad's work over the past 15 years has developed as a corrective response to what she sees as postmodern philosophy's failure to account for how materiality informs and participates in knowledge production, theoretical inquiry, and philosophical deliberations on relationships among representation, material reality, and experience. She expresses concern that postmodern approaches have emphasized the cultural and linguistic imprint on experience and meaning to the exclusion of how matter and materiality participate. Barad claims, "Language has been granted too much power" (2007, p. 132), an emphasis, she asserts, that actually reinscribes the binary historically imposed between ontology and epistemology and its assigned values that postmodern scholars find problematic, unsatisfactory, and even reprehensible. Agential realism stresses the agential participation, the "performativity," of the materiality of everything in the world – nature, humans, non-humans, social and cultural practices, machines, theories, and research – in constituting what Barad calls "social-material practices" and what counts as knowledge (Barad, 2007). Within her framework, the knowledge we think we produce as a product of our own human agency acting on a world we behold separate from ourselves, actually comes to us because of our "intra-acting" with that world, being in the world that exerts agency that acts with, on, in, and through us so that we know through being. We gain "understanding from within" the world, not by "reflect(ing) on the world from the outside" (Barad, 2007, p. 89).

To name this mutuality, Barad uses the concept of "ontoepistemology" to express how existence and knowledge, ontology and epistemology, always act together, entangled so intimately that they must be conceptualized and studied as mutually constitutive, mutually productive, and mutually agential. She conceptualizes matter; the observers of matter; the languages and grammars that describe and theorize matter; and the apparatus by which matter is observed, whether it is technological, mechanical, political, social, cultural, procedural, or physical, as intra-acting in an entanglement of mutual interdependence (Barad, 2007, 2008; Hekman, 2010).

According to Barad, no element of an entanglement can presume an independent, separate, or *a priori* reality, and neither matter nor discursivity and nor observers nor their apparatus prevail over any other. Barad's theory of agential realism removes the lines and boundaries drawn between matter and language or discursivity, and between "objects and agents of observation" (Hekman, 2010, p. 75) to conceptualize them as messily and inseparably entangled. From and through these entanglements emerges ontological reality: "individuals emerge through and as part of their intra-relating" (Barad, 2007, p. ix). Being in the world is knowing in and through the world through what Barad calls "intra-action" with social meanings, cultural practices, the weaknesses and strengths of our bodies, the political and ideological currents that flow around and through us, as well as the streets we walk on, the trees whose leaves flutter in the wind, the chairs we sit in, and the medical apparatus that measures us.

Promiscuous reading and qualitative research

Having mapped out these theoretical and contextual frameworks for this promiscuous reading, I present a more detailed explanation of what I think promiscuous reading is. Curiously enough, I begin by contextualizing promiscuous reading within the theoretical tensions between Judith Butler's post structuralism and Barad's corrective of it in her feminist materialist theory. Then I suggest what this approach offers to international qualitative research.

In the 1999 preface to her now classic *Gender Trouble,* Butler describes her analysis of feminist theory as an "immanent critique," a critique that turns a theoretical orientation's concepts and vocabulary back on itself to critically examine its premises and vocabulary in order to reveal the "presuppositions of its own practice" (Butler, 1999/1990, p. iii), in a sense betraying it. Considered broadly, promiscuous reading similarly calls for reading that uses unexpected interpretive framework/s to analyze how a text, practice, set of practices, or experiences contradicts itself, or shows interruptions or snags in its interpretation or justification. Butler characterizes her process as "intellectual promiscuity," first because of the unlikely associations among French theorists from different disciplines she calls on to build her analysis of US theories of gender – Foucault, Levi-Strauss, Lacan, Kristeva, and Wittig – "who had few alliances with one another and whose readers in France rarely, if ever, read one another" (Butler, 1999/1990, p. x), and second because of her use of "French Theory" to analyze US theory. The upshot of this, according to Butler, is "a new venue for theory, necessarily impure" (promiscuous) as it crosses traditional geographical and disciplinary boundaries as well as those attached to philosophical traditions (1999/1990, p. ix). This not only loosens theory's ties to the tradition with which it is associated, impure and promiscuous reading offers new linkages that bring new possibilities, and enhanced, even if complicated, understandings to ways to use theory in qualitative research in education.

By most accounts, Butler's intellectually promiscuous *Gender Trouble* (1999/1990) successfully critiqued contemporary feminist theories' heterosexist and unexamined presuppositions concerning gender, sexual difference, and the constitution of the subject. Furthermore, the book substantially contributed to the development and expansion of what has become known as feminist post structuralism. Barad, however, asserts that Butler, despite unraveling representationalist ways of thinking about gender and the subject, and opening up new avenues of thought, left materiality curiously untheorized (Barad, 2007, p. 64). Butler's concept of "performativity" introduced to account for agency in gender identity formation does acknowledge an association of materiality with cultural formations, the body with identity through the body's iterative cultural practices, by which specific materializations of the body are produced (Butler, 1993, 1999/1990). Yet, according to Barad, even as Butler moves away from the notion of an agency-less body as "inscribed" with cultural meaning, and proposes performativity as a materializing process whereby boundaries, exclusions, inclusions and surfaces considered to be matter are produced (Butler, 1993), her theorization still does not account for the actual connections and transactions that occur between matter and the discursive. Barad writes, "...while Butler correctly calls for the recognition of matter's historicity, ironically she seems to assume that it is ultimately derived (yet again) from the agency of language or culture. She fails to recognize matter's dynamism" (Barad, 2007, p. 64). This is where Barad offers her work as a corrective to the inadequate theorizing to the point of neglect, of the agential capacity and energy of material and cultural practices as well as human and non-human entities in ongoing and mutual co-constitutiveness.

Reading Addams' appropriation of feminist pragmatism promiscuously

Complicating existing interpretive frameworks of a text, experience, or practice by promiscuously reading through several analytic frameworks provokes new ways of thinking not only about the central focus of study, but about the intersections and contradictions among the theoretical frameworks and methodologies used in the process. For feminist pragmatism, questioning the linkages between feminist pragmatism and Addams' work provokes thinking about the qualities of each tradition's unique contribution to educational philosophy and qualitative methodology useful in education and other social sciences, and its agential suppleness in grappling with contradictions and complications in those fields of study. I ask, if Addams' work is not feminist pragmatist, what is it? What was she reaching for? For agential realism, this project takes on the challenge of exploring how to account for entanglements with agential force and impact as irreducible intra-action of the discursive and the material (matter), how material reality in its "fullness of physicality...come(s) to matter through the world's iterative intra-activity – its performativity" (Barad, 2008, p. 141).

In this promiscuous reading of Addams' work, I ask how Addams theorized how "matter matters" (Barad, 2003), and how Addams, dissatisfied with the theoretical frames available to her for examining and theorizing women's experiences as well as those of the immigrant poor with whom she worked, performed a "mattering" of the intra-actions of meaning and the material, and for feminists particularly, how our bodies matter in reciprocal social relations and in notions of inclusive pluralistic perspectivism. Addams may be particularly suited for such an exploration because she firmly rooted her philosophical and social thought in her practice and experience. She wrote of her experiences and philosophical conclusions as inseparable. In her preface to *Twenty Years at Hull House,* she explains that "each of (her) earlier books [was]…an attempt to set forth a thesis supported by experience, whereas this volume endeavors to trace the experiences through which various conclusions were forced upon me" (1961/1912, p. xxii). Addams leaves the impression that the agency exercised by the world around her, along with her past engagements in the world, "forced" the conclusions to which she came, perhaps a recognition of their agential capacity.

Addams' well-known work on behalf of laboring women, her acute sense of the particular dilemmas and challenges facing the first generations of college-educated women in an increasingly industrialized society, her efforts in collaborating internationally with women on behalf of world peace, and her controversial, "dangerous" political decisions testify to a strong and decisive mind that crossed boundaries and transgressed expectations in her pursuit of collaborative and reciprocal approaches to investigating and ministering to human needs in an increasingly violent and dehumanizing world (Davis, 2000/1973; Elshtain, 2002; Fischer, 2000, 2009; Knight, 2010). In this context, Addams worked and lived out materializations of the feminist pragmatist concepts of reciprocity and perspectivism in practice, developing them as her philosophical and methodological guides for action and theoretical interpretations. Two narrative vignettes from *Twenty Years at Hull House* (Addams, 1961/1902) will be used to illustrate feminist pragmatist reading of her appropriation of these concepts problematized through a promiscuous reading that also points to Addams' promiscuous interpretations. Then, a reading through Barad's ontoepistemological framework further complicates interpretation of the vignettes.

Reciprocity

Addams writes that after a Chicago Woman's Club meeting at which she had advocated for the "necessity" of settlement houses in the building of democratic community, one of the club members told this story as a critique of Addams' vision:

> …When she was a little girl playing in her mother's garden, she one day discovered a small toad who seemed to her very forlorn and lonely, although she did not in the least know how to comfort him, she reluctantly left him to his fate; later in the day, quite at the other end of the garden, she found a large toad, also apparently without family and friends. With a heart full of tender sympathy, she took a stick and by exercising infinite patience and some skill, she finally pushed the little toad through the entire length of the garden into the company of the big toad, when, to her inexpressible horror and surprise, the big toad opened his mouth and swallowed the little one. The moral of the tale was clearly applied to people who lived 'where they did not naturally belong,' although I protested that was exactly what we wanted – to be swallowed and digested, to disappear into the bulk of the people. (Addams, 1961/1902, pp. 203–204)

Addams recognized the woman's cautionary tale of the "danger" – life-ending for the little toad – for classes and ethnicities to inhabit proximal spaces for fear of being subsumed or destroyed by one or the other. It surely reveals the club woman's own xenophobia and elitism, which Addams critiques as she claims that the story serves as an illustration of the goals of Hull House. As an exemplar of feminist pragmatism experimentation in action, Hull House embodied Addams' central organizing idea and the key to her social theory – reciprocity. She stated that Hull House was developed, "on the theory that the dependence of classes on each other is reciprocal; and that as the social relation is essentially a reciprocal relation, it gives a form of expression that has peculiar value" (Addams, 1961/1920, p. 82). Developed as an educative institution for both those living in the house as well as the local neighborhood, Hull House, to Addams' way of thinking, fulfilled her understanding of what reciprocity would look like.

A characteristic pragmatist conceptualization, reciprocity, refers to the organic, multidirectional, mutually informing interdependence that operates, acknowledged or not, in transactions that take place at all levels of activity in the world. The pragmatist defense of *relations* between things and not *essence* or *a thing in itself* as integral to meaning, experience, and inquiry relies on this notion of reciprocity. Dewey emphasized the continuous and dynamic relation between theory and praxis based on "organicist" claims about the "antidualistic unity of subject and object" (Garrison, 2006, p. 4). Various feminist pragmatist scholars elaborate some of the types of these reciprocal relations: people to people, theory to action, social to political, domestic to social, and philosophical to cultural (Addams, 1961/1912, 2002/1902; Duran, 1993; Rooney, 1993; Seigfried, 1996, 1999; Sullivan, 2003; Whipps, 2004). According to Addams, each entity in these relationships both intentionally and unintentionally takes from and gives to the other. However, it is important to point out that the reciprocity within a community, as both Addams and the feminist pragmatists understand it, does not imply any sort of equality between its entities. This point seems to have been recognized in all of their work, as well as in the work of the male classical pragmatists, but inadequately theorized across class, race, and gender.

Reading Addams' interpretation of the toad story promiscuously points out several implications useful for thinking about how power operates within theorized reciprocal relations. First, Addams' interpretation glosses over the real differences between the power each toad exerts, not to mention their disparate sizes. Second, even though Addams does not see herself sharing the same viewpoint as the club member, as the founder of the Hull House settlement led by middle-class privileged white women placed in an immigrant community, she carried out paternalistic actions similar to those of the girl in the story. Like the girl, who assumed the little toad would be happier with the big toad, Addams made assumptions about the needs of the neighborhood into which she moved. The girl's well-intentioned and naïve actions brought about the little toad's death. Addams' establishment of Hull House in an immigrant neighborhood, for all of her good intentions, ran the risk of bringing danger and conflict to the local residents, not to mention resistance to its assimilative influences. Finally, the girl's actions brought about the reinscription of the big toad's appetites and power as it consumed the small toad. Similarly, Hull House has been critiqued as a site of a paternalistic "Americanization" of immigrants that subsumed individual cultural differences, even though considered to offer a softer and more persuasive approach (Lissak, 1989). The inevitability of power differentials in cross-cultural encounters between a colonizing power and immigrant populations, even played out in apparently friendly and supportive circumstances such as Hull House, also inevitably involves paternalistic relations. In those situations, reciprocity acts as an ethics to be worked for rather than an assumed practice.

Third, Addams' expressed desire to be "swallowed up and digested" by community subverts one of feminism's most integral, if contested, concerns – that of establishing and maintaining political identity from which concerted political action grows. To abandon that stance, to be swallowed up in community could presage a return to the status quo of being swallowed up in the male universal, a possibility Addams does not mention, and does not seem to recognize. Addams' interpretation of reciprocity as a social relation approves a loss of identity in that relation – an abandonment, an indiscriminate "spreading herself around" that complicates her appropriation of feminist pragmatism. This anticipation of a loss of identity in community could be called a transgression of feminist commitments to establish and expand women's political identity and space to counter patriarchal aggression and oppression, especially in a time when women campaigned for the vote, suffragettes suffered forced feedings in prisons, and Addams herself worked actively for women's improved working conditions through union organizing. Addams' idea of reciprocity's call for give-and-take seems to require yielding or modifying of the centering of gender or women's hard-won political identity in the name of community.

This interpretation further complicates the question of how Addams conceptualized a feminist pragmatist political identity for women from which concerted transformative and emancipatory efforts develop, could grow and emerge from social relations distorted by power. The feminist pragmatist defense of the importance of respecting and including multiple perspectives in democratic social relations and decision-making implicitly requires grappling with and analyzing the relations of power that undergird such multiplicities, a necessity Addams must have recognized and responded to, even to a limited extent. Her refusal to let the University of Chicago take over administration of Hull House emerged from some awareness on her part of the hegemony of the androcentric academy, and her commitment to retaining women's leadership and collaboration in that community (Ross, 1998; Seigfried, 1999). One wonders whether this is yet another "veiled" critique of fellow pragmatist William James' sexist comments disparaging "reading like a woman," and advocating for separate spheres for men and women as well as other pragmatists' resounding silences on the gendering of experience (Seigfried, 1996).

Reciprocity and intra-action

Moving my promiscuous reading of reading Addams through Barad's framework makes it possible to see this interpretation as a story not of Addams' anticipation of loss of identity, but of her anticipation of an identity or identities becoming through the intra-actions with which she engages in community, of knowing through mangle-like (Hekman, 2010) reciprocal processes being in community with others, the "stuff" of nature, man-made structures of all kinds, machines, habits, social and cultural practices. When Addams declared she wanted to be "digested…into the bulk of the people" (1961/1912, pp. 203–204), her desire was to become something else, something more, know something else differently or something more, to know through being in community. Addams' declaration can be read as emerging from the intra-acting of her understanding that "subjectivity develops only in social relations" (Seigfried, 2002, p. xiv) with her sense that more than just "social relations" participated in configuring subjectivities. She seemed to be responding to a sense of her own becoming and mattering through the materiality of her experiences with the Hull House community.

Although Addams stresses the human social relations through which she saw her sense of herself, her relationship with others, and the world becoming, her writing displays evidence of the agency of the non-human, both discursive and material, as the mattering of an industrializing, laboring context of smoke, fumes, ash, inescapable mechanical roars, and manufacturing detritus sustained by the economic, civic, and political policies of a capitalist society. That the intra-action of bodies, environment, cultural, social, economic practices, nature, political beliefs, and social discourses articulate and configure substantive, material, "felt" relations with the world was an expansion on ideas about reciprocity forced upon her in the course of her experiences in the Hull House community. Such were their emotional and physical impact and cognitive "perplexity," that Addams felt compelled to recognize how bodies matter, and how bodies of knowledge, economic policies, business practices, all of these and more, are involved, "implicated and enfolded in…a dynamic articulation/configuration of the world" (Barad, 2007, p. 151) we experience as materialized, physical "felt" realities.

The world Addams narrates and from which she draws her social theory is one of bodies shaped by the demands of a burgeoning industrial society and overpowering poverty with its ever-present hunger, as much as they shape and are shaped by the practices developed in response to poverty, such as the young child with his back bent from being tied to the kitchen table all day because there was no one to care for him as the whole family had to work all day to survive (Addams, 1961/1912). This child's body was bent as an articulation of the family's mangle-like intra-action with the industrial economy at large; the intra-action of the child's body with the table; and the intra-actions of the family members making this arrangement. The child's body mattered in that the family had to make arrangements for his care; and the child's body mattered in that its corporeality took on the harsh pressures and constraints experienced by the working poor. It is ironic perhaps, and deeply telling, that it is the table – used for meals for the family's sustenance – to which the child's body conforms; indeed, the misshapen child's body produced and was produced by the provision of sustenance for the family.

Perspectivism and how bodies matter

In contemplating the implications of reciprocal social relations as a requirement for democratic and inclusive social communities, the classical pragmatists made the crucial connection that for reciprocity to be working as they conceived it, the acknowledgment, visibility, and inclusion of multiplicities of experiences were integral and necessary. However, a second narrative vignette from *Twenty Years at Hull House* provides a feminist pragmatist claim that Addams' work represents a clear and unmistakable reproach to this bland perspectivism as she advocated for political and economic space for the particular immigrants', workingman's and woman's struggles and concerns, and valorized their experiences as valuable sources of knowledge (1961/1912, 2002/1902). Addams writes:

I was detained late one evening in an office building by a prolonged committee meeting of the Board of Education. As I came out at eleven o'clock, I met in the corridor of the 14th floor a woman whom I knew, on her knees scrubbing the marble tiling. As she straightened up to greet me, she seemed so wet from her feet up to her chin, that I hastily inquired the cause. Her reply was that she left home at five o'clock every night and had not opportunity for six hours to nurse her baby. Her mother's milk mingled with the very water with which she scrubbed the floors until she should return at midnight, heated and exhausted, to feed her screaming child with what remained within her breasts. (Addams, 1961/1912, p. 116)

In this vignette we see the wealthy, privileged, well-dressed, and comfortable educated woman conducting civic business encountering a young working mother miserably wet, tired, hot, sweaty, and despairing of her situation. Both women live and exist in the same environment, but the social, cultural, economic, and historic factors that position them within that context articulate the stark differences such as Addams narrates. This narrative resonates with that of a similar encounter described in *Democracy and Social Ethics*, in which a "daintily clad charitable visitor" is confronted with the "little house made untidy by her hostess, the washerwoman" (Addams, 2002/1902, p. 12). As Addams does in this late night encounter, the charity visitor realizes that the washerwoman, "represents social value and industrial use, as over against her own parasitic cleanliness and a social standing attained only through status" (2002/1912, p. 12). In this story of the late night encounter, Addams' narrative includes both perspectives, as it places both women in the same community, but it also demonstrates that mere recognition of multiplicities of experiences as integral to an inclusive community such as forwarded by the classical pragmatists does not necessarily engage the historical power relations from which these experiences emerge. Feminist pragmatists point out that the classical pragmatist stand on perspectivism hesitated to promote any one perspective or struggle for fear of marginalizing others (Seigfried, 1996). The irony is that in taking that stand, the pragmatists inadvertently maintained the androcentric Eurocentric view from the top.

Addams' writing implicitly but consistently confronted received notions of perspectivism with its own inadequacies regarding women by her unapologetic placement of women's experiences as central illustrations of moral and ethical dilemmas faced by all individuals as they engage in social, discursive, and material relations affected by the rapidly changing conditions of an increasingly industrialized society, as illustrated in her two books referenced in this paper. However, her insights into women's conditions and exploitation did not extend to all of the multiplicities of experiences, and so her critique of perspectivism was limited, as was her own perspectivism. For example, Addams greatly disappointed Ida Wells Barnett with her 1899 speech protesting lynching to a mostly African-American audience. Addams never identified lynching as a consequence of white racism; rather she condemned it for its lawlessness so that it was more a rebuke to the white southerners predominately responsible for the crimes, than an indictment of a gross moral failing of an entire nation (Knight, 2010).

A promiscuous reading of the scrubwoman's narrative challenges feminist pragmatist appropriations as an indictment of perspectivism as practiced by the pragmatists. Addams aims more broadly, and focuses this story as a social, even socialist critique of the problems of poverty brought on by an industrialized capitalistic society that does not provide for poor mothers who must work when they have young children who need them. She writes, "It is curiously inconsistent that with the emphasis...placed upon the mother and....infancy, we constantly allow the waste of this most precious material" (1961/1912, p. 116). I find her use of the word "material" very curious and intriguing. Addams' dehumanizing and industrial use of the term "material" in reference to this woman who certainly appealed to Addams' compassion seems cold and dispassionate. But it may have been purposeful. "Material" can refer to the woman's labor both as scrubwoman and as mother. Surely, it refers to the unused breast milk, that when mixed with the soapy water lost its nutritional value and became "material." Perhaps it was an unconscious play on the fact that the substance of the breast milk was wasted as well as the young woman's vitality in the service of the industrialized economy's demands at the expense of family, the building owner's demands, and her family's needs. It could also be read as a cynical comment critiquing the attitudes of those who do see such a woman and child as "material," fodder for their industrial machines.

Addams' observation of the inconsistency between the social sentiment that emphasizes and values, even romanticizes "mothers...and infancy," but allows the lives of poor mothers and children to be poured out in service to its appetite for goods and profits, reads as a criticism of the hypocrisy of male privilege in a patriarchal capitalistic society that determines whose perspectives "matter." In a foreshadowing of feminist critiques of hegemonic masculinity and patriarchy to be developed in future years, Addams laid her finger on the pivot point by which woman's reproductive capacity was the instrument of her oppression. My promiscuous approach to this narrative also reads Addams' criticism of this hypocrisy written with the sentimental and emotional language characteristic of the domestic discourse prevalent at that time, as Addams' attempt at a "one-two punch." First, she draws on the domestic and sentimental discourses of the physical and material details of the woman's experience to materialize the felt qualities of the experience for the reader. Then, once the reader is engaged in the woman's experience and the injustices so apparent, she offers her "curious" observation of the discrepancies between a society's claimed values and its actual practices, thereby challenging claims of inclusive perspectivism. Addams underlines the epistemic and moral value of this woman, the encounter, and her social critique. Finally, it allows Addams' use of the word "material" to be read as a giveaway "tell" of her sense of materiality's agential force pressing in around her and its impact for people such as this woman.

Intra-action exceeding perspectivism

The materializations of the intra-acting discursive and material circumstances Addams saw in the experiences of the Hull House community, as in this narrative, escaped and exceeded Addams' conventional knowing in social relations. I think that Adams, without access to Barad's conceptual tools, sought to express the impact this had on her as evidence of the agency exerted by both material and discursive practices as well as social relations to articulate the subjectivities that she apprehended through her encounter. I can think of few of her other stories that so dramatically illustrate how bodies, and particularly women's bodies matter through the entanglement of agential apparatus in multiplicities of perspectives within the world and how they "come to matter."

This working nursing mother's body matters in multiple ways. As a source of production, she produces children, breast milk, labor to birth her children, support her family and its labor production, all of which intra-act with the ideology, economy, and politics of production in an industrialized and capitalistic democracy. Her soaking wet body emerges from the entanglement of the means, forces, and apparatus of production. In another iteration of this entanglement, Barad's framework suggests that this young woman's body bearing scrub water, sweat, and the breast milk so imperceptibly that Addams could not tell one agent from another, emanates from the entanglement of the woman, her child's needs, her need to nurse her child, their physical needs for nourishment, the need for labor, and the exploitative demands of the industrialized laissez-faire economy. The young mother matters as *"substance in its intra-active becoming – not a thing but a doing, a congealing of agency"* (Barad, 2007, p. 151). Women's bodies matter, as material substantiated and wasted by an industrial economy, as materially supportive of their families, and as embodied and materialized phenomena emanating from the entanglement of economy, ideology, and physical and psychical forces; they matter in Addams' accounts of the unjust consequences of these entanglements. Addams reached to recognize the force of ontoepistemological entanglements of matter, history, politics, social relations, theory, and practice on existence as perspectivism from within the world, rather than from outside observations, as knowing through being, through intra-acting within the world.

Final thoughts

In placing feminist pragmatist and agential realist approaches alongside each other in a promiscuous reading, my purpose is not to criticize or disparage feminist pragmatist scholarship. I wanted to closely examine the claims of this scholarship to learn more about the possibilities and limitations of this theoretical recuperation. I also wanted to investigate the features of Addams' transgressions of feminist pragmatism through Barad's agential realism to see if Addams was trying something new that could not be claimed by pragmatists or feminists. At this point, I conclude that Addams' promiscuous methodology was not a seamless integration of feminism and pragmatism, but an irregularly stitched together and promiscuous methodology materialized from her entangled relations of theory intra-acting with practice and those each intra-acting with the harsh physical, economic, and political environment of early twentieth-century Chicago.

So, what are we to do with Jane? She remains mysterious – promiscuous – mobile – agentially trespassing to evade containment. I think Addams' transgressions betrayed an untheorized awareness of and inadequate grappling with how the material and its excesses press on our representations, trespass into our meaning making, act constitutively, and become intelligible despite our attempts to control or theorize them. Her transgressions also suggest her dissatisfactions with forms of analysis available to her through pragmatism and feminism as practiced and theorized at the time, raising the question of what interpretive framework might offer a way to reconsider and/or reconfigure the excesses with which she struggled with all her limitations.

Addams' own excesses have proven hard to contain by feminist pragmatists, feminists, pragmatists, as well as myself. Barad's work suggests that Addams is hard to pin down because during her life, she was engaged in being digested; she was becoming as she was knowing in being in twentieth-century Chicago. She lived, acted, and wrote her becoming. We who read and engage her life and work today see how she is still becoming, a becoming that challenges us to think about our own becomings – becomings in which we are all entangled that compel us to deliberate on how we become. How we come to matter. How we matter.

Notes

1. Attributed to anonymous reviewer.
2. American philosophers associated with the pragmatist tradition include John Dewey, William James, Charles S. Peirce, Josiah Royce, W.E.B. DuBois, and George H. Mead (Seigfried, 1996). Jane Addams has more recently been included in this panoply of early pragmatist thinkers.

References

Addams, Jane. (1961/1910). *Twenty years at Hull-House*. New York, NY: Signet.
Addams, Jane. (2002/1902). *Democracy and social ethics*. Urbana, IL: University of Illinois Press.
Barad, Karen. (2003). Posthumanist performativity: How matter comes to matter. *Signs: Journal of Women in Culture and Society, 28*, 801–831.
Barad, Karen. (2007). *Meeting the universe halfway: Quantum physics and the entanglement of matter and meaning*. Durham, NC: Duke University Press.
Barad, Karen. (2008). Posthumanist performativity: Toward an understanding of how matter comes to matter. In Stacy Alaimo & Susan Hekman (Eds.), *Material feminisms* (pp. 120–154). Bloomington, IN: Indiana University Press.
Behrends, Jan C. (2011). Visions of civility: Lev Tolstoy and Jane Addams on the urban condition in *fin de siècle* Moscow and Chicago. *European Review of History, 18*, 335–357.
Bilton, Chris. (2006). Knowing her place: Jane Addams, pragmatism and cultural policy. *Journal of Cultural Policy, 12*, 135–150.
Brandom, Robert. (2011). *Perspectives on pragmatism: Classical, recent, and contemporary*. Cambridge, MA: Harvard University Press.
Butler, Judith. (1993). *Bodies that matter: On the discursive limits of "sex"*. New York, NY: Routledge.
Butler, Judith. (1999/1990). *Gender trouble*. New York, NY: Routledge.
Davis, Allen. (2000/1973). *American heroine: The life and legend of Jane Addams*. Chicago, IL: Ivan R. Dee.
Duran, Jane. (1993). The intersection of pragmatism and feminism. *Hypatia, 8*, 159–171.
Elshtain, Jean Bethke. (2002). *The Jane Addams reader*. New York, NY: Basic Books.
Fischer, Marilyn. (2000). Jane Addams' feminist ethics. In Cecile Tougas & Sara Ebenreck (Eds.). *Presenting women philosophers* (pp. 51–57). Philadelphia, PA: Temple University Press.
Fischer, Marilyn. (2009). *Jane Addams and the practice of democracy*. Urbana: University of Illinois Press.
Garrison, James. (2006). The permanent deposit of Hegelian thought in Dewey's theory of inquiry. *Educational Theory, 56*(1), 1–37.
Haack, Susan. (2006). *Pragmatism, old and new*. Amherst, NY: Prometheus Press.

Hamington, Maurice. (2004). *Embodied care: Jane Addams, Maurice Merleau-Ponty, and feminist ethics*. Urbana: University of Illinois Press.
Hamington, Maurice. (2009). Feminist prophetic pragmatism. *Journal of Speculative Philosophy, 23*, 83–97.
Hekman, Susan. (2010). *The material of knowledge: Feminist disclosures*. Bloomington, IN: Indiana University Press.
Knight, Louise. (2010). *Jane Addams: Spirit in action*. New York, NY: W.W. Norton.
Lissak, Rivka Shpak. (1989). *Pluralism and progressives: Hull House and the new immigrants 1890–1919*. Chicago, IL: University of Chicago Press.
Rooney, Phyllis. (1993). Feminist–pragmatist revisionings of reason, knowledge, and philosophy. *Hypatia, 8*, 15–37.
Ross, Dorothy. (1998). Gendered social knowledge: Domestic discourse, Jane Addams, and the possibilities of social science. In Helena Silverberg (Ed.). *Gender and American social science: The formative years* (pp. 235–264). Princeton, NJ: Princeton University Press.
Seigfried, Charlene. (1996). *Pragmatism and feminism: Reweaving the social fabric*. Chicago, IL: University of Chicago Press.
Seigfried, Charlene. (1999). Socializing democracy: Jane Addams and John Dewey. *Philosophy of Social Sciences, 29*, 207–231.
Seigfried, Charlene. (2002/1902). Introduction to the Illinois edition. In *Democracy and social ethics*, by Jane Addams. Urbana, IL: University of Illinois Press.
Sullivan, Shannon. (2001). *Living across and through skins: Transactional bodies, pragmatism, and feminism*. Bloomington, IN: Indiana University Press.
Sullivan, Shannon. (2003). Reciprocal relations between races: Jane Addams' ambiguous legacy. *Transactions of the Charles S. Peirce Society, 39*, 43–60.
Sullivan, Shannon. (2006). *Revealing whiteness: The unconscious habits of racial privilege*. Bloomington, IN: Indiana University Press.
Whipps, Judy. (2004). Jane Addams' social thought as a model for a pragmatist–feminist communitarianism. *Hypatia, 19*, 118–133.

Promiscuous feminists postscript

Maggie MacLure

Education and Social Research Institute, Manchester Metropolitan University, Manchester, UK

It is a mark of liveliness of thought when new research imaginaries are named and set to work. So it has been great to witness the debut in these articles of the figure of the promiscuous feminist researcher, with her dirty theories and messy habits, her diverse and perverse commitments and her productive–seductive vulnerabilities. Of course promiscuous feminist research is not really unitary, nor is it fully formed. The authors are appropriately uncertain and provisional in their essays across boundaries. And there is not unanimity, although the editors do count themselves members of a particular generation of feminist scholars, aware of their rich inheritance, but shaped and equipped to work differently in the ruins of social science (Editors' Introduction, this issue). So there are multiple connections and resonances across the collection, and shared experiences of the material realities of academic work in North American universities. Still, although the authors are united in their aspiration to push feminist theorising in education beyond gender, each has fashioned and glimpsed her own apparition, her own vision of what the promiscuous feminist researcher might become and do. A rough trawl for verbs in the collection suggests that this work is variously to infiltrate, transgress, infect, mix, unmoor, entangle, fail and unsettle. Adjectivally, promiscuous feminisms are wild, patient, persistent, nomadic, dirty, impure, disloyal, vulnerable, impossible, destructive, constructive, creative, treacherous and mad.

The writers and texts in this special issue have necessarily assumed a variety of uncomfortable, impossible positions therefore, bent into and out of shape by the effort of maintaining a precarious, disloyal fidelity to feminist thought and practice, while at the same time twisting and pressing these into relations with other disciplines and domains. They have struggled to transgress boundaries while embracing their condition of perpetual, productive entanglement. Exercising interpretive licence, they have brokered wary alliances with partners – male continental philosophers, grant-science technocrats, pragmatists and policy-makers – whose status (big toad or little toad, predator or prey) cannot be known in advance. As Rick noted in his opening contribution, the term promiscuity is itself semantically promiscuous, and the contributors have exploited its polysemy to open up good questions about feminist methodologies and practices for new educational contexts and purposes.

In the remainder of these brief closing comments, I am not going to try to recapitulate the arguments of the contributors, nor deal with the individual articles one by one. Readers who have got this far will recognise that my opening paragraphs above are already thoroughly entangled with, or infected by, the terminology and tropes of the texts to which they refer. I do not want to drain the individual articles of their singularity. And I am certainly not going to try to interpret, explain or represent their contents. One of the liveliest currents running through the collection, which I will return to below, has been a trenchant critique of representation, explication, interpretation and categorisation in qualitative research. There would be no value in commentary that tries to frame or speak for the work and the mobile uncertainties in these texts. So I propose simply to dwell briefly on those elements in the articles that beckoned to me.

First, I was struck by the persistent, patient, dogged exposure of the colonialist logic that still structures research and educational practices. The authors identify, with varying degrees of explicitness and anger, the persistence of colonising tendencies at work in their chosen area – in the performativity and technical rationality of grant science and the NSF criteria (Stephanie); in the unacknowledged epistemic violence of 'righting wrongs' praxis (Jeong-eun); in the Eurocentrism of methodologies that reify marginalisation (Fran); and finally, deep inside interpretation itself, as the continuing legacy of a humanism that fails to address its own libidinal desires and fantasies, and renders others mute in its rage for intelligibility (Aparna). If anyone thought that the experimental ethnographers and post-structural feminists of the late twentieth century had written the book(s) on the colonialism inherent in social science methodology, these articles are here to tell us that it still works inside the most mundane and seemingly innocent of research acts.

I found the post-colonial critique of representation, interpretation and explication particularly powerful. The work of finding new, non-representational concepts and images of thought has been under way for some time, animated by the work of Deleuze (1994) and commentators such as Olkowski (1999), Massumi (2002) and Thrift (2008). But the malign effects of those deeply ingrained intellectual habits are immensely difficult to discern, and almost impossible to renounce or escape, even now, in our allegedly post-Enlightenment, post-humanist times. This special issue reminds us of the price that is paid by those who are subject to the framing and fixing work of researchers and elders, as they interpret, categorise, compare, divide and explain. Jeong-eun's tropic repetition of the phrase *it was explained* beat out the rhythm of relentless ignorance of difference and becoming, and the almost comic oversimplification that is mobilised in order to enforce fixed positions on questions such as what it means to be a good researcher, a dutiful daughter, a Korean woman. Aparna, after Klein, traced interpretation's silencing of difference to the first 'staggering' attempts of the infant and mother to find a foothold of intelligibility in the swirling stew of desires, affects, bodies and bodily substances that is the maternal relation. This suppression of the 'wild horse within us' ultimately produces symbolic and social order, but only by projecting onto the other the chaos of hate, fear and fascination that we cannot tolerate in ourselves.

Not surprisingly, given their manifold allegiances, the individual authors locate their work with respect to a range of contemporary methodological tendencies – as post-critical, post-qualitative, literary critical, post-structuralist, psychoanalytic, post-colonial (as already noted), while in many cases critiquing and creatively interfering with these labels at the same time. Then there is materialism. I was particularly interested in the attentiveness to the demands of matter, embodiment and affect – which one would of course expect of a feminist methodology that is promiscuously aware of its own fleshy parts. Some of the authors explicitly located their work within the 'material turn' in the social sciences and humanities, drawing on the 'new' material feminism of writers such as Barad (2007) and Hekman (2010) for theoretical resources to comprehend the involuted mangle of materiality and discourse in the shaping of lives. Sara wanted a material feminism that recognises the agency, affect and capacity for 'intra-action' among the entities that populate 'the field' – 'bodies, buildings, books, desks, policies, theories, and discourses'. Becky mixed feminist pragmatism and Barad's agential realism to fashion a new reading of the social reformer Jane Addams as a feminist materialist ahead of her time, moved and mobilised by the dire effects and affects wrought upon adults' and children's bodies by hunger, poverty and industrialisation. The articles were also attentive to the material conditions of research employment in the academy – conditions that are often precarious and marginal for young women scholars these days – and how these impact on research practices and research knowledge. Stephanie looked at how the colour-blind empiricism of 'grant science' was materialised in proposal-writing meetings. Jeong-eun found herself caught between the academy's demand/desire for theoretical complexity and the stark 'material simplicity' of daily living for many of those who are 'researched'. Finally, within this materialist inflection, if not 'turn', there was attention to affect: to the significance of emotions and the body's sensations. Fran argued for the clandestine force of vulnerability, as the capacity to affect and to be affected. Aparna noted how affect is silenced in the conventional research practices of interpretation and representation, and commended an 'affected interpretive practice' that might glimpse the deep complicity of humanism with colonial violence.

I liked the examples: the detail and the anecdotes. It was here that the attention to matter was often most evident in the articles, so that in reading and reflecting on them, it is often the examples that have pressed themselves upon me. Jeong-eun's difficulty in stomaching the hunger of a Korean mother who may not have eaten in order to accommodate a researcher's busy schedule. That comment about 'social justice crap' that opened up questions of colliding imaginaries for Stephanie. Fran's grandmother's sunflowers, connecting personal experience, black feminism, love, loss and William Blake. Sara's 'matter' of inquiry – books, bodies, buildings and desks. The dying children in the AIDS hospice and the 'insignificant moment of "queer misrecognition"' in Aparna's 'wild reading' of Coe. And the examples in Jane Addams'/Becky's writing. I have learned from Becky's article that Addams had a great eye for examples. Particularly striking, for me, was Addams' account of her late-night encounter with the exhausted cleaning woman, drenched from feet to chin in breast milk mixed with dirty water – a brilliant instantiation of the material-discursive 'mangling' (cf. Hekman, 2010; Pickering, 1995) of women's and children's bodies by economic and ideological forces.

Increasingly, it is the examples, the choice bits of data, that most appeal to me in research writing (cf. MacLure, 2010). Greedily, I would have liked even more of them here. I would have liked more of those glimpses of the promiscuous entanglement of the material and the discursive that are rendered by the example. I am not thinking of examples that merely illustrate, but rather of those that disseminate. Massumi, who like Agamben was a big fan of examples, writes that they have powers of 'creative contagion' (2002, p. 19). At their most lively, examples have a kind of affective agency – a power to reach out and connect forcefully with the reader, to open up questions, and to summon more than can be said in so many words. 'Every example harbours terrible powers of deviation and digression', writes Massumi (2002, p. 18), and he sees this as their strength. You could see delayed and deviated action of 'creative contagion' at work in these articles – for instance, in Becky taking off from Addams and the drenched cleaning woman, taking things further, to unfold multiple meanings in Addams' use of the word 'materials'.

Examples are important for the work of theorising in qualitative research: they anchor theory in the mundane, forcing it to the ground to tangle with the perplexing materiality of the everyday, complicating its separation from practice, or from experience, making easy abstractions or generalisations more difficult. They make it harder for those of us who work with theory to come to rest in the metaphors or figurations that are so generative in moving our thinking on. The articles in this special issue have mobilised, and been mobilised by the figure of the promiscuous feminist researcher and her familiars (the bat, the wild horse) to great effect. But there is still, always, a risk that the dynamism and challenge of the figure will drain away with use and time – as I have argued has happened with previous figures for post-structuralism such as the cyborg or the nomad (MacLure, 2012) – leaving behind, in the worst case, a romanticism that describes or dreams of transgression, treachery, dirt and madness, but cannot know what it has actually done. Have we been dirty enough? Are we promiscuous only with safe and predictable partners? I am reminded of the famous definition of surrealism (not an obvious friend of feminism) as the chance encounter on a dissecting table of a sewing machine and an umbrella. Could we be open to less thinkable, more improper rapprochements?

References

Barad, K. (2007). *Meeting the universe halfway: Quantum physics and the entanglement of matter and meaning*. Durham, NC: Duke University Press.
Deleuze, G. (1994). *Difference and repetition*. (P. Patton, Trans.). New York, NY: Columbia University Press.
Hekman, S. (2010). *The material of knowledge: Feminist disclosures*. Bloomington, IN: Indiana University Press.
MacLure, M. (2010). The offence of theory. *Journal of Education Policy, 25*, 275–283.
MacLure, M. (2012). Qualitative inquiry: Where are the ruins? *Qualitative Inquiry, 17*, 997–1005.
Massumi, B. (2002). *Parables for the virtual: Movement, affect, sensation*. Durham, NC: Duke University Press.
Olkowski, D. (1999). *Gilles Deleuze and the ruin of representation*. Berkeley, CA: University of California Press.
Pickering, A. (1995). *The mangle of practice: Time, agency and science*. Chicago, IL: University of Chicago Press.
Thrift, N. (2008). *Non-representational theory: Space, politics, affect*. London: Routledge.

Index

ab-use 5, 13, 88, 89
activism 63, 104, 105
Addams, Jane 10–11, 22, 24, 26, 27, 104–18, 121
advocacy 62, 63
affection 35
affective agency 122
affective interpretation 35
affectivity 96, 97, 99
Africa 37–9
agency 13, 20, 23, 26–8, 50, 56, 66, 88, 97, 100, 108–10, 113, 115, 121, 122
agential realism 106, 107–8, 121
aggression 32, 35, 36, 112
alienation 8, 35–6
ambivalence 3, 8, 19, 25, 33
"aporias" 100
assimilation 10
"autoethnography of methodology" 94

Barad, Karen 93, 96, 99, 106, 107–8, 121
Barnett, Ida Wells 105, 114
Baudrillard, Jean 66–7
becoming feminisms 23–4, 93–103
belonging 47–60
Berlant, Lauren 43
Beyoncé 52
black feminism 61–73; curriculum 63–4; experience 70–2; insufficiency of power 66–70; pedagogy of 61–2, 64
Blake, William 71, 121
bodies 94; material 27–8, 62, 109, 113–15; ownership of 62; shaping of 113; vulnerability 68
broader impacts criteria (BIC) 74–92; elucidation of 79–80; and ethics 78–81
Butler, Judith 108–9

can-do attitude 65
cheating on feminism 94–6
Civil Rights Act (1964) 80
Clapp, Elsie Ripley 105
classical American pragmatism 104, 105
clusters, conceptual 22–3

codes 22–3
codifications 22–3
Coetzee, J.M. 37–41
colonial discourse 40, 41, 42, 120
colonization 42, 48, 88
containment 10–12, 25, 26, 29, 32, 77–8, 85, 88, 116
contamination 8, 12, 24, 29, 77–8, 87, 88
creative contagion 121, 122
critical race theory (CRT) 4, 101, 105

Dahlberg, John 81
Derrida, Jacques 31, 41–2, 100
desires 9–12, 22, 27, 31–4, 37, 40, 42–3, 78, 87, 88, 89, 120
dirty theory 2
disability 79, 82, 86
discrimination 69, 71; gender-based 3; racial 25
diversity 19, 22, 67, 76, 80, 83, 85
Dura, Marguerite 55

education 63; non-white racial inequality in 97–9; privatization of 19; racial stratification 98, 100; urban 98
elitism 111
emancipation 4
embodied lives 29
empowerment 4
environment 106, 107, 113, 116; maternal 19, 34, 44
ethics 78–81
Ethics Education in Science and Engineering (EESE) grant program 81
ethnic bias 82
ethnic community 51
ethnic diversification 10, 19
ethnicity 26, 64, 76, 79, 111
ethnography 13–14, 29, 53, 76, 77, 82, 86, 88, 95
Eurocentrism 20, 71, 114, 120
Ewald, Francois 31
experience 70–2
explanation 50, 54, 56, 58, 70

INDEX

failure 7–8, 10, 12, 14, 47, 96, 98, 100, 101; research failure 49, 51–7
fantasy 32, 36
fear 35–6, 62, 111, 114
female anatomy 62, 68
feminism 49–50; cheating on 94–6
feminist becoming 23–4, 93–103
feminist pragmatism 106–7, 112
feminist research 4–5, 6; becoming feminisms 23–4; doing of 93–103; funding 74–92; institutional legitimacy 53; intelligibility of data 53–5; matter of 94–7; post-critical perspective 23; productive unease 24–5; research failure 49, 51–7; theoretical complexity vs. material simplicity 55–7; untenured employment 52–3; wanting and doing 57–8
feminist theory 99–101
feminists of color 3, 4, 10, 22, 23, 24–5, 27, 50, 76, 82; black feminism 61–73
fetish 36
fieldwork, materiality of 93–103
fitting in 10, 11
Foucault, Michel 62–3, 65–6, 67, 68, 108
freedom 10–11
Freud, Sigmund 33
funding 74–92

Galland, John 81
gender 25–6, 51, 94; bias 3, 82; identity 4, 25–6; theory 108
gender-based discrimination 3
gender-based oppression 5, 27
gendered privilege 70
genealogy 5–7
Gilman, Charlotte Perkins 105
grant proposal writing 81–7
grant-science 74–92, 121

habits 107
hatred 35–6
historicization 26–7
Hull House settlement 104–18
human rights 37, 57
humanity 19, 33, 36–43
Hurricane Katrina 82–5
hybridity 19, 48

identities 65–6, 71
impotence 68
inequity 21, 24–6, 28, 63, 64, 66, 77, 82, 99–100
infancy 34–5; maternal relations 34–5, 44
inquiry 23, 32, 55, 75–7, 93, 95, 96–7, 101, 107
institutional legitimacy 53
institutional oppression 9
intellectual promiscuity 108–9
interdependence 29, 108, 111

interdisciplinarity 4, 6, 19–20, 86
interpretation 24, 29, 31–44, 56, 63, 71, 74, 77, 80, 81, 83, 86–7, 99–100, 108, 110, 111–12, 120
interpretive engagement 44
interpretive practice 33–7
intersectionality 4, 19, 20, 65, 94
intra-action 97–9, 108; and perspectivism 115–16; and reciprocity 112–13
invulnerability 67

James, William 112

Kipnis, Laura 68
knowing through being 96
knowledge 43, 65–6; production 67; theoretico-active 67
Kristeva, Julia 108

Lacan, Jacques 34, 108
language 1, 2, 20, 28, 32, 36, 41, 42, 48–50, 53–5, 57, 58, 66, 83, 98, 107
Lather, Patti 7, 55, 100
law of the father 34
Lee, Spike 83–4
legacy 5–7
Leo, Melissa 52
Levi-Strauss, Claude 108
liberal democracy 28
lineage 5–7
literary engagement 33, 42, 43, 44
lived experience 25, 38, 40, 64, 83, 94, 98, 106
living differently 3

madness 8, 11, 41, 42, 122; *see also* wild reading
making of promiscuous feminism 52–3
male domination 5, 6; grant teams 81–2, 85
male feminists 5–6
March, Peter 79
marginalization 69, 114
Martin, Jane Roland 52
material bodies 27–8, 62, 109, 113–15
material simplicity 47, 49, 55–7, 121
material-discursive becoming 99–101
materiality 2, 6, 7–10, 25, 29, 49, 53, 55–8; of fieldwork 93–103; new feminist 23, 96, 102
maternal environment 19, 34, 44
maternal relations 34–5, 44
Mayer, Marissa 52
messy practice 1, 2
methodology-in-practice 1–2
misappropriation 36, 39
Mitchell, Lucy Sprague 105

National Science Foundation 74–92; grant policy 78–81
need 27–8, 35

INDEX

neoliberal scientism 24, 74, 76, 80, 83, 85–7
new feminist materialism 23, 96, 102
New Orleans, flooding 82–5
No Child Left Behind (NCLB) 97
non-action 68
"not-so-feminist" feminist methodology 3

Occupy Wall Street Movement (OWS) 28
O'Connor, Sandra Day 52
Ohio Public High School 97–9
Oliver, Kelly 35, 40
ontoepistemology 108
ontology 27, 93–103
oppression 20, 40, 57, 63, 69, 70, 71, 115; alienation of 35; gender-based 5, 27; institutional 9; partriarchal 112
outside-in feminist methodology 4–5

parrhesia (truth telling) 63
paternalism 25, 111
patriarchy 2, 5, 42, 74, 77, 115; challenges to 63, 112; law of the father 34
pedagogy of black feminism 61–2, 64
performativity 107, 109, 120
perspectivism 106, 110; how bodies matter 113–15; and intra-action 115–16
Pillow, Wanda 95
policy as practice 95
positivism 6, 7, 19, 29
post-critical perspective 23, 100
post-representational world 28–9
postcolonial studies 33–7
postmodernism 63, 94, 107
poststructuralism 63, 66, 67, 72, 76, 108, 109
power 65–6, 68; insufficiency of 66–70
power relations 66–7, 68–9, 111
pragmatism 104–18; classical American 104, 105
privatization of education 19
productive knowledge 67, 70
productive unease 23, 24–5
projective identification 33–7, 38
promiscuity 7, 8, 20, 32; definition 20–2
promiscuous feminism 1, 2, 7–8, 12, 21, 77, 87–8; as alienation 62; making of 62–3
promiscuous pragmatism 104–18
promiscuous reading 108–16
promiscuous science 77–8
psychoanalysis 26–7, 33–7
public discourse 62, 63

qualitative research 108–9
queer feminists 4, 9, 82, 97
queer theory 19, 20

racial discrimination 25
racial diversification 19
racial stratification in education 98, 100

racism 10, 25, 83–4; critical race theory 101; reverse 83; white supremacy 100
reciprocity 106, 107, 110–12; and intra-action 112–13
refugeeism 5
refusal 48, 69
representation 34, 41–2, 43, 56, 99
reproductive choice 62
rereading humanity 40–3
research *see* feminist research
research failure 49, 51–7
reverse racism 83

St Pierre, Elizabeth 95
seduction 67
sexism 1, 2, 3, 5, 6, 77
sibling rivalry 38, 41
social Darwinism 57
social justice 81–8
social relationships 35, 110–13, 115, 116
social-material practices 107
Spivak, Gayatri 3, 65, 76, 77–8, 87, 88, 89
STEM culture 19, 80, 83, 86, 87
stereotyping 36, 51
strength 28, 72, 108, 122
stuck places 23, 55, 100

"The Bat, the Bird and the Beast" 25, 47–60
"The Humanities in Africa" 37–40
theoretico-active knowledge 67
Tiananmen Square massacre 50, 51
troubling times 19–20

"un/containment" 9–11, 12
undoing 66, 107
unruliness 6–7
untenured employment 52–3
usable data 53–5

vulnerability 12, 22, 28, 29, 65, 68–9, 72, 121

wanting things both ways 47–60
wave metaphor 88–9
weakness 108
white supremacy 100
"wild horse", suppression of 8, 31, 43, 120, 122
"wild" reading 27, 31–46, 121; projective identification 33–7
"wild" writing 9–11
wildness 32–3
Wilson, Elizabeth 99
Wittig, Monique 108
Woolf, Virginia 8, 31, 32–3
"working the ruins" 6, 7
worlding 77–8, 89

xenophobia 111